HIGH VOLTAGE

ALSO BY JIM MOTAVALLI

Forward Drive: The Race to Build Clean Cars for the Future
(Sierra Club Books, 2000)

Breaking Gridlock: Moving Toward Transportation That Works
(Sierra Club Books, 2001)

*Naked in the Woods: Joseph Knowles and the
Legacy of Frontier Fakery*
(Da Capo, 2008)

AS EDITOR

Feeling the Heat: Dispatches from the Frontlines of Climate Change
(Routledge, 2004)

Green Living: The E Magazine Guide to Living Lightly on the Planet
(Plume, 2005)

*EarthTalk: Expert Answers to Everyday Questions
about the Environment*
(Plume, 2009)

AS CONTRIBUTOR

The Whole Green Catalog: 1,000 Best Things for You and the Earth
(Rodale, 2009)

Nonprofit Guide to Going Green (Wiley, 2009)

HIGH VOLTAGE

THE FAST TRACK TO PLUG IN THE AUTO INDUSTRY

JIM MOTAVALLI

RODALE.

Rodale books may be purchased for business or promotional use or for special sales. For information, please write to: Special Markets Department, Rodale Inc., 733 Third Avenue, New York, NY 10017.

Printed in the United States of America
Rodale Inc. makes every effort to use acid-free ♾, recycled paper ♻.

Book design by Christopher Rhoads

Library of Congress Cataloging-in-Publication Data

Motavalli, Jim.
  High voltage : the fast track to plug in the auto industry / Jim Motavalli.
     p.   cm.
  Includes bibliographical references and index.
  ISBN 978–1–60529–263–2 hardcover
  1. Automobile industry and trade—Environmental aspects. 2. Hybrid electric cars—Economic aspects. 3. Electric automobiles—Economic aspects. I. Title.
  HD9710.A2M68   2011
  338.4'76292293—dc22   2011014675

Distributed to the trade by Macmillan
2   4   6   8   10   9   7   5   3   1   hardcover

We inspire and enable people to improve their lives and the world around them.

www.rodalebooks.com

For Mary Ann, Maya, and Delia, my copilots on this journey

CONTENTS

INTRODUCTION

The importance of the Volt is more than a single
profit-and-loss statement.

—ROB PETERSON, GENERAL MOTORS

BY THE TIME YOU READ THIS, the showrooms will be full
of green car options that didn't exist even a year ago. You can
walk right in and buy one of several zero-emission cars that plug
into the wall and operate for just a few cents a mile. There will be
more hybrid choices than ever before, plus a new variation, the
plug-in hybrid, which extends the concept with up to 50 miles of
battery-only range. In a few more years, hydrogen fuel–cell cars
will also be ready for sale to the public.

If you're like most people, you probably have more than one
reason to be interested in the new generation of electric cars. You
know they have much lower operating costs, sure, but you also
like the idea of automobiles running on batteries—with no dependence on foreign oil and no polluting tailpipe. You're intrigued
that this new technology is enjoying a rebirth, and wondering if
now's the time to plunge ahead, be an early adopter, and put a
green car in the driveway.

Maybe you're a bit like James Brazell of Asheville, North
Carolina, who in February of 2011 became one of the first 500
purchasers of the innovative Chevrolet Volt, a plug-in hybrid

unlike anything else the sometimes technophobic General Motors has ever produced. "It's a great car, and it meets my needs very well," he says. Brazell drives an average of 30 miles a day,[1] so with the car's 35 miles of all-electric range he can mostly avoid visiting gas stations. But when he needs to make longer trips, such as his frequent 230-mile round-trip runs to Charlotte for football games, the car can accommodate that with 300 miles of range provided by the gas engine.

Brazell is 84, which made him the oldest Volt customer, but more important than that, he's the former coordinator of worldwide exploration and production for oil giant Texaco. That gives him an insider's perspective on our dwindling fossil fuel supply. And he's worried—let's make that *very* worried—about the future.

"I think we're very close to peak oil," Brazell told me. "Production might plateau where we are for a while, maybe a year or two, but then it will start to decline. If demand [especially from China] keeps rising as it has been, the stress point on worldwide production is going to be reached, and that will happen this decade for sure."

It isn't necessary to have worked for Texaco to be worried— let's make that *very* worried—about our foreign oil dependence. A 2010 Rock the Vote poll[2] showed that 86 percent of 18- to 29-year-old voters were worried about it, and a Rasmussen poll in the same year showed that it concerned 73 percent of all adults.[3] The growing alarm is bipartisan, which isn't something you can say about climate change—that splits Americans along ideological lines.

But even if you're a global warming skeptic, you're probably worrying about it at least a little bit, and when coupled with concern over rising gas prices, peak oil, and local air pollution, there's a powerful case to be made for cleaner cars. Transportation accounts for about a third of all greenhouse gas emissions in the United States. Cars and trucks are also the biggest source of our smog pollution, says the Union of Concerned Scientists.[4]

Fortunately, after a series of false starts, technology breakthroughs are enabling electric cars to compete with gasoline vehicles from the world's carmakers. Not until 2011 did consumers finally have a real range of green car choices (see the definitions below). What's unfolding today is the culmination of a historic drama that's been proceeding in fits and starts for more than a hundred years. Your great-grandparents might have driven electric cars.

We're still in a very early stage of their development, and the cars aren't yet all they can and will be. Hybrid cars have gone mainstream; though the Prius was once derided as Toyota's folly, it's gone on to sell more than 2 million units worldwide. But the Prius didn't bound out of the gate, and the new cars probably won't, either. There are challenges. Battery electric vehicles (EVs) have limited ranges (100 miles, usually) that get shorter in cold weather. Plug-in hybrids, which solve the "range anxiety" problem with a few hundred extra miles provided by the gasoline engine, are expensive—and therefore may not justify their extra cost by operating at a lower cost.

GREEN CARS: HERE WE GO AGAIN

I'm writing this book at a point in history that has strong parallels with 1900, when the fledgling auto industry was building electric, gasoline, and steam cars—each with noisy advocates and strong sales. According to the American Oil and Gas Historical Society, "Of the 4,200 automobiles sold in the United States in 1900, gasoline powered less than 1,000." When 48,000 people paid 50 cents each to see the new cars in New York's Madison Square Garden in that year, the society reports, the "most popular models proved to be electric, steam, and gasoline . . . in that order."[5]

Gas cars of the period were infernal, noisy machines that could break arms when the engines caught after owners turned them over with hand cranks. An early commentator called the internal-combustion engine "noxious, noisy, unreliable, and elephantine. It vibrates so violently as to loosen one's dentures. The automobile industry will surely burgeon in America, but this motor will not be a factor."[6]

Famous last words. The first EVs, powered by variations of the same lead-acid batteries that are under the hoods of our gas cars today, were fated for oblivion when General Motors' Charles Kettering pioneered the self-starter for gas cars (it debuted on the 1912 Cadillac). Electrics saw their market steadily shrink. Soon the plug-in cars were targeted mainly to women, whose "domestic sphere," containing home, school, and grocery store, supposedly meant that their limited range was not a factor.[7]

Maybe the story would have been different if people at the time had had any idea that cars with tailpipes polluted. The same awareness might have saved our extensive national trolley system. But EVs were sidelined without much second-guessing, and they made only sporadic and, because they were pitted against perennially cheap gasoline, doomed revival efforts until recently.

The Arab oil embargo of 1973 brought EVs out of hiding

briefly, but the entries from hopeful independent automakers were often crudely made things with very limited ranges. And when cheap gas was back and the long gas station lines were gone, the cars lost what had already been a severely limited market. Another driver was California's 1990 plug-in mandates, which, had they been put into place, would have required EVs to be 2 percent of new-car sales by 1998 (and 10 percent by 2003). The mandates, which led in 1997 to General Motors' short-lived EV1 but were ultimately much watered down, are chronicled in my book *Forward Drive*[8] and in the 2006 film it helped inspire, Chris Paine's *Who Killed the Electric Car?*

The EV1, called "the tragic hero of the electric car narrative" by *Time* magazine,[9] met its demise in 2003, with only about 800 having been leased in California and Arizona. The cars, taken back and crushed by an automaker wary of warranty claims on the battery packs, seemed to symbolize the end of an era, the death of a dream.

The EV1 was up against stiff headwinds, including the early stages of the SUV craze, very cheap gas, and its dependence on outdated battery technology. Most of the EV1s had lead-acid batteries, just like those that power the 1909 Baker Electric in Jay Leno's Big Dog Garage. In "economy" mode, the two-seater EV1 could deliver 100 miles of range with second-generation batteries, but "performance" mode cut that in half. Even with all of that, the early adopters who had briefly lived with the GM cars fell totally in love.

So what's different now? Everything. The plugs are back, and this time to stay. Battery technology has taken a major leap forward, from lead-acid to nickel–metal hydride and now to lithium-ion, and range has stabilized at about 100 miles. That's still not great—and it's provoking a lot of nail-biting—but with carmakers focused on electrics, batteries are finally getting the kind of concentrated research effort they need to make progress.

I first started reporting on the bright dream of electric cars in the late 1980s, when SUVs ruled Detroit and cheap gas seemed as inexhaustible as the boundless resources of the sea. The realization that both of these things were finite was still in the future. But we're wide-awake now, and green cars are finally making their move with impressive propulsion.

How fast can electric car sales go from zero to 60? Roland Berger Strategy Consultants projected in February of 2011 that 10 percent of new car sales globally will be electric by 2025, and hybrids will have grabbed 40 percent of the market by then.[10] That would mean that half of all new cars heading into show-rooms around the world would be at least partly electric. That sounds like a tipping point to me—the end of green cars being relegated to a little niche market while the real business of auto sales happens elsewhere.

ELECTRIC CARS: KNOW THE DIFFERENT TYPES

There are indeed levels of electrification. It's very easy to get confused by EVs, and a lot of people are misinformed about what plugging in can deliver. A 2011 IBM study determined that 45 percent of the American people said they had little or no information about electric cars.[11] It's common for people to think that battery cars can routinely travel 300 miles on a charge (an

also widely held belief, oddly enough, is the complete opposite—
that their range is 50 miles or less). So before we go much further, we need to define our terms and set the basic parameters.
Flip back to this section later if you find yourself getting lost.

There are abbreviations out there such as BEV for "battery
electric vehicle" and PHEV for "plug-in-hybrid electric vehicle,"
but I hate them because there's no agreement on which acronyms
to use, which only adds to the murk surrounding this topic. So in
this book I've used EV (for "electric vehicle") occasionally for the
general category of electrified cars, but mostly I spell out what I
mean. Take issue with this if you will, and I'm sure many of the
passionate enthusiasts will do exactly that.

⟋ **Battery electrics: Betting on the charge.** These cars have
electric motors and battery packs, and no other means of propulsion. Let them run down, and they're dead until plugged in
again. Their range is generally 100 miles, but that's not likely
to remain the standard for long. The $128,500 Tesla Roadster
Sport, a high-performance electric sports car and a pioneer on
the American market, claims 245 miles on a charge, and its
stablemate, the Model S four-door sport sedan, can deliver
300 as an optional choice. On the road, of course, your experience will differ—cold weather, among other things, nega-
tively affects battery performance, and some people (including
me) have been surprised by disappearing range when the temperature drops. Battery packs consist of groups of individual
cells, which look either like larger versions of AA batteries
(cylindrical) or flat, square panels (prismatic) about the size of
45-rpm record sleeves. The Tesla Roadster has approximately

6,800 cylindrical batteries; the Think City EV, a Norwegian battery car being produced in Indiana, uses 384 individual prismatic cells. Battery pack size is measured in kilowatt-hours, with 25 kilowatt-hours probably being about average. Battery electrics either already on or headed for the market include the Nissan Leaf, the Ford Focus, Daimler's Smart Fortwo Electric Drive, the BMW i3 Megacity Vehicle, the Honda Fit, and the electric version of the Fiat 500 from Chrysler. From the independents: the Tesla Model S, the Coda Sedan, the Wheego LiFe, and the Think City.

↗ **Plug-in hybrids: Power in reserve.** Buyers of these cars like to have options. The plug-in hybrid acts like an electric car for approximately the first 50 miles, but then can switch to an onboard internal-combustion engine that either drives the wheels directly (the Toyota Prius Plug-In Hybrid) or acts like a generator (the Chevrolet Volt and Fisker Karma) to keep the electric motor supplied with electricity. (The Volt's gas engine does drive the wheels under some circumstances.) Dispensing with range anxiety, plug-in hybrids have greater range than regular cars (500 miles in the case of the Ford C-Max Energi, 350 miles in the Chevrolet Volt). The only downside of plug-in hybrids is that they have a tailpipe, meaning that to people who care about such things, they're not technically zero-emission cars. I know, battery EVs charge off of power plants, most of which have "tailpipes" known as smokestacks, but we'll get into that later. Chevrolet likes to claim that its Volt is a "range extender" electric car, but a plug-in hybrid is closer to that mark. Nissan CEO Carlos Ghosn is clearly going after the Volt when he says that, in contrast to his company's Leaf, any car that uses gasoline is "automatically a hybrid."[12] This debate can get pretty heated.

✗ **Hybrids: Something extra for the gas engine.** The hybrid concept, using both gasoline and electric drivetrains for maximum efficiency, has been with us since the dawn of the automobile—Ferdinand Porsche incorporated electric and gasoline drives into the so-called Lohner-Porsche Mixte hybrid of 1901. The modern hybrid had to wait for electronic controls that could intelligently coordinate the two modes. The first such car on the market in North America was the two-seat Honda Insight, which offered 70 mpg on the highway in 1999. The Prius, which delivered 50 mpg combined in its 2011 version, entered the US market a year later, in 2000. Today, most automakers offer or plan to offer hybrids that incorporate such features as automatic shutoff at traffic lights and regenerative braking (which recaptures energy usually lost as heat). Hybrids either use their electric motors as assists for the gas engine (Honda's system) or allow short bursts of electric-only driving (the Prius and the Ford Fusion hybrid). Since I first kicked the tires on an early Prius, hybrids have gone distinctly mainstream.

✗ **Micro-hybrids: The affordable kick.** I've always wondered why regular gas cars couldn't have the fuel-saving auto-stop technology and regenerative braking that are standard equipment on hybrids. Auto-stop, which by itself can result in a 10 to 15 percent fuel savings, is really cool, seamlessly shutting down the car at traffic lights, then almost imperceptibly starting it again when the driver lifts his or her foot from the brake. The answer is fairly simple—it's the batteries. The lead-acid battery under the hood of a conventional car doesn't have the power to run the increasingly sophisticated, electricity-hungry systems on your car when the engine's shut down. The so-called micro-hybrid has a larger battery, and sometimes a bank of ultracapacitors (which can accept a charge quickly and discharge it just as quickly). Largely because US regulators have been slow to recognize the value of auto-stop, it hasn't taken off in the American market. But the technology gained traction rapidly in Europe, where millions were quickly on the roads. Then the American market finally began gearing up: According to Lux Research in 2010, there could be 34 million micro-hybrids on world roads by 2015, 4.6 million of them in the United States. Jacob Grose, a Lux senior analyst, told me that adding auto-stop to a car costs between $300 and $1,500—with the higher amount also fitting a car with regenerative braking.[13]

✗ **Fuel-cell cars: EVs with help from hydrogen.** The fuel cell, which produces electricity (as well as water and heat) from the most abundant element in the universe, is even more venerable a concept than hybrid technology, dating to the 19th century. Much later, the fuel cell was used to provide electricity and water for early American spaceflights, and it has long been advocated as an effective replacement for internal combustion (though hydrogen itself is an energy carrier, not a fuel). Many of the automakers who are developing electric cars (including Honda, Daimler, Toyota, Hyundai, and General Motors) also have parallel fuel-cell programs that are targeted for limited commercialization by 2014 or 2015. Hydrogen cars *are* electric cars, with the fuel cell replacing the battery pack. In early 2011, I started taking part in a long-term test of a Toyota fuel-cell car, which can refuel at a new solar-powered station near my home in Connecticut. Fuel-cell cars should be no-brainers, since we'll never run out of hydrogen, and range isn't a problem (my test car can travel 300 miles on a tank). But it's all very expensive, including the cars, the hydrogen itself (which has to be separated from other substances, usually water or natural gas), and the filling stations (well over $1 million each). That's why the much-cheaper EV charging stations are going up all around the country, while there are still fewer than 100 hydrogen outlets in the United States. But a determined entrepreneur, Tom Sullivan of Lumber Liquidators, is funding his own "hydrogen highway" along the East Coast, and my refueling station in Connecticut was his first outlet.

There is no single solution for electrifying transportation. Although advocates of some of these technologies feud openly, I see a path forward that combines all of them. These different options are finally getting past the test period and moving from the show stand to the road. The cars started rolling out at the end of 2010, very slowly and cautiously at first, but with increasing boldness as nearly all the vehicles were swallowed up by eager early adopters.

Automakers are taking a chance with these cars, no doubt

about it. Steven Rattner, who headed the 2009 auto bailout for President Barack Obama and helped steer General Motors through bankruptcy, said that the automaker would spend $40,000 building each of its early "range extender" Chevrolet Volts.[14] That's a bit of a problem when the car is being sold for $41,000. General Motors didn't deny Rattner's estimate, which he uncovered performing "due diligence" during his days as auto czar. But Volt spokesman Rob Peterson told me, "The importance of the Volt is more than a single profit-and-loss statement."[15] Contrast that with the Big Three's attitude a decade earlier, when it let cost issues derail a chance to get in early with hybrid cars.

Rattner's pessimism (he told me that "EVs are everybody's latest fantasy") and Peterson's optimism crystallize the challenge the auto industry faces as it starts a transition to electricity from more than a hundred years of fossil-fuel domination. After many false starts since the 1920s, the revival of the EV is now well underway, pushed forward by technological leaps, the imperatives of global warming, and the sobering prospect of peak oil.

I've gotten behind the wheels of nearly all of the new electric and fuel-cell cars. Guess what? They're really fun to drive, taking off like scalded cats because batteries deliver instant-on power. Are there electric drag races, smoking tires, and quarter-mile times in the 11-second range? You bet. So when I say it's been a really exciting ride so far, that's not hyperbole. Electric cars are going to jump-start our lives and do good things for the planet, too.

CHAPTER ONE

RACING FOR THE GOAL

Elon has huge steel balls. He truly does.

—JUSTINE MUSK

TO SUCCEED, electric cars will need a dash of stardust, and it helps if their CEOs and marketing people have studied the works of the ultimate showman, P. T. Barnum. We need to be *sold* on buying green, and it's good that some of the most charismatic corporate leaders are helming clean auto start-ups.

Speed equals excitement, and automakers have known that forever—that's why they spend millions on motorsports. The old slogan is "win on Sunday, sell on Monday," and it still rings true. So the green cars are at a disadvantage, right? Wrong!

Actually, it's a total myth (or perhaps a vestige of ancient history) that electric and plug-in hybrid cars are slow, with none of the neck-snapping performance that excites readers of *Car and Driver* and *Road & Track*. In fact, I've had some of my most exciting times behind the wheel in battery cars. Electric motors have many virtues, and one of the most interesting is their ability to call up maximum torque at near-zero rpm. They *take off.*

Slow? Shawn Lawless's drag-racing motorcycle, the 1,610-horsepower Rocket, set a record at 177.09 miles per hour in a quarter mile. John Wayland's White Zombie is a 1972 Datsun 1200 that relies on lithium-ion batteries to sprint from *zero to 60 in 1.8 seconds.*

I have to admit it—I like driving fast. I just prefer to do it without a tailpipe involved, and some of the new high-performance EVs allow me to do that.

Tesla Motors and Fisker Automotive are two California-based American start-up companies determined to make sure that their cars are part of a rapid transit system, and that fun is part of the package. The first time I drove a Tesla Roadster, it turned out to be a totally visceral experience: The car felt alive, and every stab at the accelerator (we can call it a "gas pedal" no longer) yielded instant response and swift progress toward the distant horizon. Who knew electric cars could be like this?

Telsa and Fisker have a lot in common, but they're also very different, and intense, bitter rivals with grievances (relating to a brief working relationship) that, instead of healing, have metastasized. Both enterprises have charismatic, outspoken leaders born outside the United States whose outsize public personas tend to dominate discussion of their prospects. And both have borrowed very large amounts of public money from a $25 billion Department of Energy loan fund: Tesla received $465 million[1] to build a factory for its all-new Model S sedan (and a separate powertrain facility); and Fisker $528.7 million for its plug-in hybrids, including, in addition to the flashy $95,900 Karma sedan, a smaller car, code-named Nina, that will be built in a former General Motors factory the company acquired in Delaware.[2]

But the differences are as big as the similarities. Tesla's $109,000 high-performance Roadster, an electric adaptation of the lightweight Lotus Elise, has been on the market since 2008, after being introduced to the public in 2006. The Roadster has phenomenal battery range and a zero-to-60 time of 3.7 seconds. If it sounds fun to drive, that's because it is.

The first Roadster went to the man now known as the public face of Tesla, the South Africa–born and still-boyish Elon Musk, often described as a "billionaire" as the result of his role in helping found, and then sell, online payment company PayPal. In the Roadster's first three years on the market, as the company began opening stores in the United States, Europe, and Asia, approximately 1,700 were sold worldwide. Tesla is firmly committed to high-performance electric-only cars—although it flirted with making its 2012 Model S sedan a plug-in hybrid, it's now unlikely to sell anything other than battery vehicles.

Fisker Automotive was launched later, in 2007. Danish-born Henrik Fisker, who founded the company with Bernhard Koehler, is a veteran and well-respected car stylist, having worked for Ford (where he specialized in cars for Aston Martin, which was then a subsidiary) and BMW. At the German company, his very first project was the E1 battery car, which was first shown in 1991 but never built.

Fisker Automotive is a marriage, arranged over dinner at an Italian restaurant, between the founder's designs and Quantum Technologies' Q-Drive plug-in hybrid system. The Fisker Karma's 20-kilowatt-hour battery pack supposedly offers 50 miles of all-electric range, followed by 250 miles with the aid of its turbocharged GM-sourced gasoline engine, which acts as a generator to supply two big electric motors, producing more than 400 horsepower. After some significant delays, early versions of the car finally met the press in March of 2011.

The Fisker Karma is the only significant electrified car I haven't driven as I write this book. Fisker steadfastly maintained an air of mystery around its car from 2007 through 2010. That's why it made headlines when (1) Denmark's Crown Prince Frederik briefly drove (or at least rode in) the car when arriving at the 2009 international COP 15 climate talks in Copenhagen,[3] and (2) I reported that the Fisker Karma test cars weighed more than 5,000 pounds—a challenge to its 50 miles of electric range.[4]

The companies' stories need in-depth telling here. I've spent time with both founders, and if they weren't real people they'd make great movie characters. Both of their companies are high-stakes gambles that you and I, as taxpayers, have a stake in.

ELON MUSK: SERIAL ENTREPRENEUR

First, a cautionary tale: At the start of 1995, there was no more promising start-up than hard-charging US Electricar, which had grown from 35 to more than 300 employees in a year. But as it announced ambitious plans to sell its General Motors–based battery cars internationally (there were joint ventures in Hawaii, Malaysia, and Thailand), the company was also burning through many investors' cash and producing very little.

The growing pains soon began to show. The US Electricar test vehicle I drove in late 1994 was a shoddy mess that broke down on the highway. By the early spring of 1995, the company's partners were shocked to discover not only that US Electricar was experiencing huge quarterly losses, but also that its CEO and senior staff had been selling off stock for months. The company, which had sent its employees around the world on Learjets, collapsed amidst recriminations.

I tell this story here not because I expect Tesla to flare out—I don't—but because it illustrates dramatically not only how hard it is to start a car company, but also how the challenge is intensified when the car in question is electric. Elon Musk himself addressed this in an interview with the University of Pennsylvania's *Knowledge@Wharton* online business journal. "As far as new companies go," he said, "the car business is such a capital-intensive business. It doesn't lend itself to start-ups very well. You need to operate with incredible capital efficiency if you are going to be a start-up and succeed in the car business."[5]

Musk learned about the importance of staying lean and mean firsthand, through personal experience at three big-league start-ups before Tesla Motors was part of his life. Tesla is still standing, and Musk's career before the company was that of a man with a seemingly sure touch in launching new businesses and selling them at the right time for fantastic payoffs.

As Musk, born in 1971, tells it, he was entrepreneurial—and tech savvy—from an early age. Growing up in South Africa in the late 1970s and early 1980s, he developed a fascination with computer games. Total immersion in the world of Atari led to programming computers, initially with the primitive 8-bit Commodore VIC-20 he bought using the generosity of his father and pocket money from odd jobs. Musk created a pair of programs (including Blast Star, when he was just 12) that earned him several hundred dollars in profit. A seed was planted.

Musk's mother is Canadian, and a strong desire to avoid the South African draft led him to emigrate there in 1989. A scholarship to the University of Pennsylvania's Wharton business school got him to the United States three years later. A second Penn bachelor's degree was in physics. If he'd stayed in graduate school at Stanford (where he was to study high-energy-density capacitor physics and materials science), he might be an academic today. But Musk made it through only a few days of advanced studies in 1995 before deferring school to start a business, Zip2, with his brother, Kimbal Musk.

Zip2, which helped the country's old-tech newspapers get online, demonstrated Musk's aptitude for attracting investment. The company, started with only a few thousand dollars and initially housed in a tiny office that doubled as the brothers' apartment, soon brought in venture funding. Investors included the New York Times Company, Knight-Ridder, SoftBank, and the Hearst Corporation. Musk, who was chairman, CEO, and chief technology officer, and his brother cashed out in 1999 for $307 million from Compaq. At the time, Musk said that it "was the largest of all cash transactions for an Internet company. That was certainly a better outcome than I had ever expected."[6]

Flush with money and convinced there was more to be done with the Internet, Musk was present at the creation of what evolved into the financial services company PayPal, which greatly eased online payments for transactions such as eBay auction buys. Again, Musk scored venture capital, in this case $25 million from Sequoia Capital. Musk was the largest shareholder when PayPal was sold to eBay for $1.5 billion in 2002.

He wasn't quite ready for Tesla, though. Instead, this serial entrepreneur founded Space Exploration Technologies, known as SpaceX, the same year he left PayPal. SpaceX, which proved a challenging sell to the venture community, builds Falcon rockets. After founding two companies that, you could say, offered brilliant, timely ideas that weren't rocket science, Musk (who is fascinated by Mars exploration) actually *pursued* rocket science.

By 2003, SpaceX had 30 employees who were pursuing the design, testing, and integration of space rocket technology, with the actual fabrication farmed out to subcontractors. The hurdles to success, he admits, are nearly as big as space itself. "As you might imagine, when somebody tries to build an orbital launch vehicle which is not really all that distinguishable from an ICBM [intercontinental ballistic missile], there's a lot of regulation," Musk told a Stanford audience. "And there probably should be, because you don't want to launch something and end up hitting LA, where I live. . . . The environmental approvals have certainly proven very difficult, much more so than we expected. . . . The fastest way to make a small fortune in the aerospace industry is to start with a large one."[7] Space investment, he said, is a job for the advanced entrepreneur.

SpaceX is still a work in progress, but it's gained a lot of ground. In late 2010, it became the first commercial company in history to reenter a spacecraft from low-Earth orbit and successfully recover it after splashdown. SpaceX is set to perform a dozen cargo missions to the International Space Station, making it a kind of high-tech delivery service. Musk has invested more than $100 million in SpaceX, and there's no cash-out on the horizon. But he's a man with a mission: "Sooner or later we must expand life beyond this green and blue ball or go extinct," he said.[8]

TESLA MOTORS: FAST, AND OFTEN FURIOUS

Elon Musk was not there at the creation of Tesla Motors, a fact that led to much dissension later on. Instead, Tesla was founded by Martin Eberhard and Marc Tarpenning in 2003 to commercialize AC Propulsion's Tzero electric sports car. So the idea of creating an ultrafast, sexy electric roadster belongs not to Musk or to either of the two cofounders, but to a behind-the-scenes company whose forte is building EVs for other people (including the electric Mini E for BMW).

In the summer of 2010 I went to Los Angeles to interview Tom Gage, one of the principals of AC Propulsion and an unsung EV pioneer. Over vegetarian food, he told me the story of Tesla's unlikely founding.

Between 1997 and 2003 AC Propulsion (using a kit car as a base) built three Tzero prototypes, the second of which (featuring 6,800 cylindrical lithium-ion batteries) was remarkably similar in concept to what became the Tesla Roadster.

"We wanted to make a car that exemplified high performance, and we did that," Gage told me.[9] "But the car we built had made no concessions to manufacturability or safety. We looked at the idea of producing it, but the hand assembly was beyond our capabilities at the time."

It was hard to ignore the Tzero because it hit 60 mph in just 3.6 seconds—something no other nonrace EV had done. But AC Propulsion hadn't built a Tzero that could be produced in quantity, and that's why the company was willing to talk about licensing the car to people who would carry the concept forward. Elon

Musk, who was already working on SpaceX and collaborating with Tesla's cofounders, turned out to be the man for the job.

"I had approached Elon about investing in the eBox [an electric Scion xB briefly sold by AC Propulsion]," Gage said. "Both Martin [Eberhard] and Elon were involved, but Elon put far more money into what became Tesla."

The lightweight body for the Tesla was adopted from the British Lotus Elise, though Musk cautions that after extensive redesign very few parts remain from that gasoline-powered car. As testing went on, Eberhard was replaced as CEO, and Musk, the major investor, took over in late 2008.

The early history was forgotten as the Tesla Roadster launched to a huge media explosion in 2008. I started covering Tesla around that time and found Musk intriguing. His public demeanor combines youthful enthusiasm and can-do spirit (he could have played Buck Rogers) with a certain level of bitterness toward his enemies, who are many. For years, one of the biggest was Eberhard, whom Musk clashed with most directly on who would get the credit for giving birth to the Tesla Roadster.

If media appearances were sales, Tesla would have been a hit right out of the box. The car, and Musk himself, were in every major magazine and all over the Internet. The car is undoubtedly sexy, and Musk's personal story compelling. Celebrities helped by buying the model in droves, with eager customers including David Letterman, George Clooney, Matt Damon, Brad Pitt, and Leonardo DiCaprio.

Dan Neil, then of the *Los Angeles Times* and now of the *Wall Street Journal*, was typical in his gee-whiz evocation of the delights of the Tesla Roadster he drove in February of 2009: "I'm bombing around Hollywood on a Saturday night in an all-electric Tesla Roadster, a sick-with-torque, carbon-fiber mosquito with a half-ton of glorified camera batteries behind the seats," he wrote. "It's a perfect night for cruising, cool and moonlit. The city lights drizzle over the silver car like Campari and creme de menthe."[10]

I got my first ride in the Roadster that same month, a car I borrowed from minder Joe Powers, who had parked a red Roadster at a Greenwich, Connecticut, hotel in the hopes of catching a stray hedge fund manager. "Erase any images you have of slow-poke, boring-as-hell electric cars presided over by a smiling picture of Al Gore," I wrote. "The Tesla Roadster blows all that to smithereens, and without creating any smoke! The bucket seats are snug, which is good because when I goosed the throttle out of the hotel parking lot, [my daughter] Maya and I were pinned like NASA astronauts. We forgot to breathe."[11]

I also complained that the steering was a bit heavy at parking lot speeds, the canvas top complicated, the storage nonexistent, and the stereo, well, terrible. None of that mattered much when the wind was in our hair and the Roadster was flying—it felt like 100 mph at 50.

But despite all that, the entry-level car cost $109,000, and sales didn't meet projections. From the beginning, Musk saw the Model S sedan (projected to cost $57,400 in 160-mile form) as by far the volume leader, with sales of as many as 20,000 a year. It offers twice the passenger utility of the Roadster at half the price, so it certainly should do better. The car, a gorgeous design evoking Ferrari and Maserati sedans, was styled by industry star Franz von Holzhausen, a veteran of General Motors (he did the Saturn

Sky and Pontiac Solstice roadsters), Volkswagen (he had a hand in the New Beetle), and Mazda.

But Musk's volume projections aren't always spot-on—he said just before the 2008 launch that the Roadster would sell 2,000 a year, when in fact cumulative sales were around 1,700 when I wrote this in the spring of 2011.

As his car was reaching the public, delayed by a transmission glitch, Musk was also distracted by a lawsuit filed in June of 2009 by Tesla cofounder Martin Eberhard. He claimed to have "formulated the idea for a fully electric sports car" and "led the development of the Roadster from its inception and design through the safety and performance testing that validated the Roadster's ability to achieve zero to 60 mph in less than four seconds, as well as its 250-mile range per charge."[12]

Eberhard claimed that Musk had slandered him (by making "defamatory, disparaging, negative and harmful statements"), erased his role in company history, and even maneuvered to damage his company car (supposedly Tesla Roadster #2). Musk immediately fired back, calling the lawsuit "twisted and wrong." He said that the decision by Tesla's board to fire Eberhard had been unanimous—largely because the car was costing twice as much to build as the then-CEO had said it would. Musk said he put in two years of 100-hour workweeks bringing the Tesla Roadster to market, and I don't doubt that he did.

It got really heated. Musk allegedly said, according to *Newsweek,* that Eberhard was "the worst individual I ever had the displeasure of working with."[13]

Musk's problem with Eberhard was more than personal—the

cost overruns in producing the car meant that the Roadster was costing more to make ($95,000) than its initial selling price of $92,000. Tesla was in deeper waters than Chevrolet with its profit-free Volt: Musk had put so much money into his car company and SpaceX that in late 2008 he was forced to take emergency cash infusions from his brother Kimbal and other investors. It didn't help that Musk's marriage to Justine Musk was falling apart, and dealing with the fallout from that was also consuming cash.

Eberhard (who was later to work briefly with Volkswagen on EV projects) quickly dropped his suit, and Musk ended up publicly praising Martin's "indispensible efforts."[14] Tesla has been involved in other legal disputes, including a particularly bitter one involving onetime collaborator Henrik Fisker. The sordid details appear later in the chapter.

Luckily, investors don't let a little bad blood get in the way. Despite continuing cash-flow problems, Tesla was on a roll. In May of 2009, Daimler announced that it had taken a nearly 10 percent share in Tesla for $50 million. The two already had a relationship, because Tesla's prowess with battery range (and the European carmaker's admitted inexperience in building EVs) had helped the company land a lucrative contract building battery packs for the electric version of Daimler's Smart car.

"We want to think out of the box,"[15] said Daimler chairman Dieter Zetsche at the time, admitting the company needed an electric-savvy partner. A second big auto investor in Tesla is Toyota, which has similarly called on Tesla to build a battery pack for its RAV4 EV. In May of 2010, Toyota bought $50 million worth of Tesla stock, amidst words of mutual praise. Musk, who has considerable charm when he wants to display it, developed a warm personal relationship with Toyota's Akio Toyoda, a scion of the founding family.

As if those big-company votes of confidence weren't enough, Panasonic (which supplies the battery cells for the Roadster) also threw in $30 million in late 2010. Again, personal relationships helped. Musk had given a ride in a Roadster to Naoto Noguchi, then president of Panasonic's battery division. When I interviewed Noguchi in Tokyo around that time, he was still talking about how much fun it was.[16] Tesla filed for its initial public offering (IPO) in January of 2010, disclosing in the process that Musk's salary was only $33,000 a year (plus $175,000 in expenses for his private plane). The IPO, launched in June of 2010, raised $226.1 million, with the stock closing at $23.89 after opening at $17. Tesla was the first American automaker to go public since Ford, and that was in 1956.

The IPO included some typical Tesla brinkmanship. An amendment to the company's registration statement cited Musk's messy domestic situation. "We do not expect the divorce proceedings to have a material impact on Mr. Musk's ability to serve as our Chief Executive Officer and Chairman," it said.[17]

But Musk also said in a filing related to the divorce that he "ran out of cash"[18] in early 2010. He reported just $650,000 in liquid assets. Justine Musk wanted a part of Tesla, but if her former husband's share of the company dropped below 65 percent he would be technically in default on the company's government loan. It's interesting to note that Justine Musk wrote on her blog that "Elon has huge steel balls. He truly does."[19]

A marital agreement protected the CEO's share of Tesla, and the crisis passed. Musk, who claimed to have put his last

$35 million into Tesla, wrote a blog post clarifying the divorce issue. "Given the choice, I'd rather stick a fork in my hand than write about my personal life," he wrote.

> What caught me by surprise, and forced me to seek emergency loans from friends, were the enormous legal fees I had to pay my ex-wife's divorce lawyers. . . . The legal and accounting bills for the divorce total four million dollars so far, which is an average of roughly $170,000 per month for the past 24 months. . . . I never said in any court documents that I was "broke" or even that I lacked considerable assets.[20]

Musk, who has since remarried, still had huge assets and he said the divorce payments caused temporary cash-flow problems.

Tesla still isn't a profitable company, though it briefly posted a profit. Musk told me in an interview at the 2010 Detroit auto show that Tesla would be profitable today if it concentrated solely on the Roadster. "If we were to hunker down and just be a roadster company and a powertrain supply company, we would be profitable," he said. "We were briefly profitable around the middle of [2009]. We are not making money right now because we have the Model S expenses, which are quite significant and growing with each passing month. It's pretty hard for a company with a 1,000-car product line to fund a 20,000-vehicle program and still be profitable."

Notice how the Roadster, expected to sell 2,000 a year, is now settling in at 1,000 in Musk's expectations. The Roadster was three years old in 2011, and had probably connected with a good percentage of the people who both wanted it and could afford the privilege. The Roadster is briefly disappearing from Tesla's portfolio as the company prepares the higher-volume Model S for deployment in mid-2012. The sedan is in alpha testing mode, hitting the road under all weather conditions around the world.

TOURING TESLA

In August of 2010, I made the pilgrimage to Tesla's headquarters. In retrospect, the trip had its comic aspects, though they didn't seem so funny at the time. I'd heard vague rumors that Tesla was moving to Palo Alto from its longtime Silicon Valley base in San Carlos, halfway between San Francisco and San Jose, but the e-mail I got from a publicist had the San Carlos address, so that's where I headed. Bad move.

A lengthy battle with my discount rental car company left me running late and taking a cab to San Carlos. The cabbie delivered me to a large, nondescript office building in an industrial section, with a bright red Tesla Roadster charging up outside. So far, so good. But then I noticed that the parking lot was empty and the big "Tesla Motors" sign had been taken down, leaving only a ghostly echo on the concrete. Uh-oh. I was in a cab with a ticking meter, and at that moment couldn't even remember where Tesla had supposedly moved.

I repaired to a nearby Starbucks for the Wi-Fi connection and let the cabbie go. I found that Tesla had indeed relocated to the tech brain-trust city of Palo Alto, and that meant another expensive cab ride. But seeing the old building followed by the new one was a great way to clarify that Tesla, banking its investments and government loan, had come up in the world. Musk may have advised other start-ups to keep their burn rates "ridiculously tiny,"[21] but the former Agilent Technologies building in the Stanford Research Park (which has hosted Facebook, Hewlett-Packard, SAP, and Xerox's PARC) broadcast the message that the company had arrived.

Tesla's headquarters combines research and assembly work with corporate offices. Tesla's white-collar workers occupy desks on a big open floor, with Musk's corner not much bigger than anyone else's. On the surface at least, the place isn't hierarchal.

I walked in on a *Wired* photo session featuring Musk and one of the few Model S cars then pretty enough for the cameras. Musk and his embryonic creation made the cover of the October 2010 issue,[22] which I would consider perfect placement for an entrepreneur who combines high-tech innovation with a big plan for industrial rebirth.

Like Fisker, Tesla is retooling an old auto plant to build its new model, but its plan—like everything else about the company—is outsize: Musk has taken on the giant, 5.5-million-square-foot New United Motor Manufacturing Inc. (NUMMI) plant in Fremont, California. The plant was a joint venture between General Motors and Toyota that churned out GM-badged Toyotas (that never sold as well as the made-in-Japan versions). Clearly, there will be room at NUMMI for more than just the Model S, and that's likely to include considerable battery-pack work for other automakers, some of it made public and the rest taking place in behind-the-scenes skunkworks.

NUMMI is a gritty factory, its echoing and empty corridors

a symbol of the Big Three's market-share shrinkage. Tesla's Palo Alto headquarters, in contrast, is a beehive of electric activity. Publicist Khobi Brooklyn took me through the photo shoot and a busy factory space where workers were assembling proprietary battery packs.

Elon Musk was having back problems when we met in a small office, and part of our meeting took place with him flat on the floor. But he was articulate anyway, and he projected an appealing mixture of youthful exuberance (he was 39 at the time) and an instantly accessible scorn for the paltry efforts of his business rivals. Much of our talk was about the Model S, which was then entering the alpha build stage. "We approach this like a high-tech or software company would," he said. "Alpha will be followed by the beta, finished in the summer of 2011, then the release candidate in early 2012 and the production car in mid-2012."

Musk said the car is on track. One of the controversial aspects of the Model S is that it will be offered in an optional version with a claimed 300 miles of range—a holy grail that duplicates what the average gas car can do. I was the first journalist to report, after interviewing Tesla technology chief J. B. Straubel, that getting there would require a very big 90-kilowatt-hour battery pack.[23] In Palo Alto, Musk told me that early Model S cars will have a 230-mile pack, and that getting to 300 miles would probably require a 12-hour charge from a 240-volt, 40-amp power supply. That's a lot of charge time, and a major development challenge since no one had built a lithium-ion pack that large.

Tesla can be boastful, but it usually makes good on its claims. A few months after my visit, the company actually moved up the schedule for the 300-mile battery, saying it would be featured in a special edition of the first 1,000 cars.

The Model S development program is a cash soak for Tesla, but it's also a pathway to profit. At roughly half the price of the Roadster and with twice the utility, it's likely to be the volume model that Tesla desperately needs. There is a waiting list with 3,000 names on it. The company is investing heavily to make the car happen, and it is also preparing a crossover SUV, the Model X, to be built on the same platform. That's how the Big Three make money (when they do): Build a platform, and then spin off several vehicles from it.

Musk told me Tesla has a healthy core business, but it is "losing money because we're making massive investments in the Model S." How big? Musk estimated the program at $500 million, with spending running at $50 million a quarter. "It is impossible for a company to be profitable in the face of that," he said. But Musk also estimated that the DOE loan and IPO had brought in 50 percent more money than the company will need to bring the Model S to market.

At the 2011 Detroit auto show, Tesla presented not the Model S but its skeleton—a so-called body in white that showcased the car's lightweight aluminum structure. Chief engineer Peter Rawlinson, a Jaguar veteran, told me that the car then weighed in at 4,200 pounds (800 pounds less than the test version of the Fisker Karma) and that his engineering team was using every means at its disposal to cut waste poundage.

Weight is the enemy with electric cars, and race cars, too. As the fierce competitor Colin Chapman, founder of Tesla partner Lotus, famously said, "Simplicate, then add lightness." He also said, "Adding power makes you faster on the straights, while subtracting weight makes you faster everywhere." If the Model S team could have legally gotten rid of the model's external rearview mirrors (which add aerodynamic drag), it would have done so. The built-in stiffness of the body and chassis enabled the team to scale back or eliminate heavy anti-sway bars. The door handles retract into the body for maximum airflow advantage.

Musk was called away for more photos, but Tesla had a surprise for me—the first journalist test-drive in the electric version of the Mercedes A-Class E-Cell, an exciting car built in an edition of 500 (no US version is likely).

The twisty roads around Palo Alto, which seemed to be going through a dry spell, were ideal for a fast run in the A-Class. I've driven several Tesla Roadsters and taken a ride in the Model S, but the A-Class was unlike either. Although it felt sporty, it wasn't an out-and-out performance car like anything Tesla-badged is. The car has really good acceleration in a wide power band, but it wasn't chirp-the-tires fast.

Typically sharp Mercedes steering helped when throwing the A-Class into curves, but the electric drive and the existing internal-combustion chassis worked in tandem to deliver a superb driving experience. Tesla's Straubel told me that putting the weighty battery pack down low in the car helped give this very tall car a more optimized center of gravity. (Mercedes had been embarrassed in the mid-1990s when a Swedish magazine flipped an A-Class during a high-speed maneuver known as "the moose test.")

Tesla does things for a reason, and it handed me the keys to the A-Class because it wanted to get its role in creating the car on the record. Straubel told me the production version of the E-Cell was nudged into being in part because of a typically bold gamble on Tesla's part.

"Daimler is a careful company, and they're always skeptical that a program can be delivered in time," Straubel said. "It was hard to get them on board the A-Class project, which we'd been discussing, without a proof of concept. So we went ahead and pushed the envelope to retire a lot of the risk."

That meant buying a European A-Class in 2009, bringing it to the United States, and working on a prototype, essentially on spec—and finishing it in only five weeks. In November of that year, a team from Daimler visited Palo Alto and was given a test ride.

"They were blown away," Straubel said. "They saw that it wasn't a science program. For them, touching and seeing was believing. The whole thing changed after that, and we moved to a real development program."

This story puts a spin on the notion of European tech supremacy ("German engineering" is a familiar phrase) that didn't play all that well at Daimler headquarters. Suppliers are supposed to stay in the background, but Tesla had made its point.

Oddly enough, Tesla told a very similar story to its visiting *Wired* reporter. The details were quite similar, but the model plugged in was Daimler's Smart car. Tesla went out and bought a gas version (they had to go to Mexico for that one), converted it in six weeks, and presented it to an astonished Daimler team in January of 2008. Skepticism that such a car was possible quickly dissolved—because there it was, right in front of them. "Let's explore a partnership," said Herbert Kohler, Daimler's head of advanced engineering.

The rest, of course, is history. Tesla has also had a hand as a silent partner in some other European electric car programs, but it managed to keep the publicity lid in place. As long as it can build battery packs with greater ranges than anyone else's, technical partnerships are likely to be a big part of Tesla's business. The company will need outside revenue, because its huge Model S investment led to a loss of $154 million in 2010—Tesla really needs for the new car to succeed. If that doesn't happen, many analysts expect Tesla to be taken over and absorbed as the electric car division of a bigger company—possibly Daimler or Toyota.

During my interview with Musk, I mentioned the fast-moving race to get cars on the road, a big difference from when Tesla had the electric vehicle market essentially to itself for several years. "There's certainly been plenty of press releases," he said, with a wicked gleam. "You can't drive a press release." I mentioned Fisker and he rolled his eyes. "Do you know anybody who's taken a test ride in a Fisker? Weren't they supposed to be in production by the end of [2010]? I find that a little sketchy."

DANISH MODERN: FISKER'S LAUNCH IN STEALTH MODE

I would love to have written a report on Fisker that is as in-depth as my Tesla account, but the company's security cordon made that rather difficult. My access probably wasn't helped by a couple of rude articles I wrote, but not even the most well-behaved journalist got access to a Fisker Karma in 2010, or 2009 for that matter.

But Fisker certainly talked about its car, and showed it—as a static display—at innumerable car shows. There's no arguing with its styling: The Karma looks even more like a high-priced

Italian sports car (with some Jaguar or Aston Martin thrown in) than the Tesla Model S. And Henrik Fisker has the credentials. A list of his greatest hits, in addition to the two cars created for his own Fisker Coachbuild, includes the lovely BMW Z8, the exterior of the BMW Z07 concept car, two Aston Martins (the DB9 and the V8 Vantage), the Lincoln Zephyr concept, and the Ford Shelby GR-1 (designed by a team under his direction).

The backlash against Fisker started when journalists got tired of looking at the Karma and started asking to drive it. The company was steadfast in refusing this, usually pointing out that it had one chance to get the car right and a botched launch would leave the kind of foul smell that's really hard to freshen up.

Born in 1963, Henrik Fisker was a wunderkind in car design. He got interested in style early on, admiring the looks of his father's cars and the family's Bang and Olufsen stereo. When he was 15, a routine excursion in the family's Saab 95 station wagon near Copenhagen turned into a life-changing experience.

"This spaceship shot past us on the road," he told *AutoWeek* in 2009. "That's the way it struck me, as a spaceship, something entirely alien to the road. I know now, because my father told me, that it was a Maserati Merak."[24] An auto obsession was born.

According to a *Design Week* article published in 2001 (when Fisker was a new hire at Ford's London-based Aston Martin division), "His design career took off the day he threw his portfolio into the back of his Alfa Romeo and spontaneously drove to the European home of the Art Center College of Design in Switzerland."[25] Luckily, he was admitted and proved a quick study.

Fisker, who is always impeccably dressed in the upscale European manner and speaks English with an accent that mixes

California surfer with Nordic skier, was hired by BMW's Munich-based advanced design studio in 1989, moving to its US office in 1998. He was still pinching himself. "I kind of like to set myself dreams which other people think are impossible," he told the *MotorWeek* television cameras. "And being a kid from Denmark, just being a designer at BMW was impossible, all the teachers told me."[26]

A year later, Fisker became president of the fast-moving DesignworksUSA, which had begun designing BMWs in 1986. The bestselling X5 SUV was designed there. Fisker's job was to grow the design business globally, a task aided by his fluency in several languages.

There was no better place for Fisker to be. BMW had purchased DesignworksUSA outright in 1995, the same year artist David Hockney created the 14th BMW Art Car, an 850CSi, in the California studio. The sojourn at Designworks, besides exposing him to the archetype of the American entrepreneur, gave Fisker a chance to work on a wide range of products, not just cars. Its current president, Laurenz Schaffer, told me the company has recently designed both local and high-speed trains for Siemens, as well as the interior of a business jet. And it's working on BMW's 2013 i3 Megacity Vehicle, a lightweight electric car (with a carbon-fiber body) designed for crowded urban enclaves.

Fisker stayed at BMW until 2001, when he left for Ford (he held positions in California and London) and the Aston Martin portfolio. "Henrik Fisker is a lucky man," wrote *Design Week* when Fisker had just arrived at Ford. "He has every schoolboy's dream job." Fisker said, perhaps recalling that briefly glimpsed Maserati Merak, "'My work is my hobby.'"

At both Ford and BMW, Fisker was able to work with and learn from celebrated designers. At BMW, a mentor was design chief Chris Bangle, the highly influential American designer whose imposing "Bangle butt" trunk look was reviled by some marque enthusiasts—but sold extremely well. Bangle's most enduring design project is his smallest car, the relaunched Mini, which somehow looked forward while it also incorporated distinctly retro styling cues.

At Ford, a major presence was and is chief creative officer J Mays, like Fisker a product of German design studios (he worked at Audi, BMW, and Volkswagen, where he headed the team that created the New Beetle). Mays's projects include a platoon of striking concept cars, as well as such mainstream fare as the Focus, Fiesta, Mustang, and F-150 truck.

Fisker brought along lessons from both when he and partner Bernhard Koehler struck out on their own with Fisker Coachbuild in 2005. The company, which continues as an arm of Fisker Automotive, produced two cars limited to editions of 150, the two-seat Tramonto convertible (a Mercedes SL55 AMG underneath) and the Latigo CS coupe.

With its designer otherwise occupied, the Tramonto will probably remain an automotive curiosity, but it's striking how closely it predicts what Fisker would do with the Karma, especially in the front-end styling. The Tramonto's lavish interior, which included carbon fiber, milled aluminum, and hand-stitched Italian leather, is also reflected in the Karma.

The Latigo, based on the BMW 6 Series, has distinctly BMW touches, especially in the roofline and rear end (though its "Bangle butt" is subdued). The Latigo doesn't make as strong an impression as the Tramonto, which may be why a low-mileage

2005 model turned up on AutoTrader in 2010 for $80,000, less than half of its original $198,000 list price.

It was partly on the basis of the Latigo and Tramonto that Fisker Coachbuild got an $875,000 contract to design what became the Tesla Model S in early 2007. According to the arbitrator's timeline in the subsequent lawsuit,[27] the work went well until the summer of that year, when Tesla learned that Fisker and Quantum Technologies, the maker of the Q-Drive powertrain, were to work together on developing a plug-in hybrid. Musk reportedly "expressed a concern" that if Fisker's car was to be competitive with Tesla, the design work should be terminated.

Fisker partner Bernhard Koehler told Tesla that there was no conflict because the two cars appealed to different markets—the Fisker car would be an $89,000 plug-in hybrid (the price later went up) and Tesla's a $50,000 all-electric sedan. Tesla bought that argument at the time, partly because the company concluded that the Fisker Karma wasn't going to amount to much. A second design contract was signed.

In October, though, Fisker and Quantum said they had gotten funding for their project and would show the car at the 2008 Detroit auto show. Musk terminated Fisker's contract in early November. The lawsuit followed several months later, in April, with one sticking point being the Motorola RAZR cell phone–based console design incorporated into some versions of the Tesla car and the Fisker Karma. Tesla had also discussed making the Model S a plug-in hybrid (like the Karma), and that too became a factor in the suit. Musk told the *New York Times*, "The styling was substandard compared to what he unveiled for his product. He gave us an inferior work product, and it's obvious why."[28]

Essentially, Musk charged that Fisker had taken on the Tesla project so that he could gain access to trade secrets as he prepared to launch Fisker Automotive with Quantum. Tesla's lawyer said at the time that the naming of the Fisker car was ironic, because Fisker's actions amounted to "very bad karma."

The suit did not go well for Tesla. Arbitrator and retired judge William F. McDonald ruled in November of 2008 that Fisker had not acted in bad faith or attempted to conceal its intentions to build a plug-in hybrid. "The evidence is overwhelming that Fisker did nothing wrong," the judge wrote. Fisker was awarded $1.14 million in court costs and fees, money that may well have been plowed into development of the Karma. The case was over, but the rift between Musk and Fisker remained.

One of the most intriguing aspects of the whole affair was the possibility that the Model S could have been a plug-in hybrid. Tesla is adamant that it is an all-electric company, but adding a small gas engine as a generator could have solved the EV range issue—and eliminated the need for a 90-kilowatt-hour battery to achieve 300 miles.

Tesla spokesman Ricardo Reyes confirmed that hybridization was talked about. "There were preliminary discussions about the hybrid option," he said in an e-mail. "Quickly, we figured out that a hybrid powertrain would add complexity, double the effort but not necessarily improve the product, especially over the long term as battery prices came down. It was also a controversial point as far as keeping our mission pure. People at Tesla believed strongly that the company should build EVs, not another hybrid."[29]

The launch of the Fisker Karma at the Detroit auto show early in 2008 made almost as big a splash as the debut of the

Tesla Roadster had. The car looked like a sexy distillation of everything Henrik Fisker had learned in the big leagues of auto design. The car was to be delivered in the fourth quarter of 2009, with a zero-to-60 time of 5.8 seconds, a top speed of 125 mph, 50 miles of all-electric range, and a base price then estimated at $80,000.

There were innumerable environmental touches. The $106,400 Eco-Chic model (using no animal products) would include a roof-mounted solar panel (providing cooling when the car was parked) and interior wood salvaged from the bottom of Lake Michigan. According to Fairuz Jane Schlecht, Fisker's color and material design manager, the wood (logging industry leftovers in the lake since the late 1800s) was given an attractive patina by its long immersion, "so we didn't have to put chemicals into the environment." Also incorporated into the interior design, she said, was recycled blue jeans used for sound insulation.[30]

Everybody loved it. "The car is stunning," said *US News Rankings and Reviews*.[31] "On styling alone, the $87,900 Fisker Karma seems a steal," said *AutoWeek*. "It looks like an Italian GT design study." *Motor Trend* praised its "traffic-stopping curb appeal."

On a roll right after the auto show, Fisker received a second-round investment of $10 million from Kleiner Perkins Caufield and Byers, a prominent green-themed venture capital firm whose partners include former vice president Al Gore. Henrik Fisker told the press the car was sold out through mid-2010, and that deliveries would begin in November of 2009. But the company would blow that deadline, raising some skepticism among the praise.

I interviewed Fisker, who was wearing a silver-blue tie that set off his light blue shirt, at the Detroit auto show in early 2009.[32] And I asked him who was the ideal customer for the Karma. "Basically I see everybody that can afford an $87,000 car and is in the market to buy a more environmentally correct car," he said. "This is a car that has the performance of a V-8 but fuel economy that's better than a Toyota Prius—so there's really no compromise with this car."

He said that the company had established 22 dealerships (toward a goal of 40) and that more than 1,300 people had ordered the car, migrating from "Lexus, BMW, Mercedes, Land Rover, Jaguar—all the luxury brands." Gas prices were dropping after the $4-a-gallon highs of 2008, so I wanted to know if the equation had changed for buyers. "Not at all," he said. "The environmental issue is still the same. . . . We haven't seen any decline in the orders, and so far we haven't felt any effect."

Asked how the relatively large car managed to eke out 50 miles of all-electric range, Fisker praised the performance of the nanotechnology-enhanced 20-kilowatt-hour lithium-ion battery pack and the good regenerative braking results. "We are easily getting the 50 miles as the base range, and then a total range of about 300 miles," he said.

At the Detroit show that year, Fisker unveiled the second version of the Karma to a dance remix of the Mamas and the Papas' "California Dreamin'." The Sunset convertible featured a retractable hardtop and was fully as stunning as the sedan. "It won't go on the market before 2011," Fisker said. He was right—it didn't.

Fisker terms the car's all-electric range "stealth mode," meaning you can't hear the car coming. But stealth mode is also what Fisker used to keep its work in progress under wraps. Fisker had leaked a video of the car driving around a test track, but that yielded no serious insights.

Even dealers didn't get to drive them. In the summer of 2009, I interviewed Santa Monica, California, superdealer Mike Sullivan (aka LA Car Guy, with sales of 180 Toyota Prius hybrids a month) who told me he was building a state-of-the-art green showroom for the Karma, complete with solar panels. "It's a sensational design, and if it drives like it looks, we're in good shape," he said. Sullivan seemed to be getting a bit impatient: "If they slap a V-8 into it, we could start selling it tomorrow," he said.[33]

Fisker did make announcements, including a pretty big one. In September of 2009, Fisker hit the jackpot: a $528.7 million Department of Energy loan. A DOE official, who asked for anonymity, told me then that investing in Fisker "seemed to be worth the risk of the loan" because it would create "a large number of jobs in America."[34]

The details of the loan are interesting because the majority of the money ($359.36 million) was earmarked not for the luxury Karma (which the company was intending to build in Finland, at a specialty factory that also assembled Porsches), but for its mysterious but more affordable ($40,000) mass-market car, codenamed Project Nina. It was a lot of money for a car that no one had seen.

Federal loans are far more politically successful if they create jobs in the United States, so the DOE was quick to point out that the Karma funding was not for manufacturing in Finland, but for "final testing and certification" of the car at company headquarters in Irvine, California, and its plant in Pontiac, Michigan.

And the Nina was to be built not only in America but also at an iconic former General Motors plant in Delaware. Vice President Joe Biden, just stepped down from his post as a US senator from Delaware, appeared at the shuttered Boxwood plant with Fisker in October of 2009. "While some wanted to write off America's auto industry, we said no," Biden said, in a not-too-veiled reference to the GM and Chrysler bailouts.[35]

I talked to Henrik Fisker for the *New York Times* right after the DOE loan was announced, and he told me that as much as 60 percent of Nina's production run would be exported, especially to Europe. "Designing cars that can appeal to Europeans has been a weakness of the American car industry," he told me. It's not, however, a weakness of Henrik Fisker—who is steeped in European design. Fisker said that the Nina vehicle, scheduled for 2012, would offer "radical" styling that will "open up a completely new segment in terms of its size."

Fisker was then estimating it would be building 75,000 to 100,000 Project Nina cars per year by 2014. Biden asked the audience to "imagine when this factory . . . is making 100,000 plug-in hybrid sedans, coupes and crossovers every single year." The vice president said he'd seen the Nina sedan and that it looked like a "four-door Ferrari."[36] The talk was interesting, because Fisker hadn't said anything about making a crossover, though that would be a sensible secondary use of the Karma platform. (At the 2011 Detroit show, Toyota announced it would be building a station wagon variant of the Prius, and Chevrolet debuted a crossover Volt.)

Perhaps predictably, the Fisker DOE loan set off alarm bells at Fox News. "$529M Gov't Loan Will Help Gore-Backed Co. Build Cars in Finland," read an on-screen headline there. It was as if Finns were heating their saunas with American energy dollars. In a lengthy and heated discussion, a Fox contributor referred to the loan as a "grant." Henrik Fisker professed to be bewildered by it all. "This was a loan, and it has to be paid back with interest," he told me. "There seems to be some confusion between grants and loans. And the money has to be spent in the US—it's a condition of the loan."[37]

MY NONVISIT TO FISKER

Especially after the DOE loan, access to Fisker became harder to get. For me personally, it would get even worse after I wrote that *New York Times* story reporting that the car weighed more than 5,000 pounds.

Weight is an enemy of electric car range. Environmental guru Amory Lovins coined the term Hypercar in the mid-1990s to describe a theoretical ultra-lightweight (weighing as little as 1,000 pounds), aerodynamic vehicle made of composite materials such as carbon fiber. Michael Brylawski, a veteran of Lovins's Hypercar project at the Rocky Mountain Institute but now an executive at Bright Automotive, told me, "Roughly two-thirds of the factors that determine platform efficiency are weight dependent. . . . Typically, the lighter you make the vehicle, the smaller you can make the battery pack for the same amount of range."[38] So reducing weight was a challenge for Fisker, as it also was for Tesla's Model S.

By this time, it was quite apparent that the Fisker Karma was not going to appear in 2009, or 2010 either. The Karma went on a "retail tour" to the dealerships in the spring of 2010, but still nobody got to drive it. "It's a chance to touch and feel the car," spokesman Russell Datz told me at the time. "A lot of our depositors have never seen the car in the flesh."[39]

Fisker was very quiet, but I was optimistic when I called spokesman Datz about a visit to the Irvine headquarters in August of 2010, on the same trip that included my visit to Tesla in Palo Alto. He said I could come, but Henrik was going to be away and access would be limited. I went anyway.[40]

Irvine presented itself as back-to-back office parks, dotted with Starbucks and delis to feed the troops. I had visited on a smoggy day, and it was sticky as I pulled into the parking lot that had to be the right one—there was, after all, a Maserati in it.

Auto companies are usually happy to show me around, but at Fisker I got parked in the lobby and stayed there. The foyer was considerably enlivened by the presence of a Fisker Sunset, its top down. I briefly met Marti Eulberg, vice president of global sales and marketing, but she was "slammed" with meetings so it was a quick hello in the corridor. I tried to set up an interview with her about Fisker's marketing plans, but it never happened. In my experience, this kind of stonewalling is unusual: More commonly, EV companies have brought out everybody but the janitor to talk with me. Instead, I went out to lunch with Datz at a nearby Whole Foods.

"Everything is going great," Datz said. The challenge, he admitted, is making all the car's systems—the internal-combustion engine, the regenerative brakes, the nanotechnology-engineered battery pack sourced from A123—work smoothly together and fit into the allotted space. "A123 is building to our specs," Datz said. "They've delivered near-to-final packs." A123 is actually Fisker's second battery supplier. It also had a seemingly settled relationship with Indiana's Ener1 but switched late in the process when A123 became an investor.

Fisker was still projecting worldwide sales of up to 15,000 in 2011, even though the car wasn't scheduled until March of that year. Henrik Fisker himself was also talking big numbers. A few months before my visit, he told *Wired*, "We'll be producing 100,000 [Nina cars] a year by 2013. And we'll have six models for sale by 2016."[41]

Asked what cars he expects to compete with, Datz points to the Porsche Panamera (that company's first four-door sedan). "[Fisker vehicles] will be seen as the responsible alternative," he said. The Panamera, of course, is able to ride on Porsche's long history of engineering excellence and considerable prestige. It's very similar in price ($89,800 in rear-wheel-drive form) and horsepower (400 to Fisker's 403), but green, it's not.

Perhaps surprisingly, Datz says a lot of Fisker customers will be replacing not a Porsche or Mercedes, but a Toyota Prius. The company's research, he said, shows that many Prius buyers could actually afford something far more expensive, but chose the Prius for its unbeatable green aspects. "It was the only thing available to them," he said. The Karma gives them another option.

I asked Datz why the company had been so secretive, and he gave me the company line about not wanting to blow its one shot at a good first impression. That's an understandable position, but it ensured a cliffhanger finish. At the end of 2010, Fisker quietly raised the price of the car (before a $7,500 federal tax credit) to $95,900. Opt for an "Eco-Chic" model, and the price was now $108,900.

I imagined a scene just beyond the bland California waiting

room in which I was sitting: Engineers were frantically shoe-horning systems into the Karma, working around the clock, as Eulberg and her troops mainlined coffee trying to finish the marketing materials. Maybe that's all wrong, but I had no other image to counter it.

A lot of companies fail to deliver their cars on time—with so many different systems, so much regulation, and increasingly tough quality expectations, it's inevitable. But Henrik Fisker has been outspoken about carmakers' slow progress and his intention to speed things up a bit. After assuring a *MotorWeek* interviewer that he'd have the Karma out by the end of 2009 ("We're ready, and we're going to do it"), he went on to talk about a better way of doing things. "The car industry seems most ripe for change," he said, "and really change not only in terms of how you develop and design a vehicle, but also the entire business model. . . . We want to . . . carve out a niche where we are about beautiful, emotional, exciting green cars."[42]

The reality is that humility helps in the car business. It's a tough racket. "It is very hard to be a full-line automaker," Britta Gross, a General Motors executive in the group tasked with bringing out the Chevrolet Volt (which did meet its deadlines), told me, "I came from aerospace, and the auto business is much more complex than rocket science—there are so many moving parts and variables, rapidly developing technology, consumer fashion trends, as well as regulation up the kazoo."[43]

Despite all the delays, the Fisker Karma finally did come out. I didn't get behind the wheel, alas, but others did. Respected technical writer Dennis Simanaitis got a turn around a California racetrack for *Road & Track*, and he described the Karma as lithe, extremely well balanced, and nimbler than either a BMW 7 Series or a Porsche Panamera. And yet he noted some behavioral short-comings, including a "gravelly roughness" and stray rattles, which could be attributed to the car's prototype status. Fisker was still working on the car at that point, and the car Simanaitis drove was a preproduction model.

In the summer of 2011, the Karma officially started production, though at a trickle at first, and there would be further delays. Fisker spokesman Roger Ormisher told me that the company's primary goal was to get quality in place.[44] The very first cars went to long-suffering dealers, some of whom had been waiting two years or more. Actor Leonardo DiCaprio got the first customer car. Production of the Karma didn't reach the full 1,500 a month until much later. Meanwhile, design work on Project Nina was proceeding.

Fisker's media package for the Karma revealed every last detail down to the wing wood substrate made with recyclable postcon-sumer pine fiber. Soy-based bio filters? Check. The one thing it didn't reveal was the car's weight, which Ormisher said might cause some people who hadn't yet driven the car to worry about the performance. "We're not trying to pull the wool over people's eyes; we just don't want them to prejudge the car," he said. "When they get behind the wheel, that will validate all of our work."

If the Karma meets expectations, nobody will worry about how much it weighs. The fact is, both Fisker and Tesla make exciting green cars. That much they agree on, and we can second it. As they surmount their growing pains, there's room in the new, environmentally conscious marketplace for both of them.

CHAPTER TWO

BUILDING THE BATTERIES

*Increased demand is critical to reducing costs and making EV
batteries affordable.*

—MARK WAGNER, JOHNSON CONTROLS

LET'S CONSIDER THE LAYOUT of the electric car. It's fairly
simple, since the wheels turn because the electric motor gets
power from a battery pack, which is under the command of a
controller (think of it as a really big dimmer switch) that supplies
electricity when you put your foot on the accelerator. The controller and motor are pretty robust, and likely to outlast many of the
parts in a typical internal-combustion engine. It's enough to make
you worry about the future of the auto parts business.

But the battery pack is something else again, and nothing if not
vulnerable. Since we don't have much recent experience with EVs
on the road, we lack a useful paper trail on battery longevity in the
wild. It's the battery pack that determines range, and the battery
pack that could need replacing a few years down the road. And it's
also the main reason electric cars carry a significant price premium.

That fact helps explain why battery companies have become the rock stars of the EV business. Most companies building electric cars, whether start-ups or mainstream players, contract out the packs or partner with their makers in joint operating agreements. It's not the auto industry's core competence. Even Tesla, whose expertise in batteries has earned it lucrative contracts with other carmakers to build prototypes and supply their EV programs, outsources its Roadster battery cells (from Panasonic).

With all that in mind, we're seeing the emergence of major battery companies with auto partners, including A123 Systems (Fisker), Ener1 (Think, Volvo), Johnson Controls-Saft (BMW, Mercedes, Ford), SB LiMotive (also BMW), Valence (Smith Electric Vehicles, Brammo), LG Chem (General Motors), NEC (Nissan), and many more. Add to that list the name Boston-Power.

Christina Lampe-Önnerud is a brisk and energetic Swede who carries the fresh air of her native country around with her. If you were to see her on stage singing with her a cappella choir, Stardust Show Chorus, you probably wouldn't peg her as an electric car battery entrepreneur. But she's that and more: She's the executive chairman of the fast-moving Massachusetts-based Boston-Power, which is plugging in not only Hewlett-Packard laptops but also Saab EVs.

Lampe-Önnerud is a splash of color among the men in dark suits, but the EV battery field is getting increasingly crowded as the cars hit the road, and many of the players have their origins far away from gritty auto factories. Some are more accustomed to making lithium-ion (Li-ion) batteries for cell phones and computers, so this new working environment—a moving target, subject to winter's chill, road salt, accident damage, and more—is a considerable challenge.

If you think electric cars are too expensive, point a finger of blame at the batteries. Modern electric cars live and (when the power runs out) die by their battery packs. Unlike gas cars that can be jump-started when they stall, EVs with dead batteries need a nice, long charge before they're back in the game. It's an understatement to say that this is a challenge.

A battery pack is a collection of individual cells housed in a flat box. It's often located under the car, where it's out of the way, to increase cargo space, help lower the center of gravity, and ease servicing. It's also the ideal location for battery switching, a concept for long-range EV travel advocated by the company Better Place. (Instead of charging depleted batteries, the company wants to switch out the packs with fresh ones at automated stations.)

Surveys show that Americans have unreasonable expectations of cars powered by batteries. The unvarnished truth is that, with today's batteries, the limitations of most of their packs mean 100 miles of range under ideal conditions. Add in bad weather (especially cold) and that range drops. Play the radio, run the heater or the air conditioner, and the range also drops. Gas cars and plug-in hybrids generate electricity as they drive, but everything you do in an EV comes out of the battery pack.

Virtually all the EVs on the market, and those slated to appear, use Li-ion chemistry because the packs are much lighter than the alternatives, have high energy density, and can hold their charges over long periods. They also will routinely handle thousands of charge/discharge cycles before needing replacement. Li-ion does have some drawbacks, including volatility at high temperatures.

But Li-ion battery packs are not only umbilically connected to their charge ports but also very expensive. The Nissan Leaf's 24-kilowatt-hour pack is variously reported to cost the company $9,500 ($375 per kilowatt-hour)[1] and $18,000 (less than $750 per kilowatt-hour).[2] Neither one is terrible, because an estimate by PriceWaterhouse Coopers put electric car batteries at about $1,000 for each kilowatt-hour installed on the car.[3] That would mean a $24,000 pack.

If the first estimate is correct, then maybe the battery-only Leaf can be a profitable enterprise for Nissan at $32,780. If it's $18,000, it's more than half the price of the car and profitability seems unlikely until battery prices drop. Brian Carolin, the sales and marketing chief for Nissan in the United States, acknowledged that Nissan expects to lose money on the Leaf, but he said that it could become profitable in about 2013,[4] which is when the company plans to switch both battery production and Leaf assembly to Tennessee from Japan.

The Chevy Volt has a 16-kilowatt-hour pack (of which 10.4 kilowatt hours are actually used). Its battery cost is reportedly coming in at $600 per kilowatt-hour, which would put the relatively small pack at $9,600. And that's certainly one of several factors in the Volt's high production costs.

According to a 2010 MIT report,[5] approximately 80 percent of the drive system cost in a plug-in hybrid with 40 miles of all-electric range is the batteries, with the rest being the electric motor, the inverter, the power control unit, and the generator.

"The battery is the most expensive component in an electric vehicle," the report said.

Certainly, battery costs are coming down, along with other improvements. The US Advanced Battery Consortium would like to reach a cost of $400 per kilowatt-hour by 2015,[6] which would be a huge help to the industry. It's a really tall order, though.

I talked to a host of battery chieftains in early 2011 about what to expect from the industry, and all danced around prospects for rapid cost reduction. Andy Chu, the director of the automotive product line at Boston-based A123 Systems (which makes the nanotech-enabled pack in the Fisker Karma), said that no huge technological breakthroughs are on the horizon. "Everyone wants to know about the next big thing, but lithium-ion will be the dominant technology for the next decade," he said, calling for more research and development efforts to move the industry forward.

Chu defends the state of the art in EV batteries, pointing out that today's packs have 10 times the cycle life of the average cell phone battery. And he addressed one of the worries most often brought up by consumers contemplating a green car purchase: Won't that expensive battery pack end up in a landfill, causing pollution?

His answer: Why would you throw out a pack that was still valuable, with a secondary buyer ready and willing to help amortize the high initial investment? "There will still be a lot of life left in battery packs after their useful life in cars is over," Chu said. Once a pack meant for 100-mile range is delivering only 70 or 80 miles, it can be repurposed, for instance by utilities, as backup power storage. When power plants produce electricity, they use it or lose it, but batteries can store electricity generated by, say, solar panels during the day or wind turbines at night (when they're at peak efficiency).

A 2010 report from the National Renewable Energy Laboratory concluded that end-of-life EV packs "may still have reasonable energy capabilities for other applications such as stationary use." The hurdles to overcome, the report said, are possible higher degradation rates in secondary uses, the high cost of pack refurbishment and low cost of alternatives, and the perception that used batteries are inferior.[7]

Despite these issues, Nissan is working with Sumitomo Electric Industries to develop a business plan for used car batteries, and Enerdel (which supplies Volvo) has another Japanese partner, Itochu, working on using end-of-life packs as energy storage in apartment buildings. Phil Murtaugh, a General Motors veteran hired in early 2011 to head start-up EV company Coda Automotive, said that he expects the company's grid power storage business to become as important as its ongoing effort to sell Coda sedans. Better Place is also evaluating secondary pack uses.

An issue for secondary uses will be determining how much that pack is then worth—do automakers or utilities absorb most of the battery's high costs? And it's not easy to project how long they will last for their primary use, though many in the auto industry were surprised when early Toyota Prius nickel–metal hydride batteries were still going strong after a quarter million miles—far longer than predicted.

Charles Gassenheimer, the CEO and chairman of Indiana-based Ener1 (parent company of EnerDel), said the game changed when, after decades of test programs and lab experiments, advanced battery cars finally hit the road at the end of 2010. "It's a lot easier to measure the development and performance of battery packs on an actual car than it is in the lab," he said. "An apt comparison would be trying to evaluate a microchip without a computer to put it in."

The field tests are trickling in. Gassenheimer's batteries are in Think City two-seat EVs, and he said a Norwegian cabbie driving one praised the lack of engine noise and vibration. "He used to get headaches at the end of the day, but now he's much more rested and his job is easier," Gassenheimer said.

Mark Wagner, vice president of government relations at battery giant Johnson Controls (which makes everything from the Sears DieHard in your Oldsmobile to the lithium-ion pack in the Ford C-Max plug-in hybrid), says the industry is struggling to get costs down. "We're tackling that from a lot of different angles," he said. "We're looking to cut the cost of making cells, and reducing the amount of scrap involved in making packs. Big goals are reducing the energy intensity of the manufacturing process and localizing our supply chain. When it comes to battery systems, we're trying to reduce the number of parts and the complexity of the system."

Another thing that will bring battery costs down, Wagner said, is scale—the more packs produced by Johnson Controls (which recently opened a big EV battery facility in Holland, Michigan), the cheaper they become. "Increased demand is critical to reducing costs and making EV batteries affordable," he said.

That's the rub, of course. Nobody knows what EV demand will be in the next few years, so nobody really knows how much a higher battery production scale will bring costs down. But high battery costs are a real drag on the goal all the players share with their automaker partners—getting more cars on the road.

ON THE GROUND: CHRISTINA BUILDS A BETTER BATTERY

I could cite dry financial analyses all day, but I'm sure you'd rather take a field trip to visit Christina Lampe-Önnerud at Boston-Power.

The company, which has 110 employees in the United States, occupies modernist offices on a bucolic campus in Westborough, Massachusetts, near Boston. The color green dominates, as does Lampe-Önnerud's Nordic aesthetic—even the office chairs look like Danish modern.

Lampe-Önnerud doesn't walk into a room—she bursts into it, radiating charm and shouldering a cell phone to her ear. It's not easy getting time on her crowded schedule, because she's apt to have back-to-back meetings and a plane waiting to take her to Stockholm.

Boston-Power makes batteries far away from Boston—it currently has manufacturing operations and 350 employees in Taiwan. Like every American battery company, Boston-Power has angled for a Department of Energy grant that would allow it to build its packs in the United States instead of Asia. Minus the government support (like the nearly $300 million Johnson Controls got to build its factory in Michigan), the economics virtually demand the much cheaper Asian capacity. California-based Coda Automotive went so far as to start a joint-venture battery business in China with partner Lishen.

Lampe-Önnerud sat down across from me, put her cell phone

down and gave me the dazzling smile that she also shines on rooms full of potential investors and swing music audiences.

"Scandinavian countries have more awareness of what it means to be green," she told me. "I was born and raised in Sweden, where my father"—who clearly was a mentor and model for her—"was very successful in business with high-energy power transmission." Wolfgang Lampe encouraged her to stick with the science that fascinated her as a child—at 12 she was conducting experiments in the basement.

She had other options, including a career as an opera singer—and medicine, too. Lampe-Önnerud was accepted into a Swedish medical school, but chose instead to study chemistry at Uppsala University, including a year abroad at Elmira College in New York (she was voted Miss Elmira).[8] Chemistry took hold and Lampe-Önnerud burrowed deep into battery technology, completing her doctorate in Sweden (it was 1995) on cathode materials for lithium-polymer batteries—a type now going into EVs.

Lampe-Önnerud got married to her high school sweetheart, fellow chemist and jazz enthusiast Per Önnerud, and the two relocated to Boston for postdoctoral work at MIT. Today, his trumpet playing complements her singing, and they work together, too—he's Boston-Power's chief technology officer.

After leaving academia, Lampe-Önnerud held posts at both Bellcore (as director of energy storage) and Arthur D. Little (as a partner concentrating on the battery market). Boston-Power was created in late-night kitchen table sessions at the end of 2004. Its first target: a better laptop battery in a compact rectangular shape.

The benefit of Boston-Power's Li-ion computer battery design was soon obvious—long life. As I've pointed out, most cells are either cylinders or flat prismatic plates. Boston-Power's design is like a combination of the two—a prismatic cylinder that's been squashed flat, if you will, with gently curved sides and with aluminum replacing carbon steel for reduced weight. The design reduces imbalances between cells in a pack, and it reduces fire risk, too.

The result is faster charging (30 minutes to 80 percent full) and a battery guaranteed to last three years at 80 percent of its original power (or 1,000 charge cycles). In keeping with Lampe-Önnerud's musical background, the pack is called Sonata.

Back in the Westborough office, Lampe-Önnerud decided to give me a walking tour. Unlike many Swedes, she is an exuberant presence, making frequent use of the word "fun," as in "Here's a fun laboratory." I can't imagine she's a big Ingmar Bergman fan.

Lampe-Önnerud stopped me in front of an HP laptop that uses her battery. There was an Asus computer too, but she didn't want to talk about that one yet. Soon after my visit, however, Boston-Power announced contracts with Asus to complement its existing alliance with HP, which dates to 2005. "We sat in a meeting with HP for two hours, and they were very quiet," she said. "We thought it had not gone so well, but then they told us that if we could deliver on the specs we promised it would revolutionize the industry."

The Sonata debuted as HP's Enviro Series in 2009 and was also made available as a replacement pack for other HP laptops. It was integrated into Asus B Series laptops the following year. It's hard for a smaller company like Boston-Power to supply enough laptop batteries to HP, Asus, and others because they produce computers in such large quantities. That was a big motivator for the company to expand with a second factory in China, west of Shanghai. The new Chinese production will give the company the ability to produce a gigawatt-hour of batteries annually, Lampe-Önnerud said.

Long-lived laptops are great, but I was there to talk about cars. Boston-Power was initially reluctant to branch out into auto batteries, simply because they're so expensive to make. "When we first looked at producing car batteries in 2005, it was totally cost prohibitive," she said. "Now it looks better, but if high pack costs mean the car will be sold for $40,000, we have to look for ways to get it down to $20,000."

We hopped into Lampe-Önnerud's car and headed over to a nearby warehouse, where workers were tidying up a Ford Escape Hybrid emblazoned with Boston-Power stickers. "We took out the existing battery in this Ford and put our own in," she told me. "With the same-sized pack, we were able to increase energy density 700 percent." The standard Escape can travel a mile or so on battery power alone, but with Boston-Power's conversion it has 43 miles of electric range.

The battery cells in the Escape were the first off the company's production line in Taiwan. The auto packs are not radically different from the computer batteries. It was Tesla Motors, of course, that introduced the public to the concept of production cars powered by thousands of laptop cells. "I love Tesla's story," Lampe-Önnerud told me. "It shows we can make small, highly efficient battery packs using consumer-proven electronics. The cells are like Legos—they're very scalable." She *would* mention Legos, but they're Danish, not Swedish.

Scalability means that Boston-Power cells could power larger vehicles, including delivery trucks, or smaller ones such as Asian-made electric scooters. I saw one of those sitting in a corner at the company's Massachusetts headquarters, and it's headed for the market in Europe. But Boston-Power is also after bigger game—it's now providing battery packs for Chinese cars.

Lampe-Önnerud told me that she was startled by how quickly Chinese companies expected her to ramp up production. "They are very eager to deploy electric cars," she said. "We did the prototype of a new design in just six months. It's inspiring."

One of the reasons Lampe-Önnerud is earning frequent-flier miles is that she's constantly on the road, negotiating with companies, including carmakers, that want longer-lasting cells. Build a better battery and the world will find you, if you don't find it first. Things got so intense for Lampe-Önnerud as she tried to run the company while traveling for meetings that in early 2011 she hired a CEO, Exide veteran Keith Schmid, to run the company internally while she's its charismatic public face. If things ease up a bit, maybe she can find some time to rehearse with the Stardust Show Chorus.

SAAB STORY: SWINGING THE ELECTRIC WAGON

If the Escape was a demonstrator for what Boston-Power could do for automakers, it worked. The car battery pack (named Swing as part of the musical series) soon had a customer—and it was Swedish, too. Saab, which went through a near-death experience as it was severed from General Motors, managed to survive with new Scandinavian owners. The company continued to have serious financial problems and production stoppages through early 2011 as it sought new funding from Chinese backers. Creditors lined up, but the one thing not in doubt is that Saab wants to be in the EV business.

Saab ownership was transferred to Spyker Cars in February of 2010, creating Saab Spyker Cars. It's an unusual arrangement because Spyker is a tiny enterprise, making only about 50 very expensive supercars annually, that took over a mainstream brand with sales of 32,000 worldwide in 2010. As it happens, I met with Saab's new owners a few months after the takeover in a boardroom at the *New York Times.* As I wrote then, "General Motors' sale of Saab to Spyker Cars, a small sports car company, was a first-class cliffhanger, and it wasn't clear until the very last minute that the deal would go through. But Spyker made a final $24 million payment for the Swedish automaker [in July 2010], and now Saab can turn its attention to producing cars and, it hopes, making a profit."[9]

We talked about the forthcoming EV, too. Jan Åke Jonsson, then Saab's CEO, told me, "On the electric side, we have signed an agreement with Boston-Power to put its battery packs into 70 electric cars in 2011. We see it as a great opportunity." Boston will always be on Saab's radar, because the company, whose American headquarters was once located in Connecticut, has New England roots, and also because the region sells a lot of Saabs.

Saab chairman Victor Muller added that an early electric test car was a convertible. "It has total torque. It's very exciting, and I would know." Indeed he would. The Spyker C8 Spyder ($288,000) is capable of zero to 60 in 4.5 seconds and able to reach 187 mph. Of course, it gets 13 mpg around town and 18 on the highway, so its green credentials are lacking.

In late 2009, Saab and its partners announced that they'd received $12 million from a Swedish Energy Agency grant to pursue electric cars—the kind of funding many American companies were seeking from their own government. It wasn't a huge amount of money, but it was enough to fund a test program with Boston-Power and three Swedish companies.

Saab, a Swedish institution dating to 1937 that frequently boasts of its background in the aviation industry, announced its very first EV, the 9-3 ePower, in the fall of 2010 at the Paris Motor Show. The car is a station wagon (based on the 9-3 Sport-Combi), making it the only EV in that form. Performance from the 181-horsepower UQM Technologies electric motor is not bad—zero to 62 mph in 8.5 seconds, and a top speed of 93 mph. The range of 124 miles from the 35.5 kilowatt-hour pack is very good indeed, and as Saab says, it "pushes out the boundaries for current EV performance" thanks to "battery cells which have an energy storage density substantially greater than the best currently used in EV applications." Recharge time is three to six hours with 240-volt AC, and 30 minutes to an 80 percent charge with approximately 480-volt DC.

Swedish families are getting behind the wheel of the ePower in a test program that extends through 2012. Cold Swedish winters will give Saab a chance to test Boston-Power's claim that the air-cooled battery pack will perform without a hitch at temperatures of –22°F. Saab hasn't made a commitment to actually produce an electric car, but Jonsson said that Saab "is determined to be represented in this important, growing segment."

Lampe-Önnerud said her mission from Saab was to produce a reliable battery with long life, high energy density, and quick recharge times, as well as the ability to take DC fast charging. She's confident that Boston-Power will eventually get costs down below $500 a kilowatt-hour.

Lampe-Önnerud was juggling her growing laptop business and the Saab launch, so that meant a lot of late meetings, 80-hour weeks, and frantic dashes to catch airplanes to Sweden and Davos, Switzerland, where she addressed the World Economic Forum on "The Next Wave of Green." She came back enthused. "The whole World Economic Forum crowd has gone from being skeptical about electric transport to completely embracing the concept," she said. "They used to say that green cars would be hard to implement, but you don't hear that anymore." The policy leaders gathered around a Nissan Leaf, and were impressed.

Lampe-Önnerud promised me that at least a few of the new Saab electric cars will come to the United States and I would be among the first to get a test ride. That, of course, depends on Saab surviving as a carmaker, a continuing worry that put one more thing on Lampe-Önnerud's plate. "I love the idea of an all-electric car," she told me. "I can charge at home or at work. The acceleration is instant, so it's environmentally friendly fun." "Fun"—there's that word again.

LEAD-ACID: THE BUDGET CHOICE

Consider the Detroit Electric Model 47 of 1914. Although you might be tempted to think of the car as primitive, it did a lot of the same things today's EVs do. Its pack consisted of 14 six-volt lead-acid batteries, and according to the company it could travel 65 to 85 miles on a single charge. For an additional $600 (a fortune at the time) buyers could request Thomas Edison's nickel-steel batteries—with a 100-mile range. The record for the Detroit Electric was 211 miles on a single charge.

Thanks to modern technology, the modern EV has some advantages over the Detroit Electric. The former routinely reaches 100 mph, while the latter was running out of steam at 20. And unlike today's cars, which can be controlled by cell phones and provide their owners with a wealth of data, the Detroit Electric offered only minimal information—you had to find your own charging stations. One lever controlled steering and the other speed, and both could be folded out of the way, easing entry to and exit from what amounted to a plush living room on wheels.

Lead-acid battery technology is fully mature now, and it's still the cheapest option for hobbyists who want a low-cost do-it-yourself EV conversion. And a lot of people are going that route and proving you can still do electric cars on a budget.

Connecticut resident James Boncek built his own electric car, using as a base the tired 1993 Toyota Tercel with 150,000 miles on it that he bought for $100 in 2004.[10] Armed with a degree from the New England Technical Institute, he installed 10 Deka lead-acid batteries in the trunk and two under the hood.

Total outlay: $10,000. "The car has a great chassis and a new heart, so it'll go for another 200,000 miles," said Boncek, a theater building manager. "It's a complete recycle." The Tercel can travel 50 miles on a charge (which takes six to eight hours) and reach 70 mph.

Portland, Oregon, engineer Bryce Nash even built his own hybrid in what was known as Project: Parts Bin. He started with another junkyard candidate: a worn-out 1988 plastic-bodied Pontiac Fiero. He left the car's V-6 engine in place, but managed to also shoehorn in the drivetrain from a parted-out electric Chevrolet S-10 pickup truck of 1990s vintage.

Nash couldn't afford fancy computer controls to switch between gas and electric power, so he simply put in two accelerator pedals, one for each form of power. He entered his hybrid in the 2009 Grassroots Motorsports Challenge.[11] The challenge consists of building the car for no more than the current year in dollars, so the 2009 limit was $2,009. No problem: Nash spent only $1,600. The Fiero came in 20th overall and won the Best Engineering award.

"It's a terrific car, with terrific packaging and really works as a whole assembly," Tom Heath of *Grassroots Motorsports* magazine told me. "For a first-year entry from a guy with no electrical engineering background, it was really impressive. And working with junkyard parts really helped: To duplicate that car from scratch would have cost many thousands of dollars."

One downside of these garage-built conversions with lead-acid batteries is that even with regular charging, the packs need to be replaced fairly often. But some companies, including Amp Electric Vehicles, are now exploring high-volume conversions with lithium batteries.

LITHIUM-ION: THE STANDARD

The interim technology between venerable lead-acid and the current Li-ion standard was nickel–metal hydride (NiMH), the cell chemistry developed by Stan Ovshinsky in 1994. Ovshinsky's Energy Conversion Devices had a joint venture with General Motors that resulted in NiMH Ovonics battery packs becoming available on later editions of the GM EV1 electric car, and they became the de facto pack for hybrid cars such as the

Toyota Prius and the Honda Civic Hybrid. But now even hybrids are switching to Li-ion.

Li-ion batteries are relatively recent entries in the field, though (in an amazing parallel to fuel cells) they have early 19th-century roots. The principle of the fuel cell was first demonstrated by British barrister and amateur scientist Sir William Robert Grove in 1839. But 22 years earlier, in 1817, Swedish mineralogist Johann Arfvedson (also a lawyer!) had first identified the lithium ion in ore from an iron mine. He named it for the Greek word *lithos*, meaning "stone." The element was isolated by other scientists the following year.

The use of lithium in treating patients with bipolar disorder was pioneered by Australian psychiatrist John Cade, who had been held as a prisoner of war by the Japanese during World War II. His experiences in the notorious Changi POW camp was said to have stimulated his interest in treating those with mental disorders. Testing the theory that mania was caused by a buildup of urea in the body, Cade injected guinea pigs with highly soluble lithium urate, thinking that it would increase their agitation. Instead, it calmed them down, and he was able to determine that lithium was the responsible agent. This inexpensive and natural mineral salt became the first effective treatment for mental illness.[12]

Cade first published his findings in 1949, but lithium wasn't approved as a prescription medication in the United States until 1970. Lithium batteries took a while to get adopted, too, because of the mineral's volatility in response to temperature changes. The first lithium-ion batteries, developed in the 1970s and 1980s, were not rechargeable for that reason. Significant cathode research by John Goodenough of the University of Texas at Austin, who is considered the father of the rechargeable Li-ion battery," solved the volatility problem to the point that Sony was able to introduce a commercial product in 1991.

These batteries led to laptops that could last longer between recharges, but Li-ion wasn't out of the woods. Sony had commercialized Li-ion computer batteries, and it was Sony that also learned the hard way about "thermal runaway" (sometimes caused by failure or puncturing of the separator that keeps the positive and negative electrodes apart). Li-ion batteries can combust or explode at high temperatures, and some laptops did just that. In 2006, Sony recalled 340,000 Li-ion computer batteries (used in Sony, Toshiba, Gateway, and Fujitsu laptops) after 16 reports of overheating, which caused minor property damage and two burns.[13] Dell recalled Li-ion batteries, too.

Getting a less-dangerous form of Li-ion into cars took a while. Volvo was a pioneer because its 3CC electric concept car of 2004 used cylindrical laptop-sized Li-ion batteries—3,000 of them, to be exact—predicting the future design of cars like the Tesla Roadster. The fire risk posed by Li-ion was one major reason battery makers chose to work with small cells that had been proven safe in computer applications.

The Toyota Vitz CVT[4] of 2005, a technological extravaganza, was the first production car with Li-ion batteries, but it was a small pack used to support the Japanese-market vehicle's stop-start system.

By 2006, Hybridcars.com was reporting that "dozens of smaller companies are racing toward a lithium payday."[14] Among these were A123 Systems, which in late 2005 unveiled an automotive Li-ion pack developed with Department of Energy funding, and Valence Technology, which started selling its Gen 1 lithium iron magnesium phosphate batteries in 2005.

Valence batteries went into EnergyCS's second plug-in hybrid conversion of a Toyota Prius in 2005, and dozens of other cars were converted. Valence batteries are now going into Smith Electric Vehicles, which was an early leader in all-electric delivery vehicles (its British "milk floats" go back more than 90 years) that is now US owned and delivering box trucks to customers such as Frito-Lay, Staples, Coca-Cola, AT&T, and Pacific Gas and Electric Company.

I didn't realize I was doing something historic when, in September of 2006, I traveled to the Solaire, an ultragreen apartment complex at the southern tip of Manhattan, to attend the unveiling of the then-DaimlerChrysler plug-in hybrid Sprinter van.[15] This not only was the first plug-in hybrid I'd ever seen from a major automaker, but also featured a hefty 350-pound, 14-kilowatt-hour Li-ion battery pack mounted under its floor. That's essentially the layout on commercial electric cars, but it would be four years before any of those would reach the market.

Quite a crowd had gathered at the Solaire because the Sprinter project was supported by the New York Power Authority and the Electric Power Research Institute (EPRI), and teams from both were on hand. Possibly because my name tag said *New York Times*, I was given the opportunity to become the first journalist to drive the Sprinter in the United States. With all of those people looking on, I twisted the key—and nothing at all happened.

I thought I'd done something wrong, but a squad of German engineers with laptops couldn't get the Sprinter going, either. It was an embarrassing end to the day. The engineers finally located a fault with the motor controller after all the dignitaries had left, but it was too late for a test drive. Instead, I had a rendezvous with the van in White Plains, New York, a few days later. This time it was running.

The Sprinter was obviously a work in progress. The 2.3-liter gasoline engine was gutless, and it was hard work getting the van up hills. The transition from electric to gas was abrupt. I was fascinated by the fact that I was getting much better performance when in electric-only mode. With the Li-ion batteries (nickel–metal hydride cells were also tested), the Sprinter had 20 miles of electric range. Clearly, this unassuming van was a harbinger of things to come.

It took two years for Li-ion to make it into a production car, the Tesla Roadster, as the sole source of power. The first car was delivered to CEO Elon Musk in February of 2008. The Roadster uses 6,800 cylindrical 18650 Li-ion batteries made by Panasonic, which is a pioneer in the EV field (though largely behind the scenes as a supplier). Panasonic formed a joint venture with Toyota, Panasonic EV Energy Company, in 1996 and provided the prismatic NiMH cells for the Toyota RAV4 EV and the GM EV1 (both of which would be short-lived on the American market). The company supplied batteries for Honda hybrids, too.

The Tesla Roadster's pack, at 53 kilowatt-hours, is bigger than any of its rivals, and that explains its 245 miles of range on a charge (347.2 miles on a record run in California). The pack, with its cells arranged in 11 battery modules, can deliver 200 kilowatts of usable power, and that, combined with its 248-horsepower electric motor, explains the car's 3.9-second zero-to-60 time. The pack is also a heavyweight at about 1,000 pounds, which is one reason the rest of the car had to be kept very light.

According to Tesla, the company purposely went with the AA-sized batteries because each cell contains such a small amount of energy that a failure would not be catastrophic. The pack also includes a liquid cooling system (using a fifty-fifty mix of water and glycol) that guards against overheating. Tesla put videos of its crash tests online to show that a combination of electronic controls and mechanical systems made its lithium battery systems safe.

Tesla did the world a favor by ensuring that Li-ion batteries were practical for electric cars, and its pioneering car was soon followed by many others that use the same basic formula. Many add phosphate to the mix to reduce the fire risk, trading energy for safety. Li-ion is settling in as the technology of choice, with no significant rivals on the immediate horizon.

Not that others aren't trying. The University of Dayton Research Institute announced in late 2009 that it had made a "quantum leap in energy storage technology" with solid-state, rechargeable lithium-air batteries. The big potential with lithium-air is 5 to 10 times the energy storage. But the solid-state lithium air batteries also use no liquid electrolyte, and its proponents claim that this eliminates the fire risk with Li-ion. "We've replaced the liquid electrolyte with a solid electrolyte that works just as well, but is far safer," claimed Binod Kumar, a research engineer in Dayton.[16]

The university said it had built three dozen lithium-air batteries, and added that it was aiming for an unheard-of 4,000-cycle life. But it's the very early days of lithium-air development, and it's nobody's idea of a near-term technology. Argonne National Laboratories, a key advancer of Li-ion technology, is also committed to researching lithium-air, and the lab's director, Eric Isaacs, offered a caveat. "The obstacles to lithium-air batteries becoming a viable technology are formidable and will require innovations in materials science, chemistry and engineering," he said.[17]

IBM is also working on lithium-air as part of its Battery 500 Project at the Almaden Research Center in San Jose, California. "Wherever you look there are challenges," said IBM's Winfried Wilcke. "It's like climbing Mount Everest."[18]

Solid-state battery technology also got a boost in 2010 when a little-known Michigan company, Sakti3, received $3.2 million in research funding from General Motors' investment arm, GM Ventures. I broke that story for the *New York Times*[19] and had the opportunity to spend some time with its dynamic CEO, Dr. Ann Marie Sastry, during a 2009 visit to Iceland.

Sastry, a University of Michigan professor and entrepreneur, is a fast talker and fast mover (like Lampe-Önnerud, she's constantly on her cell phone making plane reservations) who clearly is focused on building the world's best batteries. "The race is on in advanced battery development, with the aim of quickly riding down the cost curve," she told me. "Who can get advanced batteries to market profitably? We have a technology that gives us optimism that we can make cost-effective battery cells."

Sastry's technology, like that developed at the University of Dayton, replaces liquid electrolytes with solids, and she envisions it doubling energy density. The State of Michigan has also invested millions in Sakti3. David Cole, then chairman of the influential Center for Automotive Research and a former University of Michigan professor, told me that Sakti3's work was "a step beyond the current battery technology. It's like the transition from the vacuum tube to the transistor, promising a dramatic performance increase. GM Ventures wants to put its money where a particular technology can have a downstream impact and provide a competitive advantage."

But Sastry can't say when her solid-state batteries will be commercialized, and she readily admits that there are technical barriers to overcome. She has prototype cells, but it will be a long time before they're in cars.

Tomorrow may belong to solid-state lithium batteries, but Li-ion has plainly captured the present. That's why entrepreneurs like Lampe-Önnerud can develop a better Li-ion cell design and quickly commercialize it. She has the satisfaction of seeing her cells at work powering long-lived laptops, electric scooters, and Saab station wagons.

CHAPTER THREE

FROM COMPUTERS
TO CARS

[The EV business is] somewhere between the Altair and the Apple II right now. It's in the home-brew stage.

—SHAI AGASSI, BETTER PLACE

ELECTRIC CARS AREN'T COMPUTERS, but the two have a lot in common. Open the hood of an EV and instead of a big, greasy internal-combustion engine you're going to see a neat box that in some ways resembles a desktop PC's CPU on its side. That's the electronic controller, and inside is the same basic stuff that enables your computer to fire up the operating system when you hit the power button. In this case, it's wiring and circuitry to control the flow of electrons to an electric motor. If you want it fixed, the tech is going to look like someone from the Geek Squad, not a mechanic in overalls.

An amazing number of the key executives running electric car companies have computer backgrounds, and it really helps. The Chevrolet Volt, for instance, has 100 electronic microprocessors on board. "Software is the DNA of all intelligent vehicles," says IBM.

If he hadn't decided to start an electric car company, Mike McQuary might be signing you up for Internet service right now. He was certainly a pioneer in the field, having been present at the creation of popular service provider MindSpring in 1994, when it was founded in Atlanta with just 32 nonpaying customers and eight modems.

By the time he signed on as a vice president the following year, MindSpring had grown to 20 employees and 1,000 local customers. McQuary (called "McQ" by just about everybody who knows him) became president and chief operating officer a few months later and took the company through four public offerings and its ascendancy to the world's second-largest ISP, behind AOL (and ahead of Microsoft, Prodigy, and AT&T). In 1999, MindSpring merged with EarthLink, and McQ became president. By the time he left in 2002, EarthLink was a $1.5 billion company that had 5 million subscribers and 5,000 employees.

So what was next for the still-boyish McQ, whose wicked sense of humor sometimes gets him in trouble? Obviously, starting an EV company: Wheego Electric Cars. McQ is hardly unique in taking the leap from computers to electric cars. Silicon Valley has become a hub of EV startups, though there's still plenty of skepticism that the balance of power will shift from Detroit and the established auto companies any time soon. We'll get back to McQ's auto adventures later in the chapter.

FROM COMPUTERS TO CARS

Martin Eberhard, one of the founders of Tesla Motors, studied computer engineering and electrical engineering in college—a background that suited him for entering both the online and EV worlds. After getting his start in network computing, in 1997 he cofounded NuvoMedia, an early player in electronic books that were sold over the Internet—long before the Kindle and iPad.

NuvoMedia's timing was excellent because it was a new Internet player at a time when such start-ups could do no wrong on Wall Street. The company, with Eberhard as CEO, raised $27 million in three rounds between 1997 and 1999, then sold out to Gemstar-TV Guide International for $187 million in 2000.

The stage was then set for Tesla, with Eberhard flush with cash and wanting to do something positive with his life that also used his varied skills. "I'm not the only person that would like to buy a car that's beautiful and fun to drive but also remain on the moral high ground," the then-45-year-old told the Associated Press in 2006.[1] That same combination of cost-is-no-object indulgence and green credentials is what has put Teslas in the garages of many Hollywood celebrities.

Eberhard admitted in a 2006 Tesla blog posting that he was an absolute beginner. "Much as I love cars," he wrote, "I am the first to admit that neither I, my co-founder, Marc Tarpenning, nor our original investor (and chairman of our board), Elon Musk, is an automotive engineer."[2]

Musk, as we've seen, also came to EVs from the online world, and it was the money from the sale of PayPal that allowed him to become Tesla's original investor. Tesla had 80 employees in mid-2006, and it was sitting on $40 million raised not just from Musk, but also from Larry Page and Sergey Brin, founders of Google.

By that point, Silicon Valley had not one but three EV start-ups. In addition to Tesla, there was Wrightspeed of Woodside (which developed a high-speed prototype capable of zero to 60 in three seconds) and battery materials maker Li-Ion Cells in Menlo Park (later Imara, and since closed). The California Cars Initiative was also founded in Palo Alto in 2002 to develop and promote plug-in hybrids.

And in 2007, charging systems leader Coulomb Technologies was founded in Cupertino and the equally aggressive Better Place came to Palo Alto. A third major charging player, ECOtality, relocated to the Bay Area from Arizona in 2010. EV maker Coda is in Santa Monica, near Los Angeles, but it recently announced that it planned to put an assembly plant for up to 14,000 cars annually in the Bay Area town of Benicia. "By tapping the Bay Area's engineering expertise and culture of innovation, a cluster of entrepreneurs, engineers and venture capitalists here are racing to bring their own electric cars to market," Terence Chea of the Associated Press wrote.[3]

San Francisco PBS station KQED expanded on that idea by proclaiming, "The new automobile of the 21st century is likely to benefit from the culture of Silicon Valley, where people are used to taking a chip, a cell, an idea and working on it until it becomes something big."[4]

Shai Agassi, the Israeli-born founder of Better Place, is yet another computer guy and serial entrepreneur. He founded Top-Tier Software, Quicksoft, and TopManage, and was the president of product/technology at German business software company SAP from 2002 to 2007, when he created Better Place.

Agassi makes an analogy rooted in computer-speak: The EV business is "somewhere between the Altair and the Apple II right now. It's in the home-brew stage. Altair sold only in the hundreds, sort of like Tesla right now. But if you ask people like Bill Gates or Paul Allen, they'll tell you that the Altair changed their lives."[5]

Whether they were actually located in Silicon Valley or not, many EV startups enjoyed the patronage of and cross-pollination with Internet companies. Google's support could be direct, with its investments in Tesla and, through Google.org, plug-in hybrid delivery van maker Bright Automotive. But Google also developed an early interest in what is known as Vehicle-to-Grid (V2G) technology, which gives hybrid and electric cars the ability to feed electricity back into the grid at peak demand times. That ability could prove extremely useful as the number of EVs on the road grows and the system approaches overload at certain times of the day.

Google, which has invested hundreds of millions of dollars in clean energy projects, partnered with northern and central California utility Pacific Gas and Electric (PG&E) to demonstrate V2G.[6] In Palo Alto in 2007, I watched as PG&E engineers plugged in a specially modified Toyota Prius plug-in hybrid and recorded its accomplishment as it fed power back into the grid. Eureka, it delivered.

On the same day in June of 2007 that Google announced the installation at its Mountain View, California, headquarters of a huge 1.6-megawatt photovoltaic system supported by the California Solar Initiative, it also staged another demonstration of V2G at the campus. As Google's engineers outlined, its fleet of 4 plug-in hybrid cars (later to grow to 10) could become energy storage for the huge solar array—which would otherwise generate electricity that would have to be used or lost. "We see this as a win-win," Sven Thesen, then-PG&E's Clean Air Transportation officer, told me.[7]

Google's V2G experiments have since been throttled down because the technology to make them work reliably is still in its infancy. It's unlikely that cars will be feeding energy to the grid on a commercial scale any time soon. Utilities love to talk about its potential, though. And some home hobbyists have demonstrated that, in a pinch, the battery packs in their Toyota Prius hybrids can be pressed into service to provide electric power during blackouts.[8]

THE NEXT DETROIT?

Silicon Valley is only one of many alternative Motor Cities. Hartford, Connecticut, had an early claim, because manufacturer Colonel Albert Pope had sold 500 electric cars as early as 1897. But he bet wrong on the market for early EVs, fatefully telling anyone who would listen that "you can't get people to sit over an explosion."[9]

Ohio has a long automotive tradition, and so does Indiana, which is working to revive its dormant manufacturing capacity with both EV and battery companies. But the auto plants that haven't fled overseas are now scattered across America, with many in southern states that offer carmakers favorable economic conditions (including union-defying right-to-work laws).

There are some convincing arguments to be made that Silicon Valley *won't* be the next Detroit—that the seats of power will remain right where they are. Despite the bankruptcy and restructuring of two of Detroit's Big Three, longtime auto analyst and consultant Maryann N. Keller argues that the momentum remains with the established players. Speaking of the government loans to Tesla and Fisker, she claims, "We're pouring $1 billion into two companies without a future. The economics of the industry favors large companies."[10]

Keller's argument is worth quoting at length, because it speaks to the heart of whether companies like Tesla, Coda, Wheego, and Fisker will be household names 10 years after I write this in 2011. "The theory is that entrepreneurs can quickly integrate new technologies (mostly electric propulsion systems) and cobble together cars from outsourced design and components," she wrote in *Businessweek*. "But assembling cars this way cannot reach the scale necessary for mass volume. Small production volumes result in high prices that can't compete with those of the large auto companies. Although they might be late in adopting a technology, they will have the advantage of scale."

According to Keller, "the future of the auto industry will look like the past. . . . Upstart entrepreneurs will never achieve the mass scale necessary to produce vehicles at relevant prices for most consumers. While the startups may pioneer the use of some technology, any successes will be copied by the large manufacturers, which have greater resources, including government support, as well as an existing infrastructure. The startups will fail or remain relegated to niche markets."

It's impossible to know if her prophecy will come to pass, but early signs are that veteran automakers will indeed have a big advantage. General Motors was so encouraged by early orders for its Chevrolet Volt that it decided to ramp up production from 10,000 to 16,000 in 2011. And 2012 volume has increased from 30,000 to 60,000.

Keller isn't the only one arguing against the California start-ups taking root and displacing the industry as we know it. John Voelcker, a senior editor and principal in High Gear Media (which runs GreenCarReports.com), says that Silicon Valley is the wrong place to build an auto industry, and he cites several reasons.[11] The Valley culture, he said, is built around fast turn-arounds, as was the case with eBay, Google, and Facebook. Instead of the large $1 billion plus investment for factories and tooling required by any type of automaker, those companies could be started with an office and few workstations. Car companies can take a decade to break even, which is anathema for venture capitalists.

Voelcker also argues that the Bay Area is indeed full of electrical engineers, but they're the wrong kind, skilled at building integrated circuits for consumer electronics products rather than the big-scale electric motors, battery packs, and control electronics that EVs require. It's interesting how many of the engineers at EV startup companies come from major automakers, not electronics companies. As I'd noted, the chief engineer of the Tesla Model S, Peter Rawlinson, came to the company from Jaguar and also spent time at Lotus. His background is working on cars, not computers.

And Voelcker also points out that California is a highly regulated state and an expensive place for manufacturers to operate. Some of the carmakers with assembly operations in California, including both Wheego and Coda, solve this problem in part by doing a great deal of their heavy work in China.

The former joint GM/Toyota NUMMI factory in Fremont, California, taken over by Tesla for the Model S, was vacant for a reason, and it wasn't just that General Motors pulled out. The average production wage among the unionized workers still at the plant in 2009 was $28 an hour. Once NUMMI closed, Toyota moved production for the Tacoma pickup to its Tundra facility in San Antonio, Texas, where not only were production facilities much newer, but also wages often lower. A skilled tool and die maintenance person hires on in San Antonio for $18 to $21.50 per hour, according to a job posting, and unskilled labor starts at $15.50.

Tesla, meanwhile, will have to figure out how to build the Model S affordably at the 5.5-million-square-foot NUMMI plant, using California workers. Fremont is on the edge of Silicon Valley, with an average median income of $93,000, so that will be a challenge. NUMMI was the last full-size auto plant on the West Coast, which will always lack Michigan's central location for shipping cars nationwide.

In an interview,[12] Voelcker asked me to name the last American car company started from scratch by entrepreneurs whose brand is still with us today. The answer, of course, is Chrysler, which was founded in the 1920s. "You can't count supercar companies that just make a few vehicles, or Jeep, which got its start in weird ways," he said. "The fact is it's really hard to start a car company—it's a brutally expensive business with long production cycles."

Voelcker predicts that Tesla might be a brand 20 years hence, but it is quite likely to have been absorbed by a major automaker, with perhaps a dozen capable of such an acquisition. "If the Model S does well, that's the point where the venture capitalists will want to monetize their investment," he said. Tesla could end up as a division of one of its existing investors, Toyota or Daimler, or part of one of the Big Three. BMW or Volkswagen, German companies just getting their hands around the electrification thing, might want to acquire it, too.

For Tesla to remain independent, you'd have to imagine Elon Musk as a Mark Zuckerberg figure, cooly turning down a $1 billion offer so he can continue to control Facebook. The conditions of Tesla's Department of Energy loan ensure that Musk will remain a major shareholder of Tesla through the launch of the Model S in 2012, but he's got a lot of interests and anything could happen after that.

But if Silicon Valley does not become a center of EV manufacturing, it will certainly become ground zero for EV *deployment*— and that's in part because the area is so tech-friendly. The Bay Area crawls with the early adopters who filled the waiting lists for electric cars.

California overall has a bunch of natural advantages, including the best possible climate for battery cars, serious subsidies (including a $5,000 cash rebate from the state government), and a receptive audience—it's already the biggest US market for hybrids.

Nearly every EV company is targeting California in their initial launches, and Coda initially deployed its electric sedans nowhere else. Several federally supported programs will put free EV chargers in the state, and a $3.4 million grant from the California Energy Commission is installing 1,600 charging stations (half public, half home based) in key state markets: Los Angeles, Sacramento, and the San Francisco/San Jose area.

Coulomb Technologies, based in the Bay Area, is installing those stations, and cofounder and former president Praveen

Mandal told me, "For one thing, on the West Coast there's a lot of interest in saving the environment and getting off oil. There is also concern about how electric cars perform in cold climates, so it's more challenging in Chicago than in, say, Los Angeles." That state rebate is a big help, too. "Now we're talking about a Nissan Leaf battery car at less than $20,000," he said. "At that point, it becomes a mass-market car."[13]

The Bay Area was the number one launch market nationally for Nissan Leaf reservations, despite the fact that it was initially passed over by the federally supported $230 million EV Project, which subsidized 15,000 home chargers for the Leaf and Chevrolet Volt in six states and the District of Columbia. (The project added San Francisco in February of 2011.) A further challenge for EVs in San Francisco is the fact that more than half of all cars there (51 percent) are parked at the curb—the home garages that are ideal for charger installation are relatively rare. But that obstacle too is certain to be overcome, with chargers installed in condominiums and apartment buildings, public parking lots, shopping centers, and workplaces, too.

In late January of 2011, I caught up with Felix Kramer, the indefatigable San Francisco–based founder of CalCars.org and a tireless advocate for plug-in hybrids since 2001. Without Kramer's work, the Toyota Prius and Ford C-Max plug-in hybrids might never have happened, and maybe not the Fisker Karma or Chevrolet Volt, either.

While we talked, Kramer was at the wheel of his then-new Chevrolet Volt, on the way to Lake Tahoe to pick up his Nissan Leaf. Yes, Kramer and his wife were about to become a two-EV family, with a battery car and a plug-in hybrid. "I love my Volt—it's a better car than I thought it would be," he told me. "It's really stable and comfortable, with incredible amounts of pep. It's the car I've been dreaming about for 10 years."[14]

Kramer agrees that the San Francisco Bay Area isn't likely to become a big manufacturing center for EVs and that it will be perhaps the key market for electric car sales. Although there were still only a few public charging stations in San Francisco when we talked (including those I'd recently seen in front of City Hall), by 2012 he predicted there would be 700 to 1,000 of them. Imagine the city's wall-to-wall Toyota Priuses as electric cars, and you have a vision of Bay Area transportation in the next few years.

WIRING CARS: A CODER'S PARADISE

Cars today are computers on wheels. There are an estimated 30 to 50 electronic control units (ECUs) in a typical car (more in luxury vehicles), and often millions of lines of software code. Frost and Sullivan business researchers estimate that could soon grow exponentially—to as much as 300 million lines. It takes more than 20 million lines just to program the radio and navigation system in an S-Class Mercedes-Benz.[15]

That's why automakers now need to hire as many computer programmers as they do brake engineers. Writing in *Slate* at a time when many Americans were worried that the electronic "throttle by wire" systems in cars might be responsible for runaway acceleration in Toyotas, Farhad Manjoo noted, "Even though it sounds scary, integrating computers into cars brings more upsides than downsides. For one thing, cars will begin to advance at the same pace as computers. The beauty of software is that it can be updated from afar. A cell phone you buy today will keep getting better as it ages, constantly picking up new functions through downloads. Now the same will be true of cars. Through software patches, they'll keep getting better fuel economy and better safety systems. When something goes wrong, they'll be easier to fix."[16]

We all appreciate it when our car tells us of an impending fault (though the nonspecific messages from the "check engine" light drive everybody nuts), and systems like OnStar can now find a car in a crowded parking lot and track it when it's stolen. Plug a USB hard drive into Ford's Sync system and it instantly catalogs, arranges, and plays the songs on it. Today's sensors and microprocessors can react much faster than humans can, and that led to innovations such as antilock brakes (which automatically pulse the pedal up to 16 times a second) and adaptive cruise control (which controls the distance between your car and the one ahead, reacting instantly to perceived danger). Electric cars are a field day for programmers, since their range-anxious drivers will thrive on information. Many of the EVs on the market will allow owners to set up preheating and precooling from grid power through their cell phones or Web pages. Stepping into a warm or cool car without having to run a gas engine is a perk not to be dismissed lightly. A huge variety of applications will track your car's state of charge. And near universal is the ability to dial in preset charging times, so electric cars can recharge at low-demand times after midnight.

If EVs are otherwise evenly matched, apps like these could be a deciding factor for some buyers, particularly the young drivers who show more interest in their cell phones than in their cars. According to a 2010 poll by the Zipcar car-sharing company, 54 percent of 1,025 18-and-overs (966 of them drivers) surveyed said they'd rather spend time online with friends, communicating through social media, than driving to visit them. Only 18 percent of people over 55 say that. I had my driver's license the day I turned 16, but my 17-year-old, iPad-obsessed daughter is taking her time.

You might expect that the EV startups headed by Internet veterans would be the savviest when it comes to onboard apps and cool technology, but that isn't always the case. Nissan's Leaf and Ford's Focus EV excel in this area, with enticing graphics and a variety of views to measure state of charge and find an available place to plug in. But those are both old-guard auto companies. I'm still wondering why, despite its Silicon Valley origins, the Tesla Roadster doesn't have a better stereo. Couldn't Panasonic, which supplied the batteries, have helped? And the Wheego LiFe . . . well, it's got an onboard Eco Meter and a USB input.

WHEEGO: CAN IT GO THE DISTANCE?

Tiny Wheego is based far from Silicon Valley, in Atlanta, but its assembly plant is Hi Performance in Ontario, California, east of Los Angeles. Wheego is one of the more unlikely stories in the EV world, more like a shoestring Internet company than a brick-and-mortar auto manufacturer. It is, in fact, the very illustration of Maryann Keller's notion of upstart carmakers whose plan is to "cobble together cars from outsourced design and components."[17] Its fate will be either a cautionary tale they'll tell in business school, proving her point, or a highly unconventional success story. Given the realities of a cutthroat business, you're more likely to read its obituary than hear that it set a sales record.

Wheego is a spinoff from electric all-terrain-vehicle maker Ruff and Tuff, which Mike McQuary headed from 2007 to 2009. The highway-capable LiFe is a step up from the company's low-speed vehicle (LSV). The company has just five and a half employees. And McQ isn't exactly full-time himself—he has a few other things on his plate.

McQ calls the LiFe a "United Nations car." It starts out as a Chinese-made gasoline-powered vehicle called the Noble, which is made by Shuanghuan Auto, two hours outside Beijing. As Shuanghuan will tell you, the two-seater is a "romantic mini car with style of the inner originality, fashionable, lively and sport." And "the trench of postmodernism" is fully on display.

The Noble had a rough start in life, since the car closely resembles Daimler's Smart Fortwo (itself now available in electric form). After the Noble was marketed in Europe through China Motors, Daimler took Shuanghuan to court, but—probably to its surprise—lost the case in 2009, with a Greek court ruling that "an informed buyer would not confuse the Noble with the Smart Fortwo." The court said that they were very different under the hood (the Noble is front-wheel drive; the Smart rear-wheel drive) and, in any case, all mini-cars are bound to look alike.[18]

But the Noble makes a pretty good lightweight base for an electric commuter car, just as the Smart does. It's all outsourced: The 28-kilowatt-hour Li-ion battery pack comes from Flux Power in California, the 60-horsepower electric motor from Leeson in Wisconsin. Range is about 90 miles, and top speed a just-highway-friendly 67. "It's a real car," says McQ frequently, as if assuring himself.

An earlier LSV version of the car, called the Wheego Whip,

sold for $19,000 and was a surprise hit in, of all places, Oklahoma. Nearly 300 Wheegos were sold there (two-thirds of the entire production) because of a little-known state law that offered a 50 percent tax credit on electric car purchases. Yes, 50 percent, half the cost of the car. "It was the most attractive state incentive, and everybody was clamoring to get out to Oklahoma and put a stake in the ground," said McQ.

McQ considered opening an assembly plant in Piedmont, Oklahoma, but the legislature ended the tax credit at the end of 2010 and the gold rush was over. Wheego is still contemplating a second assembly plant more centrally located, and Alabama, South Carolina, and Louisiana have all prepared incentive packages.

Wheego was an early loser in the bid for Department of Energy cash, perhaps because it didn't ask for enough money (only $16 million to help develop its second model, a China-sourced five-seat crossover) and didn't project enough job creation. "I was perhaps too much of a Boy Scout about that," McQ told me. "I was told we wouldn't have any credibility unless we asked for $30 million to $50 million, but we didn't need that much. And I was told if we redrafted the application and put in more jobs, we'd have a better chance. But we're not going to create 1,000 jobs—it's not the way we're set up. We had to be real and honest—we weren't going to just take the money and run."

Remember, this is a lean-and-mean Internet-type operation. The total outlay to get the Wheego LiFe on the market was just $5 million, virtually all the money the company raised. I'd say that's unprecedented: The Chevrolet Volt program has absorbed more than $1 billion. But one result is that Wheego could be profitable with a volume that's like a rounding error at General Motors. Wheego wants to have a new four-door crossover SUV model on the road in 2012, and if that happens, McQ would be more than happy with 3,000 combined sales annually.

In his back-and-forth with the Department of Energy, McQ said the $5 million development figure was, frankly, met with disbelief. "'That's impossible,' they said. But I told them, 'I'm looking at three prototypes right now, and I'm more than willing to load one of them up on a car carrier and bring it down to the DOE tomorrow.' The first hurdle was credibility."

There are some parallels here to Tesla's car-that-could strategy—build a driving prototype (as Tesla did with the Mercedes A-Class) and they'll believe that impossible is possible.

McQ says he learned to outsource during his days at Mind-Spring and EarthLink. "A lot of the ISPs felt they needed to write their own browser," he said. "But we just took the best software components available—FTP client, newsreader, and browser—and bundled them together. Our job was to create the interoperability that allowed them all to work together." The challenge with the LiFe is exactly the same.

With all the parts in place and crash testing done, the Wheego LiFe might actually have hit the market in 2010. That became important because President Obama had committed the federal government to buying 100 electric cars from the first company to get one of the new vehicles on the road. It was obvious that the feds were thinking of the Chevrolet Volt, but Wheego thought it could be first in line. "If President Obama was serious, then the White House should be buying 100 Wheego LiFes next month," McQ said.[19]

The federal General Services Administration didn't pay much attention to Wheego's claim, and as it happened the LiFe was not on the market before the Volt. The car was ready, but held up by a vital piece of paper—a Department of Transportation waiver that would allow the LiFe to be sold, like the Tesla Roadster, without an expensive advanced passenger-side airbag. Without that, the 50 or so cars that had been completed sat idle through the last months of 2010, while the first 350 Volts were loaded onto trucks. If you were conspiracy minded you might see something in the timing of all that, but there was unlikely to be much of an outcry if tiny Wheego didn't get justice.

THAT'S LIFE: DRIVING THE WHEEGO

In March of 2010 I was the first journalist to drive the highway-capable LiFe, in Atlanta, where the company is based. Wheego shares an unassuming office building in an industrial district with Brash Music, McQ's record company. Wheego may have only a few employees, but Brash is smaller still—just two. Still, it has a surprisingly strong roster that crosses the boundaries between rock, techno, folk, and R&B. Twenty artists have issued nicely packaged CDs, and Brash is surviving despite a steadily shrinking music business that can put an album at number one with just 40,000 weekly sales.

McQ and I slide easily between talking about cars and talking about music. He's fun in conversation, with a mouth that sometimes gets him into trouble. In Atlanta, he displayed few qualms about flipping me the keys to the sole LiFe prototype, despite a freak snowstorm.

I enjoyed the squeak-free ride and the ultratight turning radius. Acceleration was adequate, if hardly in Nissan Leaf territory—it responded to my foot, but not with instant-on readiness. I experienced some wheelspin on the wet roads, the result of a too-light front end. Wheego addressed this soon after by moving the heavy batteries forward.

Chinese cars I've seen have retro interiors, and not in the good sense. The LiFe follows suit and is laid out like a nicely equipped 1995 Toyota Corolla, a two-seat version. As with the similar Think City and Smart electric-drive EVs, it has a lot of room behind the seats but limited utility, with room for only two passengers. Tesla is convinced that its Model S sedan will be the volume leader, and that's true of Wheego and its four-door crossover, too. Still, as McQ is fond of saying, the LiFe is a real car, and you can tell where every dime of the $5 million went.

I drove the LiFe again the following November at the 2010 Los Angeles Auto Show, where it made its official debut. This time the company's president, Jeff Boyd (who has since left the company), was my copilot. Boyd is the closest Wheego got to an old auto hand—the company cited his "over 25 years of automotive experience." Boyd was CEO of Miles Electric Vehicles, parent company of Coda, and also served as chief operating officer of a dealership organization with 32 outlets in four states.

The car now had better weight balance, but otherwise was much the same. Delivery was scheduled for a few weeks hence, but Boyd told me he was still tweaking a few things. The price had been set at $32,995, slightly more than the original price for the five-passenger Leaf, a much more sophisticated car, especially when it came to electronic apps. The lack of cool apps was a bit ironic, considering McQ's computer experience, but at the end of 2010 the company was operating on very thin margins. Nissan had a cushion to lose some money on every car sold, but McQ told me just before the car's launch that he was "running on fumes."

The bottom line: Wheego was going to need a heck of a marketing strategy to reach sales targets. Boyd told me he had 500 advance orders, and McQ offered a rather novel approach to getting the car into consumers' hands: The company will purposely seek out markets that are not in the initial launch plans of the big players. "It's not that we are trying to avoid the major automakers," he told me. "We will sell in the same half-dozen markets that Nissan and GM are going to launch in. But that leaves about 90 percent of the population of the US that will be our exclusive selling domain for at least a year." Stealth marketing!

Wheego's Los Angeles stand was in the auto show's basement along with the other specialty companies, but there was still some foot traffic, and the usually casually dressed McQ, now wearing a suit, interrupted our interview when a young couple came by to kick the tires.

"We're not focusing on being big, we're focusing on being great," McQ told me between sales pitches to prospective buyers. Later that day, Wheego held its press conference, and it did not go particularly well. Maybe McQ was nervous, but he made a bunch of jokes at the expense of Chevrolet and Coda that some reporters interpreted as snide. "I was trying to be provocative enough to get people following our story," he told me later. "I guess I made a few comments that some interpreted as inflammatory." McQ actually does sincerity much better.

As he sat in Atlanta waiting for the DOT to release the LiFe to a wider world, McQ might have been expected to bask in his achievement ("It's a real car!") and tout the direct line from the Internet to the automobile. But he didn't. "Silicon Valley excels at intellectual capital, more than any mechanical know-how," he said. "Companies like Apple outsource their manufacturing. And there are steep hurdles to manufacturing anything in California. It's not a manufacturing hub, the cost of real estate is high, the location is hardly central for shipping around the country, and there are a lot of regulatory requirements on manufacturers. There are a lot of other places to look first."

But McQ said he's glad his cars' final assembly is near Los Angeles, since he agrees that half or even more of early EV sales will be in California. "The state has the mind-set and the incentives," he said, "and it also allows electric cars with only one passenger to ride in the HOV lanes."

If you think that's a trivial motivator, consider my cousin, Charles Mark-Walker, who lives in the San Fernando Valley but works in Santa Monica. Traffic is brutal, and he's been above it all in his HOV-friendly Honda Civic Hybrid. But the once-precious yellow sticker became useless on June 30, 2011, after which only zero-emission battery cars and plug-in hybrids could ride in the HOV lanes. So guess what? Charlie signed up to buy a Leaf.

CHAPTER FOUR

THE BIG PLAYERS

The Volt is an electric car 95 percent of the time, but when you need to go to Vegas or San Francisco, it turns into a regular car—that's the key.

—JAY LENO

BEFORE PICKING UP THIS BOOK, it's unlikely that you'd ever heard of Wheego, Coda, Fisker, or Think. These electric car start-ups are not under the radar by choice, but because their tight budgets are going into getting the cars out the door, not marketing them. Of course, they've set aside some money for publicity and advertising, but it's minuscule compared to the clout enjoyed by the big, established companies, including Nissan, Chevrolet, and Daimler. And that's one reason the start-ups are unlikely to blow the big players out of the water in terms of volume. In the long term, the latter's chances are better.

Nissan's launch of the Leaf could be taught in graduate business seminars. The Japanese automaker knows how to put on a party, and few TV viewers could have escaped the fact that it was going electric. When CEO Carlos Ghosn was not being interviewed on network TV, he was signing off on big ad budgets. If you saw the Super Bowl, you saw the Leaf. Nissan's marketing

dazzle was on full display when the Leaf reached its first customers in California.

The polar bear had big black claws, just as real polar bears
do. And just as he does in the Nissan Leaf TV ads, this polar
bear was giving the Nissan Leaf electric car (white like him) a big
bear hug. He hugged me, too. The scene was the plaza in front of
San Francisco's City Hall, and Nissan had taken it over in mid-
December of 2010 to celebrate the delivery of the first Leaf battery car to the first customer, Olivier Chalouhi, a tech
entrepreneur from Redwood City.

One down and 20,000 to go. That's the number of people
who put down $99 to make a Leaf reservation, and Nissan said
they would all have their cars by the end of the summer. The
Japanese earthquake and tsunami threw a loop into that schedule, but it seemed doable then. Many of Nissan's customers are
the "early adopters" that California has in great numbers—
young, tech savvy, possessed of disposable income (the 2012 Leaf
starts at $35,200 before rebates, after all), and very green.

Earlier in the day, up north at Northbay Nissan in Petaluma,
Chalouhi had been handed the keys to his black Leaf. Although
he was the first person to sign up for the car, the company
couldn't have found somebody more media friendly—Chalouhi is
a photogenic (as are his wife and two kids) 31-year-old French-
born entrepreneur whose venture-supported start-up company,
Fanhattan, has just the right kind of high-tech buzz.

"I love it," Chalouhi told me when his ownership was five
minutes old. How did he become the first Nissan Leaf customer?
"Luck, I guess."[1]

The first Leaf really was a media occasion, and film crews

from all over the world had made the trek to Petaluma. Chalouhi did interviews in several languages. Also giving interviews was Nissan Americas' then-chairman, Carlos Tavares, the car's number one fan after Ghosn. "This is a great moment, a dream come to reality," he told me with his trademark wall-to-wall Cheshire cat grin.

The Portuguese Tavares has been with the Leaf from the beginning, and it is indeed a dream come true for him. As the program unfolded, it was Tavares (at events in New York and Los Angeles) who revealed new details about the car—that Nissan was going to let customers separately lease the battery packs, and then that it wasn't. It was Tavares who told me that Nissan expected that 10 percent of new car sales by 2020 would be of electrics, a category that includes hybrids. "I believe that in a few decades, zero emission will be the cost of admission to the automobile market," he told me in a video interview.[2] "I'm very confident that will happen, but as to when the auto fleet will be fully electric I would not dare to predict."

Tavares proved his value to the Renault-Nissan Alliance with his work on the Leaf, and shortly after it was introduced, in May of 2011, he was promoted to chief operating officer of Renault, where he will supervise an electric car rollout even more ambitious than Nissan's. It includes a sedan with swappable batteries that will be widely deployed in Israel, a panel van, and a tiny city car.

From Petaluma, four of us got to drive Leafs to San Francisco. It was a great opportunity, and by far my longest time to date behind the wheel of this celebrated car. I had driven it through New York City's Central Park, but this was a trip of more than 30 miles.

I was paired with the Leaf's chief marketing manager at the time, Trisha Jung, who told me during the ride that the company's challenge is not to sell the car to early adopters—they were already on the waiting list—but to the people she called "the pragmatic majority." According to Jung, the pragmatic majority is the mass-market customer, represented by the 260,000 "hand wavers" who had by then registered on Nissan's Web site to make their interest in buying a Leaf known before the launch. How many can be converted into buyers?

"The pragmatics are not quite as willing to take risks as the early adopters," Jung said. "They're looking to see the early adopters prove out the EV concept. These people are somewhat green—they take out the curbside recycling—but they want the car they buy to be a good value."[3]

The value thing is a challenge for Nissan. Although consumers can be shown how much money they'll save per mile by charging their cars instead of filling them at gas pumps, they still have to adjust to a high purchase price. Paul Hawson, Nissan's product planning manager for electric vehicles, says the Leaf will cost just 2.6 cents per mile on the road, or $390 over 15,000 miles. A comparable 25-mpg gas car running on $3 a gallon gas would cost 12 cents a mile, or $1,800 over that same 15,000 miles. Of course, before rebates, the Leaf also costs about double the price of a new 2010 Honda Civic DX.

Consumer Reports conducted a 2010 survey[4] that found a disconnect here. American car owners told the watchdog publication that they're really concerned about cutting our dependence on fossil fuel. They don't like their gas dollars funding terrorists, which is something everyone agrees on, including the Tea Party. They're willing to do their part by purchasing green cars, too, but when they talk about their expectations it goes totally off the rails—they want far more than the market can deliver right now.

A majority in the poll, 59 percent, cite a lower purchase price as a reason to buy a greener, more fuel-efficient car. That would be fine if we were talking about traditional compact cars—the very affordable Toyota Yaris and Honda Civic, for example. EVs offer zero emissions and the equivalent of more than 100 miles a gallon—but they cost more. The Leaf cost $32,790 before a 2012 price rise to $35,200, which would buy you a nice Lexus, or at least a used one.

Eric Evarts, associate *Consumer Reports* auto editor, told me, "No doubt consumers are responding correctly to the current reality—expressing an interest in Honda Fits and Chevy Cruzes, perhaps. But the reality of really high-fuel-efficiency cars coming down the pike is that they're going to cost more than people expect."[5]

It's interesting to note that, despite the fact that it adds more than $900 to the bottom line, more than 90 percent of early customers opted for the Leaf SL package that includes a back-up camera and fog lights. But I think it was the solar panel (which trickle charges an accessory battery) that these true-blue green early adopters really wanted.

I agree with Nissan's Jung that the battleground is in the second stage, with the pragmatic buyers. They're the people who will look closely at the numbers. They're not likely to get blown away simply by driving the car, which was my own experience. I got to pilot the car over the Golden Gate Bridge, a spectacular test drive in anyone's reckoning. Our caravan of cars lined up at the entrance to the bridge, providing a stirring sight—a veritable fleet of EVs heading to the city that loves them more than anywhere else.

The Leaf is pretty much what you would want it to be—fast accelerating and smooth, exceptionally well built, and quiet to the point that the team had to add a special sound to warn blind people and pedestrians of its presence. It offers a wealth of data about the charging process on colorful screens, and your cell phone is just aching to interact with it.

The only thing the Leaf *doesn't* offer is long-range travel (it's good that Petaluma isn't farther from San Francisco). Nick Chambers of PluginCars.com got 116.1 miles out of a charge,[6] but most drivers report the range is from 60 (especially in cold weather) to 110 miles. The official range of the Leaf is 73 miles, says the EPA, which also rates it at the equivalent of 99 mpg.

In the city, the Leafs became enmeshed in lunch-hour traffic, and I was reminded that one drawback of EVs is that, although they emit no tailpipe emissions when in gridlock, if the heat or air conditioning is on, they do consume valuable electricity that would otherwise go toward extending the range. Owners will probably be tempted to shut off the climate control for extra miles of travel.

A huge crowd had gathered in front of San Francisco's City Hall, which features a row of charging stations. The polar bear was posing with the Leaf, and politicians who'd championed state EV subsidies were taking a victory lap.

Also there was Leaf customer number two, Tom Franklin, a Southern California clean-tech patent attorney with three kids who was scheduled to pick up his car in San Diego the next week. "Those of you looking for a used Toyota Prius, please see Tom because he's about to upgrade," Tavares said.[7] Franklin told PluginCars.com, "I'm excited about not using foreign energy to power my car. We go to war and do all kinds of crazy things, certainly influenced by our great need for foreign oil. To be able to power a car domestically, it's a huge deal."[8] Other first cars were being delivered that week, undoubtedly to equally motivated buyers, in Arizona, Oregon, Washington, and Tennessee.

The polar bear proved a lousy interview subject, but his doppelganger was Steve Amstrup, the chief scientist for Polar Bears International. Amstrup's presence served to remind us of why we were there, and why we care about electric cars in the first place. In Los Angeles he told me that melting sea ice could make polar bears extinct in the wild by 2050. "They're dependent on hunting seals from sea ice, but the ice is melting because of climate change. And as the sea ice goes, so goes the polar bear."[9]

I caught up with first Leaf owner Olivier Chalouhi a couple of months later, and by then he'd put 1,300 miles on the car.[10] He still loved it. "As I drive it, I get more confident on the range issue," he told me. "The first week there was a learning curve, and I worried about running out of electricity on trips to San Francisco. So we took my wife's car. But now that I have more confidence, I've been driving it everywhere."

Chalouhi had had a couple of close calls when the bars indicating range had all disappeared, but he's also found that when return trips are mostly downhill he can gain back some miles with the regenerative braking.

It's interesting that Chalouhi reports no significant jump in his electric bill with 600 miles of EV travel tacked on to it. The former Honda Accord driver is sold on electric cars. His next car? "I plan to keep the Leaf a long time, but maybe I'll eventually buy a second, bigger car. Perhaps the Tesla Model S. It will definitely be an electric car."

PLUGGING IN THE VOLT

My first real experience of the brave new world that is the Chevrolet Volt (after some fun with "test mules" in Michigan) was on Pier 92 on the West Side of Manhattan.[11] It was April Fool's Day, 2010. Though the setting was picturesque, conditions weren't ideal for test-driving a high-tech car like the Volt—we were allowed to drive it around the on-ramp of a parking garage. The short distances meant we never got out of all-electric mode, but I was able to determine that (a) the steering is in sports sedan territory; (b) the brakes work; (c) the electric motor offers instant-on torque; and (d) my test car, despite being a hand-built model intended for durability testing, was squeak- and rattle-free.

But I wanted a real date with an actual production-line Volt. The highlight of the 2010 Los Angeles Auto Show for me was getting picked up at LAX in a shiny new Chevrolet Volt and getting to drive it all the way to Santa Monica. This was one of the first cars that actually rolled out of the Detroit-Hamtramck factory. My copilots were Rob Peterson and Britta Gross of GM, both of whom played big roles in the Volt story (Rob as its principal spokesperson and Britta as the point woman for making sure the car has somewhere to plug in).

The four-passenger Volt is a game changer, no doubt about it.

It sells for $41,000 (but costs perhaps $40,000 to build) and has from 25 to 50 miles of electric-only range, followed by another 300 miles with the gas engine running. GM initially gave the impression that the gas engine never actually drives the wheels, but after filing some patents, the company had to backtrack on that, revealing that the 84-horsepower, 1.4-liter four-cylinder engine does indeed power the car at certain times when the battery power is exhausted. The gas motor also runs on very cold days to enable the heater to work.

The car is a techie tour de force, and during my drive from LAX I was constantly stealing glances at the displays, which offered multiple views of my state of charge, as well as the song playing on the radio. My favorite moment came when we lost our way and Gross was able to use the OnStar system to ask for directions, which were then downloaded into our car.

Volt drivers will know they're not driving a 1915 Detroit Electric. They can equip their cell phones with Volt-specific apps that will interact with the car to set charge times, display the battery pack's state of charge, and tell them how many recent miles were electric only. Through a partnership with Google Maps, owners can search for a destination, pinpoint where it is in relationship to the car, then download the directions directly to the screen through OnStar.

The Leaf has a sophisticated navigation system that includes easy prompts to find charging stations, but with a 100-mile range it needs it—charging is not nearly as central to the Volt. In fact, GM told me that it expects 80 percent of its customers to be satisfied with charging the car from house current—they won't even need to install $2,000 240-volt units in their garages.[12] The Volt has a 16 kilowatt-hour pack, but in its effort to preserve battery life (and the integrity of its eight-year, 100,000-mile warranty), it uses only 10.4 kilowatt-hours. And with 110 electrical service, the pack recharges in just eight hours.

THE VOLT'S NUMBER ONE FAN: JAY LENO

The initial response of Volt owners to their cars bordered on euphoria. I talked to *Tonight Show* host Jay Leno, probably America's number one car enthusiast, soon after his Volt was delivered. He'd picked up the car in Northridge a few days earlier and had 248 miles under his belt by then. "I'm impressed from a quality point of view," he told me. "I had a club date that was 60 miles away the other night, and the car just switched to gas when the electric was depleted, with no range anxiety, no problems— the Volt just becomes a regular car, without any compromises."[13]

But Leno is skeptical about battery cars, despite owning a few of them (among his 200 cars and motorcycles). He told me, "Electricity has always been the best way to power a car, but unfortunately battery technology has some issues. I have a Baker Electric [1909] that will get 85 to 100 miles on a charge, which is the same as a modern electric car."[14]

For Leno, the Volt is the smart one because it "uses electricity at the point of generation. The BMW Mini E, the electric drive Smart, I don't get those. With the Mini, they took a fine car and ripped out the rear seats, put batteries in it, made it more expensive, slower and heavier, with less range than the gas car. What's the advantage of that? Most people won't buy a car like that unless they're a really green sort of person. The Volt is an electric car 95 percent of the time, but when you need to go to Vegas or San Francisco, it turns into a regular car. That's the key."

Leno has a point. With the Volt, you have options. Britta Gross says that public charging won't matter as much to the Volt. "We want some infrastructure, but we don't want large amounts," she said. "We expect public charging to be under-utilized. It's going to be a lot of cost for [what] potentially could be pretty severe under-utilization."[15]

The Volt is the car you're least likely to see plugged into a charge point downtown. It's going to make it home, no matter what. But regular battery EVs may not need that much public infrastructure, either. All EV drivers, including those dependent on their charging ports, are likely to acclimate to their cars and what they can do. That will mean fewer panic-induced stops at chargers while on the road, and much more reliance on plugging in at home.

I heard a similar opinion from Roland Hwang, the transportation program director for the Natural Resources Defense Council and a veteran green car guy. "BMW's field trials with the Mini E electric show that people get used to the range, and what their cars are good for and what they aren't. Once people understand how EVs actually drive, the whole issue of range tends to go away."[16]

Some 450 BMW Mini E cars, converted to electric by Tom Gage and AC Propulsion (the same company whose Tzero led to the Tesla Roadster), began their field trials on the East and West Coasts in 2009. There were speed bumps: Deliveries were delayed, European cables were incompatible, and some owners reported that their range was reduced in cold weather. Despite all that, the cars were great fun to drive. And a 2009 study of 150 Mini E drivers by the Plug-in Hybrid Electric Vehicle Research Center at the University of California, Davis found that, in real-world conditions, most found the 80- to 100-mile range adequate. After a yearlong field test, UC Davis updated that study in 2011 and reported that 60 percent of the Mini E drivers queried "agree very strongly" that electric cars are fine for daily use.[17] The upshot is that the Volt, by answering range anxiety up front, will have an initial marketing advantage that could diminish over time as people adjust to battery-only cars.

GM sent a fleet of cars across the country for what it called the Volt Unplugged tour in late 2010 to rub in that range advantage.[18] When the Leaf is running on empty, the Volt will have another 250 miles to go. Volt's product and marketing director at the time, Tony DiSalle, told me that his car was "the only electric vehicle able to drive such long distances under a variety of driving conditions and climates without having to stop to recharge."

The Volt and other plug-in hybrids will always push that selling point, and they should. But if people get comfortable with battery limitations, and charging stations become ubiquitous, opinion is likely to change. We probably won't know how this will play out until EV owners have logged a lot more miles than they have now.

FORD'S BETTER IDEA: A GREEN STRATEGY

On a cold night in Detroit, Ford's green brain trust gathered at the Rattlesnake Club for an on-the-record dinner with journalists. Executive chairman Bill Ford was the lead attraction, but also on hand were Sue Cischke, group vice president for sustainability and the environment; Barb Samardzich, a global products vice president; and Sherif Marakby, director of the company's electrification program.

Earlier in the day, at the 2011 Detroit auto show, Ford had introduced the Energi, the car that finally ended years of speculation about which platform would host the plug-in hybrid the company planned to introduce in 2012. It's a C-Max, and there will be a C-Max hybrid, too. The C-Max is a five-passenger crossover imported from Spain, and a good choice for a green makeover. A few days before, Ford had unveiled its long-awaited Focus battery car at the Consumer Electronics Show in Las Vegas, and in Detroit it had set up a tiny test track for it on the show floor. With an anxious Ford tech in the passenger's seat, I piloted the Focus up an incline. The car briefly stalled on the dynamometer, and after the Ford guy muttered something about a "reset" we were on again. It wasn't a real test, but at least now I could say I'd driven Ford's new battery car.

The Focus is part of a strategy that will include the introduction of five new hybrid and battery electric cars by 2012, including the Focus and C-Max cars, plus the Transit Connect electric van. "It's been a hell of a ride over the last four years," Bill Ford said at the dinner, pointing out that a similar event three years ago was much more somber. "We've been through good and bad times, and you never declare victory."

Ford is the only one of the Big Three to escape bankruptcy and reorganization, thanks to some timely planning by CEO Alan Mulally in 2006—he mortgaged company assets and built up a $23 billion cash war chest that at the time he called "a cushion to protect for a recession or other unexpected event." That act, considered folly at the time, proved so prescient given the horrific year the automakers experienced in 2008 that Mulally has been the golden boy ever since. At the dinner, there was speculation about how the company could replace him should the unthinkable happen and Mulally move on. "When he gets to 98 or 99 we can talk about retirement," Ford said.

He likes to say that Mulally has imbued the company's culture with smart thinking, so it will now keep its eyes on the prize no matter who's in the executive suite. And its green strategy has remained remarkably consistent over the years—a suite of hybrid and battery EV offerings, with something for every buyer.

Bill Ford brought green to the table when he took over for his own stint as president and CEO in 2001. Ford said that his early efforts (which included championing electric car and hydrogen pilot programs) were met with skepticism from company engineers, and it has sometimes been hard to see the green cars through the thicket of SUVs, from Expeditions to Excursions, that lined the dealerships. That's in the past, though. "This is an exciting time, although with big challenges," said Cischke.

In Detroit, Ford called for a national energy policy that could give the company some clarity about where the United States is going as a country. The outlook for green cars is a bit like "throwing darts," he said, because the market is buffeted by external factors—and especially the price of gas. Ford started talking about the need for a gas tax 10 years ago, but passage of a comprehensive energy and climate bill would be pretty useful, too.

Ford is developing its range of environmentally friendly options for an uncertain market. "There's a lot of prognostication about car sales being 25 percent electric by X year, but really, who knows?" Ford said. The company has very modest goals for the Focus electric (up to 5,000 cars worldwide the first year), but Samardzich points out that it could ramp up production quickly because the car is a Focus, which is built on a high-volume assembly line. That's a big built-in advantage the established carmakers have, and it speaks to the point made by Maryann Keller about challenges for start-ups.

Marakby said that hybrids have been on the market for a decade, but still represent only about 2 percent of the car market. Ford itself entered the hybrid sweepstakes in 2004 with the Escape. That was late in one sense, since the Prius debuted in 2000, though it was ahead of other American companies. But Toyota defined the market: In a good year, Ford (with some parts availability limitations) sells 15,000 to 20,000 Escape Hybrids in the United States, but Toyota sells 10 times more Priuses. The newer Fusion hybrid has sold well, however, sales build geometrically: "Eighty percent of new cars bought by hybrid owners are hybrids," Cischke said.

Like other carmakers, and in particular European ones, Ford would build green cars even without a vote of confidence from the public because it needs to meet a tightening regulatory regime. The Obama administration's combined climate and fuel economy regulations call for a fleet average of 35.5 mpg by 2016, and that standard rises to 54.5 mpg by 2025. The *Jalopnik* blog, performance oriented like most of the auto press, declared that the new standards "killed all the fun cars."[19] In Europe, cars are required to meet a very strict emission standard of 120 grams of carbon dioxide per kilometer by 2012, and 95 grams by 2020.

Samardzich said that Ford is working to meet the targets by taking as much as 500 to 700 pounds out of some of its cars. "And that allows the engine teams to keep driving down the size of engines," she said. "There's no limit to what we can achieve." The company is also working with low-emission biofuels.

At the end of the dinner I brought up the prospect, advanced by many environmental groups, that carmakers should have been held to a 60-mpg fuel economy standard for 2025. Automakers think that it's overreaching, and it didn't go over all that well at the Rattlesnake Club. But Ford concluded by saying that the company will be ready for any standard that comes down the turnpike, and 60 mpg may look like child's play by then.[20]

ELECTRICS EVERYWHERE YOU LOOK

Nearly every mainstream carmaker on the planet is talking electric, showing electric cars and hybrids, and finally giving them actual street dates. There are electrics, at least in show-car form, from Volkswagen, Audi, Daimler, Honda, Toyota, Chrysler, BMW, and more. Some are serious efforts, others public relations exercises. But it's encouraging to see the activity.

Let's start with Chrysler, because any EVs have to come out of a radically reorganized company, with a majority share owned by the Fiat Group and headed by that company's CEO, Sergio Marchionne. The company that had to absorb German culture when it was DaimlerChrysler now needs to go to Berlitz to learn Italian.

Chrysler's near-death experience killed its ambitious plans to launch electric cars under the ENVI banner in 2009. Among the ENVI vehicles was the snazzy, bright orange Dodge Circuit that was first shown in 2008. The very small Circuit, based on a Lotus like the Tesla Roadster, offered similarly high performance—the 200-kilowatt electric motor promised 268 horsepower and a zero-to-60 time of less than five seconds. Range was 150 to 200 miles from a lithium-ion battery pack. The car was tight for two passengers, just like the Tesla, and suffered from poor rear visibility.

A version of the Circuit could be coming back, as might the plug-in minivan and Jeep the company showed. But Chrysler is pinning its hopes on an electric version of the tiny Fiat 500. Chrysler is hoping that lightning will strike twice and Americans will take to the retro 500 as they did to the Volkswagen New Beetle. The 500 name doesn't have the resonance in the United States that it does in Europe (where the tiny 1957 version was a design icon), but the gas version of the car, which starts at $15,500, is definitely cute and fun to drive.

The electric 500 has lithium-ion batteries from SB LiMotive, a joint venture between Samsung and Bosch that is also supplying BMW's Megacity Vehicle. Earlier reports had said that ENVI supplier A123 was doing the packs, but that company's CEO, David Vieau, said it had pulled out of the deal in part because the project's volumes had gotten too small.

The 500 is green in a number of ways. A neat aspect of all American 500s is free Eco:Drive software that can be downloaded to the car via USB.[21] Candido Peterlini of Fiat Group told me that the system records driver behavior related to acceleration and deceleration, braking, speed, and gear changes. It measures that performance against eco-driving ideals, which include early gear changes, maintaining a steady speed, smooth acceleration, and efficient deceleration. Early tests of the system in Europe led to controversial ratings that gave the highest marks for eco-driving to British and German drivers and the lowest to the French, Italians, and Spanish.

Marchionne said in 2009 discussions of Chrysler's new product plans that expensive batteries make electric cars a difficult business proposition. And he predicted that less than 2 percent of its vehicles would be electric by 2014. That, coupled with the expected low volumes of the 500, doesn't give much confidence in Chrysler as an emerging green car leader.

An amusing aspect of the EV phenomenon is the number of automakers that initially dismissed electric cars but then got on the bandwagon when they saw momentum building. In that box I would put Honda (which said for years it was betting on hydrogen fuel–cell cars and produced the spectacular FCX Clarity) and all the German automakers, which repeatedly stressed the advantages of diesel over electricity to reluctant American buyers. I've had many German fingers waved in my face in defense of diesel.

But BMW has that carbon-fiber-bodied i3 Megacity Vehicle (MCV), an urban electric with 100-mile-range, on tap for 2013. It has built electric versions of both the Mini and the 1 Series Coupé, and these are on the road in global test programs as rolling research beds for the MCV. Ulrich Kranz, director of the Project i team that is building the MCV, told me that the rapid growth of megacities—those with populations of more than 10 million— pushed the project to the fore. "We went out and talked to city planners," Kranz told me in 2010.[22] "And we visited potential customers living in megacities such as Los Angeles, London, Tokyo and Shanghai. We lived a couple of days with them. We wanted to see not only what they said about their driving habits, but also what they actually did when they drove to work."

A *McKinsey Quarterly* report in early 2011 predicted "big clusters of potential early adopters" in big cities.[23] That could include 30 percent of all car buyers in Shanghai and 20 percent in New York. The study said that, by 2015, battery cars could account for 16 percent of overall new car sales in New York City, 9 percent in Paris, and 5 percent in Shanghai. "That's true even with today's financial incentives and limited public charging facilities," the report said.

BMW has a sensible approach to building an EV. It's using lightweight but tough carbon fiber, which will reduce weight and result in a smaller battery pack that will reach the 100-mile range. After all, if the Megacity Vehicle isn't affordable in the megacity, what good is it?

I own a Honda Fit, so I was gratified to see Honda electrify that versatile model. I talked to Ben Knight, a vice president of research and development at the company, about why it had plunged ahead with an electric Fit. "Why not?" he replied. That's as good an answer as any, but until recently Honda was far more dismissive of electric cars. I'm more used to having the company tell me why plugging in doesn't make sense. Honda's R&D president, Tomohiko Kawanabe, said in the spring of 2010, "We lack confidence [in the electric vehicle business]. It's questionable whether consumers will accept the annoyances of limited driving range and having to spend time charging them. . . . We are definitely conducting research on electric cars, but I can't say I can wholeheartedly recommend them."[24]

Uh, okay. Honda had been somewhat soured by its experience

with the EVPlus battery car, a contemporary of the General Motors EV1 that sold no better. But then, in the fall of 2010, Honda CEO Takanobu Ito signaled a change. He told Reuters, "It's starting to look like there will be a market for electric vehicles. We can't keep shooting down their potential, and we can't say there's no business case for it."[25]

The company acted quickly. At the Los Angeles Auto Show soon after, Honda unveiled both an electric Fit for 2012 and a bare platform that will become a new plug-in hybrid car.[26] The Fit electric uses lithium-ion batteries and shares its electric motor with the FCX Clarity hydrogen car, attaining 100 miles of realistic range. The Fit is already being produced in a hybrid version, though not for the US market.

The electric Fit, which has three drive modes—normal, sport, and economy, with the latter adding 17 percent battery range—will go into California test programs at Stanford University, Google (where it'll be part of the company's GFleet, whose environmental performance is being tracked online), and the City of Torrance.

"The Fit is a great package, small but with enough room for a band with all its equipment," Knight told me. "We learned from the EVPlus that people want to use their electric cars for all their errands, and the Fit is the perfect platform for that." Indeed it is, which is why I bought one.

Toyota, another battery-car naysayer, is also getting with the program. The company's loss leader for 2012 is a plug-in hybrid version of the Prius with 9 to 13 miles of all-electric range and a price only a few thousand dollars more than a standard Prius. Roland Hwang of the NRDC told me the Prius plug-in hybrid is the green car he expects to buy. "It has a lot of potential because it's an incremental improvement on well-proven technology," he said. "In the short term, plug-in hybrids are going to have bigger market share than pure electrics."

I spent a week with a Prius plug-in hybrid and liked it a lot. Because I work at home, my daily driving didn't strain the 13 miles of all-electric range. Having the car meant it was pressed into service for my Dad's Taxi Service, and the kids were in back, chattering with one of their friends. "Kids, this is your first-ever all-electric ride," I told them. "It's historic!" Their chatter stopped for a minute. I tried to explain what a plug-in hybrid is. "So it isn't really an electric car?" they asked, and then went back to texting and horsing around. They weren't going to share my sense of moment.

Yes, the plug-in Prius, with a small 5.3-kilowatt-hour battery pack, is an electric car some of the time. The small pack size means that it can recharge from house current in three hours, and it was dead easy to plug it in. And the car is also a regular Prius when the standard hybrid drive kicks in. In my experience over a week, the plug-in hybrid Prius had about 12.5 miles of all-electric range and delivered something over 60 mpg if you look at it that way. We don't yet have a good formula for figuring out the mileage of plug-in hybrids, because they can be driven mostly or not at all electrically. The Volt claimed 230 mpg, then dropped the idea. And the Volt's first government rating is on the gas engine alone, not its entire cycle that includes electric-only driving.

Toyota has shown some small urban electric car prototypes, but it never did much with them. But it's serious now. Planned for 2012 are both an electric version of the diminutive iQ for city driving and a larger electric RAV4 that it developed very rapidly in partnership with Tesla Motors.[27]

Tesla's Elon Musk and Toyota CEO Akio Toyoda (a grandson of the company's founder) hit it off over a ride in the Tesla Roadster, and the plug-in RAV4 was one of the fruits of that friendship. Toyota liked the test version Tesla built and quickly slated it for production. The RAV4 had been electrified in an earlier incarnation. Its many fans succeeded in keeping it out of the crusher, like the EV1, and it retains a loyal following to this day (with several celebrity owners). Toyota spokesman John Hanson told me, "We looked at many different combinations, but the RAV4 made the most sense from the beginning. It's a small SUV, and it gives us a lot of flexibility with packaging."

The Audi E-tron electrics run the gamut, and certainly look the part. The A1 E-tron is really cool, looking much like the European production car but a serial hybrid under the skin, with a 60-horsepower electric motor driving the front wheels for 31 miles, after which an outlandish 20-horsepower Wankel rotary engine mounted under the load deck kicks in to extend the range for another 124 miles. As in the Fisker Karma and Chevrolet Volt, the engine acts as a generator and doesn't power the wheels directly. I'd buy one, but I'd like to see more gas-powered range.

The electric A1 is no speed demon. Car magazines prefer the high-speed version of the E-tron, a kind of mini and lightweight (less than 3,000 pounds) R8 that would give Tesla a run for its money. Michael Dick of the Audi Management Board told me that the E-tron's four electric motors produce a peak output of 313 horsepower, which can get the car to 62 mph in just 4.8 seconds. The big 53-kilowatt-hour battery pack weighs more than 1,200 pounds, so it's a good thing the rest of the car is light. Range is 155 miles.

Audi will sell a limited edition of the R8 E-tron starting in 2012, after which, according to Dick, "the customers will decide what happens next." The customer has to be deep-pocketed, because this car is expensive.

I briefly rode in the Volkswagen Golf Blue-E-Motion electric car in Santa Monica, California, at a gala VW party that featured *Gossip Girl* Jessica Szohr.[28] Although it had decent performance from its 26.5-kilowatt-hour Sanyo Li-ion battery pack (and 93-mile range), it was a work in progress. Doug Skorupski, a consultant to Volkswagen, said that four design teams are working on the e-Golf. The test programs go through 2012, followed by the production car in 2013.

I've heard that VW has a prominent silent partner in its battery-car program, but understandably nobody wanted to confirm that. It makes sense, because VW is new to the electric car business, doesn't have its own technical base in the area, and was definitely one of those companies wagging its fingers about diesel. VW announced a limited association with Chinese battery- and carmaker BYD on electrics and plug-in hybrids in 2009. The company is clearly conflicted, as Honda is, about electric cars. On a recent electric mobility tour of Germany, the company spent a lot of its face time with journalists explaining why battery cars don't make sense.

Electric has momentum now, so it's hauling just about everyone along for the ride.

CHAPTER FIVE

CHARGING AHEAD

The players involved don't realize how complex this
is going to get.

—CHELSEA SEXTON, EV ADVOCATE

FOR 100 YEARS, automakers and the oil companies vital to their enterprise have maintained cordial but largely separate businesses. There never was much reason for them to actively collaborate. We have a different paradigm now. For electric cars to work, the auto companies *have* to work closely with utilities. As soon as the flow of electrons stops, so does the car. That's true of gasoline, too, of course, but as soon as the basic exchange had been worked out—stations in every neighborhood dispensing gas and oil—the two industries could go their separate ways.

EV charging is still a work in progress, and it won't be fully evolved until the cars have been on the road for a few years. Consumer preference will determine how often people will plug in at home and how often at public stations. Lots of people have put in their two cents on this—and the general assumption is that 80 percent of charging will be done at home. But it's just speculation.

It's critically important that we get charging right, and electric cars can live or die based on how it plays out. From what I've seen, not enough of the hard work has been done to ensure a smooth transition to electric transportation. There are still a lot of questions, many of them relating to how charging will unfold in the urban settings where EVs work best. People who live in apartments don't have garages.

Will the stations be on the street? In parking garages? Dusty state and local regulations also complicate EV charging, and that obstacle should have been cleared away before the cars rolled out. Even something as basic as standardizing fast-charging ports dragged on well past the point of EV introductions.

Another really basic issue puts charging stations up against battery swapping. Suppose you could just drive into something resembling a gas station without attendants and have robots switch your battery pack for a fresh, charged one in just minutes? It's not science fiction, it's here now, and it offers a solution that's particularly useful for the long trips that battery EVs are ill equipped to deliver.

In April of 2010, I sat in a Tokyo hotel conference room with Shai Agassi, the founder of global charging company Better Place. Agassi is an intense, driven guy, and one-on-one he's overwhelming, with a vision of an all-electric transportation future that leaves little room for doubt. EVs are not going to be "10 percent of the market. By 2025, maybe even 2020, nobody will sell a gasoline car," he told me with the certainty that has rallied whole countries to this Israeli-born entrepreneur's side. "[Electrics] will be the only market. Then you realize that there's a billion electric cars about to be sold. . . . You don't go into denial, you get excited about it."[1]

I was certainly excited. Agassi goes his own way, and in

Tokyo he was presenting a whole alternative vision for electric cars. Instead of plugging them in for 16 hours on 110-volt house current (known as Level I), six to eight hours on 240 (Level II), or 20 minutes on 480 (Level III), he was proposing to bypass charging stations and swap batteries in an automated process lasting less than a minute.

The process works—I saw it demonstrated in bustling downtown Tokyo, with standing room only for the international press. I was on board one of the three taxis in the program (Nissan Rogues converted to electric) when it drove into a station about the size of a double-wide house trailer. With a mad whirring, the robots took over—dropping down the depleted batteries and replacing them with fully charged units.

"What we're now demonstrating is that you can have an electric car that will go and go and go, and you'll only need to switch the battery every 100 miles or so, with the whole process taking less than a minute," Agassi told me. "You end up spending less time than you would at a gas station, because fills there take five minutes. We will see cars operating for 100 days, putting on 10,000 to 15,000 miles, without ever stopping for a recharge."

Had Agassi just changed the rules? Will Mr. and Mrs. Jetson drive their Futuremobile down the interstate of tomorrow stopping only for pee breaks and quick battery swaps? It might be nice to think it will be so, but I'm skeptical. What works well for taxis is unlikely to suit the fantastically varied auto fleet, with cars in all shapes and sizes and battery packs following suit.

The Israeli plan will put 45,000 Renault Fluence ZE electric cars with swappable batteries on the road. It might work well if drivers stick to the Fluence (they'll all have the same pack, of course), but it's likely that the public will want some diversity.

The Fluence is a sister car to the Nissan Leaf, and the Leaf doesn't have swappable batteries. Agassi's challenge is to convince more EV companies to get with the program and at least make versions of their cars with switchable battery packs.

Still, Agassi has lined up an impressive list of customers for Better Place's charging formula, which includes conventional charging stations for short-distance travel along with battery swapping for longer trips. Israel, Denmark, and Australia are all signed on, as are Hawaii and four regions in California. The plan to wire Israel is well under way, working toward a commercial launch in late 2011, and the company had signed on 92 corporate fleet owners there (representing half the country's fleet cars) by early 2010. Denmark actually got there first, opening its first Better Place showroom early that year.

Agassi thinks that, as EV volumes grow, battery packs will be standardized in a few basic sizes—making swapping a lot easier. That's possible, but it's pretty far in the future. These days, automakers are fitting their packs into every available square inch of the car to try to squeeze out as much range as possible. And they're expecting their battery packs to be charged, not swapped. Agassi could wire his charging partners without the battery swap piece, but he's a visionary, and that's part of the vision.

One of the reasons that electric cars are finally going into commercial launch mode is because a robust network of public charging stations is being installed as the cars ramp up. Two federally supported programs, the EV Project and ChargePoint America, are putting charge stations in the ground, and their plans include some fast 480-volt DC chargers, which can fill up an electric car nearly all the way in just 20 to 30 minutes.

The chargers are being installed in home garages and

municipal parking lots, at gas stations and at big-box retailers (with Best Buy being the most enthusiastic). Earlier EV rollouts were stillborn in part because the charging infrastructure never achieved liftoff, despite pioneering efforts by retailers such as Costco (which had 90 stations installed as of 2006). It didn't help that in the late 1990s, with the General Motors EV1 struggling for traction, automakers adopted two mutually exclusive charging types—inductive and conductive. Today, that's sorted out and every automaker in the American market is using a standard conductive plug tagged with the ungainly name J1772 (sometimes called the "J Plug") by its sponsor, the Society of Automotive Engineers.

And major charging players have emerged, including not only Better Place but also ECOtality, Coulomb, AeroVironment, EV Connect, Clipper Creek, and home electrical equipment giant Leviton, among others. Some operate internationally, as Better Place does. And General Electric's entry into the market with the designer-enhanced WattStation was a sign that big companies are getting into the game, too.

WIRING THE WORLD

It is early 2010, and I am at the Greener Gadgets conference in New York, listening to a curly haired young Swiss, Yves Béhar, talk about changing the world through design. Béhar, described as a design "superstar" by *Fast Company*,[2] was up at the podium describing his vision for the "hackable" electric car. It would be, like Linux, on a very simple open-source platform that people could improve, and to save money the front half would be essentially the same stamping as the back half. On the roof: A solar panel, of course. The headlights: LEDs.

Béhar is most famous for designing the Jawbone Bluetooth headset and (with MIT's Nicholas Negroponte) a laptop computer that could be built for $100, so it was interesting to hear his ideas for shaking up the auto industry. A fan of the $2,500 Tata Nano mini-car from India (he called it "awesome" in an interview), Béhar said his EV design could easily be transformed into a pickup, SUV, or station wagon. Established auto companies are "very much stuck in a design rut," he said. "They need original design briefs and 21st-century business models."[3]

In an e-mail, Béhar told me, "The famous brief for the [Citroën] 2CV was to allow two peasants to drive 100 kilograms [220 pounds] of goods to market at 60 kilometers an hour [37 mph], across rutted fields without breaking eggs. While wearing hats. And of course, that brief led to a vehicle that was insanely hackable. And in fact, the models that have existed largely unchanged for decades in automotive history often have that in common—the Ford Model T, the 22R-based Toyota pickup, the Citroën 2CV, the Volkswagen Beetle and Bus, the Series Land Rovers and the Jeep CJ. And people have done things with them the designers and engineers behind them never would have considered."

I love it when people think out of the box, and Béhar plainly wants to smash the box to bits. Despite that, he's lined up major contracts to design everything from headphones to LED lamps, chandeliers, and dog accessories. Béhar developed a reputation for stripping down long-established products to their basic functionality, then proposing a better way of making them.

So it was perhaps inevitable that Béhar would get the brief to design the General Electric WattStation, a charger for both home and public use that set off a mini revolution. After the ultrasleek public WattStation debuted in July of 2010,[4] other charging companies imitated it with designer-enhanced models. Considering the plain, industrial-looking chargers that had been the norm (think the blinking-light panels in 1950s science-fiction movies), Béhar did the world a favor.

Traditional public EV chargers look like scaled-down gas pumps; Béhar's WattStation is more like a parking meter or an automatic teller machine at a bank. The round display is angled toward the user, and the charging cable retracts when not in use. Like many modern chargers, it is designed to integrate with the smart grid and with online billing systems—swipe a card and the station can access your account. The design is so pretty that I worried it might be vulnerable to vandalism, but Béhar assured me it was tough—and the retractable cord is a security measure.

The public WattStation was soon followed by an oval, wall-mounted home version, designed to sell for approximately $1,000, that makes it simple to choose a late-night charging time with the lowest possible electricity rates. The company said it would recharge an EV with a 24-kilowatt-hour battery pack in four to eight hours. The environmental equation gets better when solar panels are added to the mix, and GE showed off a large photovoltaic array with charging for 13 cars daily at a company parking lot in Connecticut.

My first thought about the home version of the WattStation had to do with marketing. Most chargers are being offered by the companies—Coulomb, ECOtality, and others—that are also wiring municipalities, giving them a built-in market. But GE had that base covered—in September of 2010 it announced a partnership with Better Place[5] that should help get WattStations into public places and garages all over the world.

I reconnected with Shai Agassi, who told me that GE's public chargers are likely to be seen at sports arenas, movie theaters, and other places where people spend hours at a time. "We're seeing less interest in charging at retail locations where people are going to be spending just 10 or 15 minutes," Agassi said. "It might not justify the hassle of connecting the cable. There's more opportunity at places where you park for two or three hours."

GE's David Searles, director of the company's Ecomagination program, told me that his company likes Better Place's battery-swapping plan because "it allows the EV to become a vehicle with all the same functionality as an internal-combustion car—it won't be limited by range."

Like Agassi, GE goes for game-changing moves, and it certainly created one of those when it announced in November 2010, just four months after unveiling the WattStation, that it would buy 25,000 electric cars by 2015, including 12,500 Chevrolet Volts, for its own use and that of fleet customers. The company was, in effect, creating its own market for the WattStation, and jump-starting the vital corporate fleet business for electric cars. I was soon informed that GE CEO Jeffrey Immelt was driving a Volt and charging it at company headquarters in Fairfield, Connecticut (just down the road from where I live).

GE equipment generates a third of the world's electricity, and Immelt's announcement about the car purchase was a practical one. "Wide-scale adoption of electric vehicles will also drive clean-energy innovation, strengthen energy security and deliver economic value," he said in a statement.[6] Immelt is an outspoken clean energy advocate who supports putting a price on carbon emissions, and his ability to influence the public debate was enhanced in early 2011 when he was named to succeed Paul Volcker as head of President Obama's Council on Jobs and Competitiveness. Perhaps he'll drive to meetings in his Volt, which could make the trip from Fairfield to Washington without either refueling or recharging.

CHARGING AHEAD

Few charging companies have the market clout of General Electric. But two big players, Coulomb and ECOtality, got a boost from federal funding in programs that have put chargers in home garages and public places. The EV Project, announced in 2009 and managed by California-based ECOtality, is a $230 million effort that includes $115 million from the Department of Energy. With partners Chevrolet and Nissan, ECOtality was to put 14,000 chargers in 18 cities and metro areas in six states (Oregon, Washington, California, Arizona, Tennessee, and Texas) plus the District of Columbia at no cost to the municipalities or homeowners. For people lucky enough to own a Leaf or Volt, it meant a totally free garage charger worth approximately $2,000.

Most of the chargers in the program are 240-volt AC units that can charge a car in four to eight hours, but the project also paid for more than 300 of ECOtality's own Blink DC fast chargers with 20 to 30 minutes to full. Fast chargers are incredibly expensive, priced at $15,000 to $50,000. So federal help makes a difference, and could also enable EV charging at gas stations—the place we're accustomed to going to refuel our cars.

How much time do you spend at a gas station? Five to seven minutes? That's probably about average, and it explains why even a 20-minute charge time is a challenge for gas station EV refueling. The key questions are not only the need to find something productive to do in that time, but also the fact that you would be tying up the charging station for that amount of time.

A few things to keep in mind, though: Most cars won't be pulling into the gas station (or other fast-charge location) with an empty "tank," so filling up won't take the full 20 minutes. And, as Mark Perry, director of product planning and strategy for Nissan, pointed out to me, drivers could end up pulling in for a quick jolt, adding 10 miles of range in five minutes at the station. A McDonald's in Cary, North Carolina, became the first fast-food restaurant to offer free 240-volt charging—the stopover there is probably just right for topping off.

What's the prospect for fast chargers at gas stations? A landmark deal was announced in November of 2010 when ECOtality said that it would install its 480-volt Blink stations at 45 BP and Arco gas stations in five states as part of the EV Project. Given the oil spill, BP needed a green makeover, and if Shai Agassi is right, by 2020 BP will need to be in the EV business anyway. We'll return to the challenges and opportunities of fast charging later in the chapter.

The second of two federally supported programs, the $37 million ChargePoint America, was launched a little later, in the summer of 2010. Coulomb Technologies was chosen as the manager of the initiative, which secured $15 million in Recovery and Reinvestment Act funding administered by the Department of Energy. This program paid for 5,000 chargers in nine regions, from San Francisco to Orlando. ChargePoint's partners are Ford, Chevrolet, and Smart, supporting a range of electric vehicles.

These programs geographically target regions that are also in the glide path of early EV introductions. The Nissan Leaf, for instance, rolled out in roughly the same places identified by the EV Project. It obviously makes sense, when EV numbers are still very limited, to concentrate resources that way.

The Electrification Coalition, a Washington, DC–based EV advocacy group that includes both utility leaders (among them David Crane of NRG Energy, who let me drive his Tesla Roadster) and carmakers (including Nissan's Carlos Ghosn), envisions in its widely distributed *Electrification Roadmap* report that 75 percent of transportation miles traveled by 2040 could be "electric miles." That's not quite as optimistic as Agassi's projection, but it's still in the upper reaches of what's possible. The coalition puts a small asterisk by that prediction, cautioning that it's likely to happen only if its policy initiatives are realized. And those proposals include an ambitious federal plan to subsidize EV deployment communities.

The plan, codified into the Promoting Natural Gas and Electric Vehicles Act of 2010, sponsored by Senator Harry Reid (D-NV), would have supported 400,000 EV introductions, with $500 million in funding through an increase in oil taxes. It went nowhere in the 111th Congress, but received a new lease in the 112th early in 2011. Vice president Joe Biden mentioned a modified version in a speech at battery company Ener1 headquarters in Indiana the day after the State of the Union address.

Biden renewed President Obama's call for a million "advanced technology" cars by 2015, and also put the executive branch behind a plan to "provide grants to up to 30 communities that are prioritizing advanced technology vehicle deployment."[7] The 2012 federal budget proposal included $300 million to provide $10 million each to the 30 communities. It would not only help install chargers, but also work to remove the regulatory headaches that are a barrier to fast EV adoption. Electrification Coalition CEO Robbie Diamond praised the deployment community idea as the best way to get electric cars beyond early adopters and deliver the keys to "millions of typical American families."[8]

Biden also endorsed a bill, introduced by Senator Debbie Stabenow (D-MI), that would provide $2 billion in new electric car battery funding and turn the $7,500 federal tax credit for electric cars into a rebate—paid to the dealer at the point of purchase. Given the high cost of the cars and the wait for tax credits to kick in, this would undoubtedly increase sales. "You won't have to wait," said Biden, who compared the proposal to the successful Cash for Clunkers program.

ROLLING OUT EVS:
BARRIERS TO ADOPTION

Installing an EV charger in a home garage is not a huge job. Any home with an electric clothes dryer already has a high-voltage circuit that can be extended to the appropriate location. Older homes may have inadequate electric service, requiring an upgrade to 200 amps or above. That can be expensive, but including the cost of the charger itself, the bottom line is usually about $2,000.

But that's not accounting for the fact that such installations are administered locally, by towns that may never have heard of electric cars and aren't familiar with the procedure. You'll need a municipal permit to install your charger, and that means a visit from a local inspector and scheduling an electrician. It's not that complicated, but there are often unnecessary paperwork delays. Installations that could occur in just one day are stretched over a month. Utilities and some municipalities are working on streamlining the process, and some have joined with Project Get Ready (a spinoff of the Rocky Mountain Institute) to share information. Richard Lowenthal, chief technical officer of Coulomb Technologies, told me it took a month to get everything in order to install the charger for his BMW Mini E—and he's in the charging business!

There is no more committed EV advocate than Chelsea Sexton, who is best known as the angry former General Motors employee in Chris Paine's *Who Killed the Electric Car?* and went from boosting the launch of the EV1 electric car to mourning its crushing at the company's hands. She later served as the first director of advocacy group Plug In America.

But Sexton has come full circle. Like director Chris Paine (whose successor film is *The Revenge of the Electric Car*), she became a GM insider. Paine was allowed into GM's Detroit-Hamtramck factory to film the first Volts rolling off the assembly line, and Sexton became the only female member of the Chevrolet Volt Customer Advisory Board.

A perk of being on the advisory board was that Sexton got a free Volt on loan, which meant installing a 240-volt charger at her Los Angeles–area home. The only problem is that she lives in a condominium. It didn't go well.

In October 2010, the GM team descended on Sexton's multi-family home in El Segundo, California, to install the charger.[9] It should have been an easy job, because Sexton has a garage and a 200-amp panel. And, indeed, there were no problems until Sexton brought up her need for a "time of use" electric meter. A little background is helpful here. California utilities have taken the lead in offering their electricity users the option of pricing categories based on their electric usage. Because Sexton used what she calls a "stunningly low" amount of electricity, she was on the lowest tier. But charging the Volt would edge her into a higher bracket, making it likely that, for her, EV charging "would be more expensive than putting gas in my Saturn." With the time-of-use meter, the EV would be billed separately and wouldn't count as part of her home use.

But California's public utilities commission required all of its customers' electric meters to be grouped together, and that meant installing the time-of-use meter would require a one-inch-thick metal conduit along the face of her building. The other option was to punch through three neighbors' walls. "I can just see the homeowners' association going for that," Sexton said. California's complicated electricity rules have left a lot of state residents scratching their heads. "I get questions about EV charging in multifamily housing almost daily," says Paul Scott, who sells the Leaf at Santa Monica Nissan (a job that grew out of his role as vice president of Plug In America).

According to Sexton, "There's nothing about my installation that they shouldn't have seen coming. . . . And the point is that it happened to me, someone who understands the process as well as anyone, who has access to all the right people, who's been party to hundreds of installations. So the average person is likely to get incredibly frustrated and may end up walking away—unless they're so enthusiastic that they'll put up with it."

Sexton didn't blame GM or her Southern California Edison

utility provider, either. After everything was installed and her Volt was plugged in, she told me, "All the stakeholders "need to be thinking more creatively about how we can get around some of these logistical difficulties, as well as how to streamline the over-all process to be shorter in general." The players involved don't realize how complex this is going to get, Sexton said. "Even when there are no hurdles, it can take weeks to get done, between the customer, dealer, electrician, city planner/permitter, utility, city inspectors and so on involved. . . . I find it a little funny that I of all people [ended up with a] challenging installation."

I'm also dubious that such advance planning has in fact occurred, particularly in cities with many multifamily dwellings. Installing charging in home garages is the easy part. In 2010, I attended a Columbia University conference in Manhattan with the lofty title New York and the Electric Car. As I reported then, "Instead of focusing on the nuts and bolts of how the city's many apartment-dwelling electric vehicle owners will plug in, the forum celebrated the prospective role of electric cars in changing the world."[10] That's all well and good—I think EVs will change the world, too, but we still have to address the many unanswered questions on the ground.

It's not a capacity issue. At Columbia, Arthur Kressner, then the director of power supply research and development at Con-solidated Edison, said that, except for relatively rare peak demand times, "the grid is more than capable of meeting the demands of electric vehicles." It probably is, but the logistical challenge of locating charging spots in a city with some of the world's most valuable curbside real estate wasn't addressed. But Kressner did say Con Ed had met with charging companies, including Better Place, and with parking garage owners. Parking garages, including those at larger apartment buildings, are likely to host a lot of urban charging stations.

PAYING THE PIPER: PUBLIC CHARGING COULD BE EXPENSIVE

The public chargers, such as GE's WattStation, ECOtality's Blink, and the ChargePoint Network from Coulomb, all contain high-tech features. Coulomb stations, for instance, can be located using smartphone apps, which are also capable of starting and ending a charging session. The owners of those stations can set pricing via a Web-enabled user interface that will also manage grid load and billing for energy providers.

Public chargers are designed to be accessed by smart-card-owning car owners, who will then get billed for the electricity they use. But a lot of early public charging was actually free to users, because the details of billing hadn't been worked out yet. At issue is a thicket of state laws and uncertainty over what the traffic will bear.

One complicating factor is that, by early 2011, only one state, California, actually allowed third-party companies (other than utilities) to charge customers for electricity by the kilowatt-hour. It sounds like a technicality, but it's actually a pretty big deal. If charging companies have to bill simply by the hour or per session, it's an issue because EVs take up electricity at different rates depending on the ratings of their onboard chargers. The Nissan Leaf was launched with a charger that could take on 3.3 kilowatts in an hour, but the Tesla Roadster gobbles up 7.2 kilowatts in that same time.

The other route is through deregulation of electricity: Companies in some electricity deregulation states can become licensed resellers of electricity (and charge by the kilowatt-hour), but getting such certification is a long, arduous process.

The Florida-based Car Charging Group (CCG), whose business model is based on installing chargers at its own cost in partnership with business owners and then sharing the profits with them, is an early player in New York City, where it signed a deal to put 240-volt chargers in garages and lots owned by Icon Parking. How much will it charge for a charge? Michael Farkas, the company's CEO, told me $3.50 an hour if it can't charge by the kilowatt-hour[11] or 50 cents per kilowatt-hour if it can. That's a fair amount of money when New Yorkers pay 25 cents per kilowatt-hour for electricity during the day and only 10 cents at night.[12]

At 50 cents a kilowatt-hour, the Think City (a small, two-seat battery car) would still operate at 12 cents a mile, versus 17 cents for a 20-mpg gas car. But it's not the huge advantage in operating costs that EV enthusiasts have touted. And for cars with bigger battery packs and longer charging times, public charging could get very expensive very quickly.

Those are, of course, early rates, dictated at a point when the company was feeling its way forward. The prices were not yet affected by what the traffic will bear, and those numbers will reflect burgeoning competition. "The industry is still in a nascent stage, still jockeying for position and working out pricing," Michael Lew, a research analyst at Needham and Company, told me.[13]

But that high preliminary pricing is an indication that a lot of public charging will be on a for-profit basis, and mostly cost more than simply plugging in at home. It could become a choice of last resort, when all the charging bars have disappeared and it's either stop or run out of juice. Given how convenient home recharging is, it's not surprising that experts such as Nissan's Mark Perry predict that 80 percent of all EV charging will be done at home, at night.

Although it's partnered with ECOtality on the rollout of public chargers, Nissan is working with a long-established company, AeroVironment, on its all-important home units. AeroVironment was founded in 1971 by the late Paul MacCready (described by *Time* as one of "the greatest minds of the 20th century"). When he wasn't designing the famed Gossamer Condor and other human-powered and lighter-than-air planes, he was coming up with the Impact, the General Motors electric car that evolved into the EV1.

AeroVironment's name isn't featured on the home chargers— they're branded Nissan—but its long expertise is behind them. AeroVironment's Kristen Helsel, vice president of EV Solutions, told me, "I think what sold Nissan is that we're an established company, not a start-up. And they liked not only the design of the charger itself but that we had the whole package: The installation, plus the customer service piece."[14] AeroVironment later added BMW as a customer, too. Customer service is going to matter a lot here, which is why Ford is teaming up with Best Buy's Geek Squad for its EV charger installation and quick-response service. "Though there's a lot of media attention to public charging, it's really important to get the home part done right," Nissan's Perry told me. It's crucial, in fact.

FAST CHARGING: A SOLUTION WITH CAVEATS

Public fast charging would seem, from many angles, to be the answer to fixing the long-charge-time blues. Why charge for eight hours at 240 volts AC and up to 30 amps when you can be done in 20 minutes at 480 volts DC and up to 200 amps? But it's not as simple as that. Fast charging is well established—we do it every day for airport vehicles and forklifts—but homes are not, and will not in the near future be, equipped to deliver that much current (seen any 480-volt outlets lately?).

Andrew Tang, at the time we talked the senior director of customer care at the California utility Pacific Gas & Electric, pointed out to me that fast charging "is a big load. Homes are equipped with 200-amp fuse panels, [but] that's for the whole house."[15] The chargers are also hugely expensive at $15,000 and up, plus installation (compared to less than $10,000 installed for a Level II station), and there are personal safety issues and concerns about overloading the grid should such charging become commonplace. And not all battery packs are equipped to take the shock of such a fast fill.

As Shai Agassi said, it's logical that public charging will be set up in places where people stop for extended periods, from Starbucks and Barnes and Noble to big-box electronic retailers. And even if high-voltage DC charging takes only 30 minutes, people are not going to want to stand around and watch the meter ticking. Do you watch your car get a lube job? Best Buy, whose rows of shiny consumer gadgets make for some easy distraction, recognizes an opportunity there, and that's one reason it's in the vanguard of parking lot EV charging, including DC fast charging.

In the summer of 2010 I broke the story that Best Buy would offer EV charging in its parking lots.[16] The chain had experimented with four Mitsubishi I-MiEV electric cars (since renamed the "i") as transport for its Geek Squad, and the company was enthusiastic.

"We like what we see," Rick Rommel, a Best Buy senior vice president of emerging business, told me back then. "They're pretty good and our agents like them. Those vehicles are parked at our stores, and so we'll need to have charging capacity for them. It's not too big a leap to see that we can re-purpose the charging infrastructure to make sure our customers can charge their cars too. 'Golly gee, if we have an electric fleet and charging stations already. . . . '"

It seemed like a no-brainer to me, and to other industry watchers, too. According to Jack Nerad, an executive market analyst at Kelley Blue Book, "This is great public relations for Best Buy. They get their name out there in a positive way connected to a real leading edge kind of thing, and at very little cost to them. It shows that companies like Best Buy are really feeling their way forward with how to respond to electric cars."

Chelsea Sexton, an informal advisor to Best Buy and other players in the EV space, said that she expects many big retailers to offer EV charging, a lot of it free to customers. "EV charging will be a very cheap marketing value," Sexton said. "For a

$10,000 installation cost, the companies will get years' worth of loyal customers and goodwill."[17]

Given the amount of time consumers might want to browse in a store, DC fast charging is a good fit. If you get in line to buy a cup of coffee and then sit down and drink it, the elapsed time is probably 20 to 30 minutes. So it's not surprising that Best Buy said its plans would include fast chargers, though because of the cost they're likely to be located only at "select" stores. "Level III is optimal for consumers who have something else to do for 20 to 30 minutes while waiting for their cars to recharge," Rommel told me.

Coulomb is installing fast chargers as part of its ChargePoint Network, and CTO Lowenthal said he doesn't expect a very large early market for the $40,000 units. Contrary to the expectations of BP for its ECOtality fast chargers at gas stations, Lowenthal is skeptical that the model will be effective. "Gas stations are designed to move cars out in 90 seconds," he said, indicating that truck stops along major highways might be a better location—after a quick visit to the food court, you're charged.

Is safety a serious concern? Jonathan Read, CEO of ECOtality, told me that DC fast chargers are "overengineered and overdesigned" to ensure safety and that his company, with 5,000 units deployed, has never had an injury. ECOtality is partnered with longtime fast-charging player Aker Wade, which also told me it had never had an injury related to the service vehicles and forklifts it charges.

The Underwriters Laboratory cautions that, both because of the heavy cables and because of high-voltage dangers, some DC fast-charging stations might need an attendant.[18] But that would be problematic for companies because they would have to pay that operator a salary without having much hope of making their money back through charging revenue.

THE JAPANESE EXPERIENCE

Fast charging is somewhat late to the EV party, particularly in the United States. The pioneer is the Tokyo Electric Power Company (TEPCO), which developed a whimsically named DC fast-charging protocol, CHAdeMO, in conjunction with Nissan, Subaru, Mitsubishi, and (later) Toyota. According to the CHAdeMO Association, formed in early 2010, the name is an abbreviation of "charge de move" or "charge for moving," but it's also a Japanese pun, because "O *cha demo ikaga desuka*" in Japanese translates as "Let's have a tea while charging."

Why DC instead of AC? Jeff Taylor, CEO of fast-charging company Aker Wade, told me that's because converting high-voltage AC to the DC actually used by the car would require expensive and bulky onboard equipment.

In early 2011, there were 539 CHAdeMO-compliant fast chargers in Japan, with the first having been installed in 2008. TEPCO believes the availability of fast charging greatly enhances the usability of electric cars. According to Takafumi Anegawa, group head of mobility technology at TEPCO, when a DC rapid charger was installed at a company branch office, use of available Mitsubishi i (formerly "I-MiEV") and Subaru Stella EVs increased by a factor of seven. TEPCO also found that after fast-charger installation in 2008, its experienced employees were allowing their EVs to run down well below a 50 percent state of charge because they were increasingly confident in the wide availability of charging—they knew they'd make it back to the office. TEPCO surveys found that awareness of the facilities' availability was more significant than their actual use.

The fast chargers have moved well beyond TEPCO's parking lots. In 2009, the popular Lawson convenience store chain announced that it would install fast charging at 25 locations in Japan to be used with its own fleet of 40 Mitsubishi i cars. Fast chargers have also been installed at apartment buildings, Mitsubishi dealers, and Japanese government offices.

In part because the standard is Japanese, it's mostly Japanese-market EVs that have been routinely equipped for CHAdeMO fast charging, including the Mitsubishi i, the Nissan Leaf, and the Subaru Stella. In the case of the Leaf, the port door in the nose opens and the 480-volt DC and 240-volt AC charging ports are right next to each other. Not all US-model Leafs come with fast charging—it's a special order for regions that have gotten fast chargers as part of ECOtality's EV Project.

In late 2010 I borrowed a Mitsubishi i in Los Angeles and fast-charged it via a CHAdeMO-compliant charger mounted on a truck operated by a company called Real Power, whose specialty is mobile power solutions. It wasn't any harder than using a slower AC charger, though the plug was larger and heavier. It was noisy, though, because the heavy-duty truck had to be running while the session was in progress. It was kind of anticlimactic, actually. We stood around talking for 10 minutes (actually, shouting to be heard over the truck), and when we took a look, the car was almost full. Fast charging is a powerful option for EV owners, but its adoption in the United States is taking some sorting out.

FAST CHARGING IN THE
UNITED STATES AND EUROPE

The simplest option, favored by many, is to simply adopt CHAdeMO. That would be easy enough to do, but there's a "not invented here" syndrome at work. US charging standards are overseen by the Society of Automotive Engineers (SAE), in consultation with Underwriters Laboratories (the "UL" that certifies electric appliances). It was the SAE that won wide praise for coming up with the "J Plug" J1772 240-volt charger, which debuted in 2009 and has been universally adopted for US-market electric cars. That erases bad memories of GM and Toyota (paddle-type inductive charging) battling it out with Ford and Honda (rectangular wand-type conductive).

But rapid charging moved slower, and when the first EVs began meeting customers at the end of 2010, no US standard had yet been worked out. The SAE, with a lot of input from the car and charging companies, was split between advocates of CHAdeMO and a made-in-USA protocol that incorporated DC fast charging into a new version of J1772. In other words, multiple charging types, from 110 to 480, using the same charging port.

Some early EVs, including the Mitsubishi i, came with separate charging ports, one on each side of the car. And that could be confusing to consumers wondering which side to plug in to. "It's easier for consumers if there's a single, universal port," said Michael Mahan, a global product manager at GE Energy, which makes the WattStation.

Domestic automakers also like the universal port idea. Gery

Kissel of General Motors is also chairman of SAE's international J1772 task force. "The idea is to go to one spot on the car with an ergonomically friendly coupler," he said. "If it can't be connected in a friendly manner, we won't use it."[19] The universal port could become standard equipment by the 2013 model year, but the SAE could also decide to simply adopt the CHAdeMO standard.

Europe is working on its own standard, called IEC 62196 and maintained by the International Electrotechnical Commission. It's probably more important that a pan-European standard be adopted—so EV owners can cross borders without worry—than that charging standards be synchronized for the United States and Europe. After all, we all know to bring plug adapters and transformers when we travel abroad. European 220-volt house current is ideal for charging EVs, so installing home and public units will actually be easier there than in the United States or Japan.

Plug design for Europe has deviated from J1772 in part because safety laws in many countries dictate a protective shutter that guards against accidental shock and affects how the plugs look and function. The EV Plug Alliance[20] was established in early 2010 with French and Italian utility members, but it has since grown to include members from all over Europe, including 21 manufacturers. Its launch goal was standardized European plugs and sockets at three levels of charging, and it has already achieved that with products on the market.

It would have been easier for everyone if the question of a US fast-charging standard had been settled back in 2009, along with J1772. If that had happened, 2011 and 2012 model cars wouldn't have any question marks. But the SAE's timetable could result in early electric cars needing a retrofit before they can plug in to standardized fast charging. And it's unclear how much that would cost and who would pay for it. Questions like this help explain why a number of American-market EVs, including the Ford Focus, were rolled out without fast-charge ports. (Some cars, including the Chevrolet Volt, probably won't ever need fast-charging ability because their battery packs are small and charge quickly even with house current.)

Fast charging shouldn't hurt battery packs that were made to accommodate it. But Nissan suggests that, to extend battery life, its EV owners get a CHAdeMO-type charge only occasionally, not on a daily basis.

ONE CHARGER AT A TIME

On a cold day in January of 2011, I stood around as a shivering group of EV owners, government officials (including the city's mayor), and executives from the Car Charging Group inaugurated a pair of Coloumb 240-volt chargers at Connecticut's South Norwalk Railroad Station.[21] Also on hand were no less than three Chevy Volts, a Tesla Roadster, and a Smart Fortwo Electric Drive. Here we had a true "intermodal" green transportation solution: Commuters could now drive their zero-emission cars to the station, plug in, and hop on an environmentally friendly Metro North train, offsetting the gridlock on I-95.

The CCG's Michael Farkas, sporting a deep tan and a *Miami Vice* haircut, was on hand to cut the ribbon. He told me that the company had 20 to 25 poles in the ground, scattered from Florida to Manhattan and the Mall of America in Minnesota. Norwalk was only its second municipal contract, and the launch came after six months of negotiations.

For budget-strapped cities like Norwalk, where major infrastructure expenses are huge hurdles, the CCG solution looks like a godsend because they don't have to underwrite station installation. And if towns are looking at multiple installations at several convenient locations, it can get expensive.

Farkas estimates that a Level II installation can cost $7,000 to $8,000, including $5,000 for the charger itself. The variables, in addition to the headache of getting all the paperwork in order, include the "run" of the electric cable that has to be installed or buried to connect the station. Brian Golomb, a sales executive at CCG, told me that installing the Mall of America chargers involved a 700-foot run.[22]

Charger installation costs will come down. CCG installed Coulomb chargers because at the time they were the only ones available with full electronic billing capability. But many other wired chargers were coming, including those from ECOtality and GE, and competition will reduce costs. CCG will sell Watt-Stations, and offer fast charging, too.

Farkas and Golomb mused that when EV charging is ubiquitous, pricing might come to resemble that of competing gas stations: If it's $3.25 a gallon on one block, it might be $3.42 on the next one. CCG's prices are always going to be higher than those offered on a nonprofit basis (a concept that doesn't exist for gas stations, as far as I know), but competition ensures those rates will fall.

In fact, a company with a very similar revenue-sharing business plan, 350Green,[23] is providing that competition already, initially in the San Francisco area and then to be extended to the city of Chicago, which granted the company a $1.9 million wiring contract to install and maintain 73 charging plazas. According to Tim Mason, the company's cofounder and president, the answer for urban charging (where garages are a rarity) is to strategically locate both Level II stations and Level III fast chargers at key destinations, especially large grocery stores and shopping malls.

Like CCG, 350Green is all about deploying chargers—it doesn't make them. Revenue will come if people actually plug in to the stations. That makes it critical for 350Green to think strategically about how people actually live. At shopping malls the average stay is 90 minutes, Mason said, so the company plans to sell charging in 90-minute installments. And people visit the grocery store 2.5 times a week and stay for 28 to 34 minutes—which turns out to be perfect for fast charging, which will be sold in 15-minute intervals. 350Green plans to offer subscriptions, so you could pay for a month of public charging (with a surcharge added only for peak hours between noon and 5:00 p.m.). This makes sense to me. CCG and 350Green both became providers when the Walgreens drugstore chain announced that it would add charging at an impressive 800 stores. In the summer of 2011, that was the biggest corporate committment to date.

The bright orange Tesla Roadster Sport at the Connecticut charger rollout was an eye-catcher, and it connected me to its owner, Lukasz Strozek, a young hedge fund technology specialist with magnetic blue eyes and a warm smile. Originally from Poland, Strozek came to the United States in 2002 to study math at Harvard. With a degree in computer science, he of course got interested in Tesla, which he described as "a tech start-up that happens to make cars."

Strozek put in an order during the spring of 2008 and took delivery of the car in late 2009, 16 months later. Through the magic of working for a hedge fund, Strozek could afford a $128,500 Tesla and says it was worth the wait. "I was worried that the car would be overhyped," he said, "but when it came it exceeded my expectations." Strozek and I took an invigorating test ride, and he actually let me drive his pride and joy.

I'd driven a Tesla Roadster before, but not the upping-the-ante Sport model. It was, well . . . more. The Sport handles corners beautifully with uprated suspension that can be set to the customer's order. But it's even more fun on a straight road. Press the accelerator and you're rewarded with a jetlike *vroom* from the electric motor, which in this version features a hand-wound stator that with high-performance Yokohama tires helps it gain a two-tenths-of-a-second edge—zero to 60 comes up in 3.7 seconds.

Strozek owns only one car, the Roadster, and he hasn't had any trouble driving it winter and summer. He charges at home in Stamford, Connecticut. As he points out, Tesla provides two charging options: To preserve longevity, drivers can choose a setting that keeps the battery between a 10 and 90 percent charge. But for longer trips they can flick a switch, fully charge and deplete the battery, and go for 245 miles. Strozek does both. "I've been concerned that the battery performance will deteriorate over time," he said. "But for a year and a half and 12,000 miles, I haven't seen any degradation from repeated charging cycles."

A charging station at the South Norwalk train station, one town and a couple of highway exits from where he works in Westport, gives Strozek options when he wants to green his occasional trips to New York City.

I stood outside the new charge stations, each of which was plugged into a Chevy Volt. A question occurred to me. After the charge is done, isn't it a waste of a charging station to leave that car plugged in until its owner returns hours later on the train? One advantage of attendants would be their ability help with moving charged cars out of their spaces.

CCG's Farkas had thought of this. The charging station has an 18-foot cord, and a new user parked nearby should be able to see that the connected car is done and remove the cable and plug in. As with a lot of things related to electric cars, the etiquette of this will need to be worked out. EV users in California have already developed some protocols, and Plug In America may produce dashboard cards for vehicles. But at minimum the interloper should shut the other car's charge port door.

CHAPTER SIX

THE SMART GRID

We managed two computers in every house, and we handled
air-conditioning. . . . Plug-in vehicles will be manageable, but
I don't want to minimize it as an issue.

—MIKE ROWAND, DUKE ENERGY

AS THE HUGE PILES OF SNOW FROM a record 2011 winter finally melted, my local utility came by and installed a smart meter on the side of my house, replacing one whose design had changed little for a half century. It's great that this state of affairs employed thousands of meter readers, but there was no reason for them in the modern era—my meter should be readable from the billing office. And now it is.

A smart meter not only enables the utility to measure my electric usage and note the bump when I plug in my EV, but also empowers me. On my computer, I can now dial up software that shows me exactly how much juice each of my appliances is using, and choose to shut some of them harmlessly down during peak power demand times (heat waves, for instance).

Smart meters are a huge advance and are fortunately going mainstream at the same time that electric cars are hitting the road. The two can work together closely. When it's plugged in, your electric car is just another household load—and a pretty big one, sometimes doubling electricity consumption. If we get really smart about this, we can create home networks that empower consumers to manage and reduce their power needs—and save money in the process. The smart home is finally coming to America, and it's also making huge strides in Japan.

The car I saw parked in the garage at Panasonic's Eco Ideas House in downtown Tokyo was a plug-in hybrid Toyota Prius, and it's part of a singularly green home energy management system. The house, presided over by a poised tour guide with a singsongy delivery, combines a five-kilowatt solar panel on the roof and a one-kilowatt hydrogen fuel cell in the backyard to generate electricity, and a stationary five-kilowatt-hour lithium-ion battery to store it. The net result: zero carbon emissions.

Holistic systems that use sophisticated power management electronics like this are all the rage in Japan, thanks to a combination of a growing green consciousness, corporate commitment, and financial support from the government.

If one of your worries is that electric cars will fuel up from a dirty grid powered by a lot of coal, reducing "zero emission" claims to "lower emission," then it's worth taking a closer look at the smart home of the future, which may make all of its own electricity in a completely green energy loop. As it turns out, even coal-fueled EVs are cleaner than today's 25-mile-per-gallon cars, but electricity with far fewer emissions attached is clearly helping to drive international support for EVs.

Nobuo Matsuo, manager of Panasonic's strategic planning office, told me that the company hopes to produce all the technology in the smart house by its 100th anniversary in 2018.[1] It makes a lot of it now, including the energy-efficient home appliances in the Eco House's laundry room and kitchen, the solar panels, and the fuel cells.

Even wilder appliances are in the planning stages: I'd love to have Panasonic's smart air conditioner, which can scan the room it's in, determine how many people are present and what they're doing (because, for example, reading needs less cooling than working out), and adjust the temperature accordingly. How about a refrigerator that learns its family's patterns and goes into eco-mode during low usage times?

Americans may think of 3-D televisions and cameras when the name Panasonic comes up, but the company has a different image in Japan. I visited a sprawling recycling facility where Panasonic dismantles many of its home electronics products, and strolled through its environmentally themed displays at the giant CEATEC electronics show.

Panasonic has sold 2,000 of its home fuel cells, which can supply 60 percent of a family's power needs. General Electric, in cooperation with a company called Plug Power, had planned to sell its own home fuel cells to Americans in the early 2000s. Plug Power even had its own version of the Eco House, entirely powered by hydrogen. But without federal subsidies, the economics weren't there—the fuel cell would have produced electricity at a cost higher than that of grid power.

The Japanese Ministry of Economy, Trade and Industry subsidizes a third of the $34,000 price of the home cell. But even with that support, the savings in electricity and gas costs are only about $500 annually, so it may be several decades before the fuel cells pay for themselves.

Panasonic is in no way alone in its smart-grid approach. In September of 2010, Toyota (with Hitachi and Panasonic as partners) unveiled its Smart Grid Village in the tiny Japanese hamlet of Rokkasho.[2] The complex includes six eco-efficient homes and eight Prius plug-in hybrids. The homes are equipped with ultrasophisticated energy management systems and smart meters, as well as efficient EcoCute water heaters. The village, a two-year experiment, uses electricity exclusively from renewable sources, including wind turbines.

Toyota's village incorporates a version of its Smart Center home smart-grid system, which allows homeowners to easily monitor the consumption of all their appliances via computer, and manage their cars' charging, too. Toyota claims that a well-managed home energy management system that seamlessly incorporates a car like its plug-in hybrid Prius could result in a 75 percent reduction in electricity consumption.

Looked at in one way, the Prius in the Eco House garage was just one more energy consumer, using up approximately 30 percent of total family consumption. And there will be lots of different approaches to feeding it the electricity it needs, helped by what many hope will be a smarter grid. Without that, EV charging faces some challenges.

THE GRID: UP TO THE CHALLENGE?

Britta Gross of General Motors says that a Chevrolet Volt, charging from a 240-volt, 3.3-kilowatt charger in a garage, will present a load roughly equivalent to that of an electric clothes dryer—but a dryer that's on for four hours at a time. It's a big load, but not an unmanageable one—the Volt incorporates, as do most electric cars and plug-in hybrids, a feature that lets the owner easily dial in a late-night, off-peak charge time that takes advantage of underutilized grid capacity.

A 2006 Department of Energy study estimated that the existing power grid could fuel as many as 180 million plug-in hybrid cars, assuming that they plugged in at night when a lot of the generated electricity goes unused. Those 180 million are 84 percent of the country's vehicles.[3]

The study looked at plug-in hybrids, though, and they don't need as much electricity as battery electrics. President Obama wants a million electric cars (including plug-in hybrids) in the United States by 2015, so what would that do to the grid? According to a 2010 assessment by a coalition of US and Canadian companies, it's quite doable.

That study says that if 684,510 electric cars all charged at the same time, the load would total 3,785 megawatts, or the output of three or four large power plants.[4] But if that same load were spread out over an eight-hour period, it would be reduced to 819 megawatts at any one time. Stagger it over 12 hours, and only 546 new megawatts need to be found. As Treehugger points out, "That's nothing! One medium-sized power plant could provide that, and if it's during the night, you won't even have to build a new power plant since there's more than enough extra capacity off peak."[5]

JD Power and Associates, the respected rating firm, doesn't think the United States is going to get anywhere near 1 million plug-in cars by 2015.[6] In fact, it predicts that electric vehicles globally will total 500,000 that year, with half of them in China.

Add in regular hybrids, which don't plug into the grid, and you get to 3 million worldwide sales annually, or 3.4 percent of global light-vehicle sales, Power said. A Department of Energy study based on manufacturers' stated intentions is much more optimistic, predicting that the United States will succeed in reaching President Obama's goal of a million plug-in cars by 2015.

There's still some dispute over volume, but it helps to consider the power requirements of battery cars as equivalent to those of 2 million plasma television sets, spread across the global grid. A two-kilowatt EV charge load is roughly equivalent to four or five of those sets. And those TVs aren't only on late at night. Utility executives from Bangkok to Boston aren't likely to lose sleep over that scenario—in fact, they're eagerly anticipating it, because their product, not the oil companies' gasoline, will become America's transportation fuel.

Mike Rowand, director of advanced customer technologies at Duke Energy, told me the utilities can handle millions of EVs without breaking a sweat. "We managed two computers in every house," he said, "and we handled air-conditioning—two things that had a bigger impact than EVs. Plug-in vehicles will be manageable, but I don't want to minimize it as an issue."[7]

Duke's load will be manageable, but I was curious what utilities in California would say, since EV deployment is going to hit hardest there. Doug Kim directs the EV readiness program at Southern California Edison, which is a big green car booster, and he told me that his 50,000-square-mile, 400-community service area could have 450,000 EVs plugging in by 2020. But he's also confident the utility can handle it, especially as it rolls out rates that give consumers big incentives to charge in the evening.

WELL TO WHEELS

I've had dozens of people, at forums and across dinner tables, wave their hands dismissively when I tell them I write about electric cars for a living. "They're just replacing the tailpipe with a smokestack—how can they be clean when the power comes from coal?" That analysis is lacking in anything akin to facts, but that factor hasn't stopped Americans from holding opinions in the past.

So here are some actual facts. In 2009, the US electric grid was 44.6 percent coal, 23.3 percent natural gas, 20.2 percent nuclear, and, despite the often-touted transformative capability of the technologies, only 6.9 percent hydro and 3.6 percent other renewables, such as wind and solar.

That's a lot of coal, and some parts of the world are still building many new coal generation plants—the Chinese have been adding approximately one coal plant a week, but that growth is likely to slow dramatically. The grid is cleaning up its act everywhere in the world, including in China, where new regulations are giving priority to wind and other renewables. And, in December of 2010, the EPA imposed sweeping greenhouse gas standards for US power plants (and petroleum refineries, too) that will make coal power a lot cleaner. That's why plug-in-car advocates say EVs are the only cars that will have reduced emissions as they get older—the power grid is cleaning up its act.

The United Nations informed us in 2006 that livestock production actually causes 18 percent of global warming emissions worldwide, more than transportation (I know you probably don't believe that, but the report came out in 2006).[8] Should we be putting catalytic converters on cows? Coal is a huge contributor by any analysis, producing (according to the Pew Center on Global Climate Change) 20 percent of the world's greenhouse gas emissions.[9]

There's surprisingly little data about the emissions produced by EVs when they're plugged into a grid with a lot of coal in it. A study by the Electric Power Research Institute (EPRI) and the Natural Resources Defense Council looked at plug-in hybrids and found that they are cleaner than gasoline cars in each of nine scenarios.[10] In the best version of events, with high penetration of plug-in hybrids, they would reduce greenhouse emissions by 612 million metric tons by 2050. They would also reduce non–greenhouse gas emissions that can be filtered more easily from a few power plant smokestacks than from millions of car exhausts.

As I've said before, though, plug-in hybrids and full electrics are different. I couldn't find any scholarly studies of the greenhouse impact of battery EVs, so I called Eladio Knipping, an EPRI senior technical manager for the environment, for some quick "back of the envelope" calculations. And after a few minutes with a calculator, he came up with a tentative figure, subject to a wealth of caveats: Battery cars are 30 to 40 percent cleaner than average gasoline cars in terms of greenhouse gas emissions.[11] That means a battery EV has about the same global warming impact as a hybrid, which isn't terrible.

Of course, results will vary in the real world, depending on your local grid. The states with the cleanest grids are Washington, Oregon, and Idaho (because of their clean hydroelectric generation) and the dirtiest are North Dakota and Wyoming (big coal states). California, which will probably host as many as half of the country's EVs in the first few years, is fairly clean, 25 percent better than the national average. In fact, a 2011 Center for Automotive Research study estimated that the state could actually have more plug-in-car sales by 2015 *than the next five states combined.*[12]

Knipping's figure is for the US grid as it is, but it is getting dramatically cleaner every year, because of both government regulations and market conditions that, as of this writing, favor natural gas plants over coal. A number of mammoth coal plant projects have been canceled in the United States in recent years. "We have an evolving grid," Knipping told me. "In the Midwest it's primarily coal, but there are inputs from nuclear and it's transitioning to cleaner coal technologies, natural gas, and renewables. Even in areas that are primarily coal, there is a diversity of sources."

An analysis by John Voelcker for *IEEE Spectrum* magazine also concluded that plug-in cars (operating on a fifty-fifty gas and electric duty cycle) emit approximately 105 grams of carbon dioxide per kilometer, almost exactly the same as a standard Toyota Prius.[13] And, he pointed out, that's before the "well to wheels" analysis, which according to MIT adds a third more carbon dioxide to the gas car's ledger from oil pumping, transporting, and refining.

This isn't a complete answer to the dinner table philosopher who thinks he has the electric car's number, but it goes a long way toward that. So if EVs are not going to overwhelm the grid any time soon, and if they are in fact much cleaner than gasoline cars on a well to wheels basis, what hurdles do they actually face? Apart from the fact that they're expensive, range-challenged unfamiliar technology—did I mention expensive?—not many. But they do represent a threat to the local grid because of the "clustering" phenomenon.

Think about it—who among your circle of friends is likely to buy or lease an electric car? The better-off folks, right, the people who have the luxury of worrying about the environment? So, for instance, $41,000 Chevrolet Volts are quite likely to be concentrated in certain zip codes (and certain states, especially California). With our current dumb grid, there's no way of tracking the load beyond the local transformer. If there are five Nissan Leafs on one block and they blow that transformer by plugging in at the same time, utility operators won't know exactly why it happened. That's a really powerful argument for extending the smart grid, because it will make that kind of information readily available. But the smart grid is very expensive, and available only in small pockets of utility customers.

Doug Kim of Southern California Edison said he expects to see considerable EV clustering in his utility's coverage area (the 90210 area code, for instance, because every celebrity will have an EV in the motor pool). It's a challenge being addressed with tiered pricing schemes that give preference to night charges. "We want to ensure seamless service," Kim said, "so that means an EV-only rate that is a third lower than peak-rate electricity."

Edison actually has a program encouraging potential EV buyers in its coverage area to identify themselves so the utility can map where the clusters are likely to occur.

In Chattanooga, Tennessee, I visited local utility EPB, which has installed not only a blazingly fast 150 megabytes-per-second, 100 percent fiber-optic smart grid 200 times the speed of the national average, but also 300 EV charging stations for the Nissan Leaf. (The Leaf is to be built in nearby Smyrna).[14] Ryan Keel, an EPB assistant vice president, told me that utilities are always trying to reduce what they call "truck rolls"—vehicles sent out to find why the grid is malfunctioning. Keel said that his company has done better than most utilities in monitoring the health of its 115 substations (each serving 2,000 customers), but its prospects are vastly better now that it has smart metering and an upgraded grid.

"Smart meters will allow us to collect incredible amounts of data," said Danna Bailey, another EPB vice president. Before the smart grid, EPB took in 2 million data points per year, but in 2012 that will jump to 6 billion data points. The company is installing 1,500 smart meters per week. "People will be able to monitor the electricity use of their toasters if they want," Bailey said. And that will make owning a Leaf a lot easier in Chattanooga, but it will still be problematic in a lot of other places that could have denser EV ownership. (Smart meters have generated some controversy over their accuracy and the possibility of harm from electromagnetic emissions, but no analysis has confirmed either concern.)

How serious is the clustering problem? According to Nissan, more than half of the 350,000 "hand raisers" who had expressed interest in the Leaf by June of 2011 are current or previous owners of the Toyota Prius, which has high population density in certain neighborhoods. Southern California Edison is using neighborhoods with high Prius density as a cluster template—the assumption is, if you see a Prius, you may soon find a Leaf. The "zero emission" Leaf is the next step up. And some eager EV fans, including Felix Kramer of CalCars.org, actually own both a Leaf and a Volt—two plugs! The upshot of this is that utilities are going to have to anticipate such heavy load areas and upgrade local distribution equipment.

THE SMARTER GRID

We desperately need to modernize the American energy grid. According to a Department of Energy report, *Grid 2030*, what we have now, despite being "the supreme engineering achievement of the 20th century," is "aging, inefficient, and congested, and incapable of meeting the future energy needs of the Information Economy without operational changes and substantial capital investment over the next several decades."[15]

Power outages and blackouts cost the United States $80 billion a year, reports the Lawrence Berkeley National Laboratories. If the grid were made even 5 percent more efficient, we'd save more than 42 gigawatts of electricity, the equivalent of 42 coal-fired power plants, said the Federal Energy Regulatory Commission in a 2007 report.

GE is investing $100 million in smart-grid research. The Recovery Act added $6.5 billion for modern electricity transmission lines and $4.5 billion for smart-grid research projects, but it's not enough. The smart grid will be very expensive, with full investment estimated as high as $1.5 trillion over the next 15 to 20 years. Smart meters cost approximately $250 in the United States.

I wanted to see the smart grid under construction. At the tail end of 2009, I was standing in a barren industrial area of northern New Jersey near New York City, where the view includes I-95, the Goethals Bridge to Staten Island, and the kind of gasoline refineries that Bruce Springsteen wrote about in "Born in the USA." I was just 15 miles from Menlo Park, where Thomas Edison invented the phonograph and, arguably, the lightbulb. It was as good a place as any to experience the transformative power of the smart grid.[16]

General Electric was unveiling a new smart connection between New Jersey and energy-hungry New York City that would allow it to move 315 megawatts of electricity, enough for 300,000 homes, in just a second. The technical details were complicated, but essentially it meant installing three variable frequency transformers so that GE could tap into power generated by the Pennsylvania–New Jersey–Maryland (PJM) transmission system and ship it, via an ultrafast new cable, under the Arthur Kill River to New York.

So that was cool, but what did it have to do with cars? Stephen Whitley, president and CEO of New York City's New York Independent System Operator grid, told me that the new system will enable grid operators to move, for instance, wind power (generated mostly at night) to regions of high EV demand, which will also spike late at night because variable pricing will give people incentives to plug in then.

"We are adding 8,000 new megawatts of wind, and right now we don't have demand at night—which means some of that renewable energy is wasted," he said. "We need to use the smart grid to send price signals to EV owners that will lead them to charge at night from wind power." Okay, I got it. Wind is one of the fastest-growing (and cleanest) energy sources we have, and it's strongest at night. It's serendipitous that clever management can deliver it to charge electric cars at precisely the time when the grid is least stressed.

The electric car is tailor-made to interact with the smart grid, and some clever apps can maximize the efficiency of what is already a very efficient process.

IN THE DRIVER'S SEAT:
THE KILLER APPS

The first time I heard Microsoft CEO Steve Ballmer speak, it was on a screen at the New York International Auto Show in 2010. Microsoft is the name on my Windows operating system, and it had seldom entered the world of my car reporting. But there Ballmer was, talking about a partnership with Ford that would bring Microsoft's free "cloud-based" Hohm application for managing home utility bills into play to help charge the new Focus electric car.[17]

Microsoft and Ford had already partnered on the Sync audio system, but the idea here was to manage the electric car along with the rest of the homeowner's electric load. The more sophisticated EVs, including the Volt and Leaf, all have variations of this, with state of charge and start times able to be maintained on the home computer, and on the smartphone, too. Derrick Kuzak, a Ford group vice president for global product development, said at the show that household energy use can double when an electric car is plugged in. And that the EV is likely to be the home's largest single power draw. No wonder it's important to manage charging.

Ford and Microsoft showed a picture of a home that echoed the concept of Panasonic's Eco House, with solar panels on the roof and an electric car charging down in the garage. Upstairs, a shadowy figure hunched over a computer, scheduling a late-night charge, no doubt. Hohm was later killed, but the charging principles laid out that day were sound.

By early 2011, when Ford introduced its Focus electric car in Las Vegas, it was obvious that the company was expecting its versatile apps to help consumers get the most out of limited range. Why debut the Focus in Las Vegas, at the huge annual International Consumer Electronics Show (CES), when the auto industry's showplace, the North American International Auto Show in Detroit, was just a week away? The answer became clear when Ford's Alan Mulally, the former Boeing executive who became the star of the domestic industry when he avoided the need for the company to take a government bailout, delivered his keynote talk at CES. "This is our first-ever gas-free, zero carbon dioxide emissions car," said Mulally, pacing the stage with his usual coiled intensity. "[It's] a great step forward in electrification."[18]

But Mulally's speech soon left the car itself behind; he made it clear that the Focus wasn't Grandpa's Ford—now it was all about the apps. Ford has relentlessly courted the youth market with a campaign that has included loaning out its smaller Fiesta to bloggers in exchange for regular social media postings. Mulally and the other presenters zoomed in on the company's MyFord Touch entertainment console. The Focus Electric display includes blue butterflies to tell owners about their charging status, and Ford makes available a downloadable smartphone app that locates charging stations (with the help of MapQuest), finds the car, and assists in posting EV driving milestones to Facebook and Twitter.

We even got a visit from Best Buy's Geek Squad, which will be installing Ford's charging stations (as Best Buy itself starts selling them, and maybe someday electric cars, too). The new Focus "just felt more at home at CES," Ford product head Derrick Kuzak told the assembled tech heads.

After the Las Vegas presentation, I took a closer look at the electric Focus with Sherif Marakby, Ford's director of electrification and engineering and fully Mulally's equal in intensity. The doors were locked, but anyone looking in could see that the car bristled with electronic aids.

"I've had a steady stream of young people tell me they're going to buy the car just because of the apps," Marakby said with a mixture of amusement and exasperation.

The Nissan Leaf comes with tons of this stuff, too.[19] Its onboard transmitter connects through mobile networks to a data center that can send out details such as a map of charging stations in range of your remaining charge, and it should eventually be able to tell if those stations are in use, too. Users can get alerts on their cell phones when a charge is complete, and they can even check on the current temperature inside the car. Even better, they can preheat or precool their cars from the grid while they're plugged in. Imagine that, no freezing until the car warms up or burning delicate parts of the body on broiling seats. It's enough to put remote starters out of business (and good riddance, because they cause a lot of pollution).

Heating and cooling are a big issue in battery cars, because they don't have the gas car's ability to generate electricity on the fly. When you use the heater in the Nissan Leaf, for instance, you're shortening its range. Plug-in cars have less range in the winter both because you're using that heater and because battery range is less in cold weather. (Seat heaters use less power than electric cabin heaters, which is why some EV makers are using them as primary heating in special eco-modes.) Four seat heaters, as well as a battery pack warmer, became standard equipment in the 2012 Leaf.

I was one of the first journalists to drive Daimler's Smart Fortwo Electric Drive (available for lease in the United States) and to test its smartphone technology, too. In this case you plug your existing phone into a special dash-mounted cradle and activate the Smart app, which provides useful information on state of charge, expected completion time, and location. When you park, you take the phone with you, and if you forget where you parked the car, the system will locate it for you.[20]

The Chevy Volt bristles with tech, including most of the useful tools we've detailed here. But it also has the OnStar system, so owners can push a button and dial the call center for GPS directions that are then downloaded to the car. You can also do this from your cell phone using the Volt's mobile app, so the directions will be there in the car when you climb aboard. And if you can't find the car in a parking lot, press the app's navigation tab and GPS will find the car and show where you are in relation to it.[21]

The Volt has the best graphic presentation I've ever seen on a car, with displays you'll never get tired of looking at. It can also precondition its interior from the grid (a process you start from the key fob), and readouts on the dash show battery life, electric-only miles traveled, and scheduled charge start times. I like it that when you start the Volt, the car emits software start-up noises and tells you it's "initializing." The matte white dashboard finish reminds me of my Sony Vaio laptop.

If I detailed the neat features on every battery EV on the market it would get a bit redundant, so it's sufficient to say that virtually every automaker is tying into the explosion of smartphone usability. It's the kind of thing that makes you realize that electric cars are happening now for a reason. There's no getting around the fact that battery vehicles are range challenged, but onboard computers and mobile technology make the most of what's available.

My GE smart-grid visit in New Jersey included a tour. A million miles of wire were installed as part of the project. I had trouble picturing a million miles of wire. We visited an eerily deserted control room that looked like the nuke command post in *The China Syndrome*. And we said hello to the three giant transformers, which had to be lifted into place by crane. The cooling fans are 36 feet across. "Go ahead and touch it: This is what 100 megawatts feels like," shouted tour guide Dan Walsh, vice president of GE Energy Financial Services, over the deafening roar of the machinery. What does 100 megawatts feel like? It felt warm.

Electric cars are enabled by 50-year-old technology (picture all those coal-burning power plants) and an outdated grid, but with an increasingly large smart layer on top. The good news is that the grid is evolving, and as it does, it makes EVs look better and better in terms of their impact on our beleaguered planet.

CHAPTER SEVEN

CHINESE PUZZLES

*It would be very hard to beat both the management and the
workforce, and the government cooperation and the
momentum BYD has.*

—WARREN BUFFETT

WHEN ANYONE TALKS ABOUT THE FUTURE of the auto
industry, China is the elephant in the room. It has newly become
the world's largest auto market, and it's growing rapidly at the
same time that Western auto sales have gone through some pain-
ful constrictions.[1] What we've seen so far is just the beginning,
because China's top-down economic management has decreed
that the country will motorize and provided for huge subsidies for
automakers and an ambitious plan to build roads.

Western visitors who saw Chinese cities choked with bicycle
riders in the 1970s and 1980s have since been shocked to see
them replaced with cars and motorized two-wheelers. Annual
sales of electric bikes in China were 40,000 in 1998 and 10 million in 2005.[2] And auto sales there have surpassed those in the
United States—the Chinese bought 18 million cars in 2010. The
smog was already bad 30 years ago, but it got much worse; still,
some people looked into the dim light at noon and saw progress.

China is no longer an afterthought in global auto planning. It's a huge opportunity, and increasingly an electric one. That's because the same party planners who want to put the country in cars are also dictating that a lot of them be electric. Chinese industry has reacted with its usual enterprise, and now many of the new models on display at Beijing and Shanghai auto shows come with plugs.

In September of 2010, Warren Buffett and Bill Gates went to China, where they visited the huge complex of BYD (Build Your Dreams), the battery and auto giant. Buffett has more than a passing interest in BYD because he owns 10 percent of the company, a $232 million investment that has had its ups and downs (at one point it had quadrupled in value).

BYD, China's largest battery maker, also wants to be the world's biggest automaker. Yes, the world's biggest. It has a huge head start because of its leadership in lithium-ion battery production. China is the dominant player in the sector: Intel counts more than 33,000 people employed making Li-ion batteries there, compared to 1,100 in the United States.

BYD builds gas vehicles and also both hybrid and electric cars. One of the latter, the E6 S crossover (with 200 miles of range), is targeted at the US market. Gates and Buffett are quite a tag team. The pair took a ride in a BYD M6 van, and liked what they found. "It was fantastic. I am amazed at the quality of that vehicle," Gates said. Buffett added, "If I had a car like that in high school, I would have had a lot of dates!" He told an assembled group of car dealers, "BYD is the right choice for me, and I hope it'd be the same for you."[3]

Buffett is a great salesman when he wants to be. Riding on

his private plane during the China trip, he told CNBC that BYD is "working on . . . some very important developments for the planet, if you're talking the electric car, if you're talking solar energy. . . . It would be very hard to beat both the management and the workforce, and the government cooperation and the momentum BYD has."[4] He left open the option of buying a larger stake—"10 percent is all we got offered," he said.

BYD is definitely the highest-profile Chinese company with an eye on the American market. The company opened a head-quarters in downtown Los Angeles, and at the end of 2010 it announced that it would put a fleet of its F3DM plug-in hybrid sedans (the first on the world market) into a test fleet with the Housing Authority of the City of Los Angeles.[5]

To demonstrate its commitment to the renewable energy Buffett spoke about, BYD is working with the city on solar solu-tions and a storage battery for storing wind power generated in the Tehachapi Mountains. The E6 electric car, after numerous delays, is slated to go on sale in 2012. It's already in Chinese taxi service.

The E6 and the F3DM are the cars on my radar. The F3DM (introduced in 2008 and initially sold only to fleet customers and government officials) made a splash because it was so early on the plug-in hybrid market. It offers 40 miles of all-electric range (approximately the same as the Volt) and was put on sale in China at a very low price—starting at approximately $21,900 (later raised to $24,859). The car has a BYD-built lithium-iron-phosphate battery pack and a solar panel on the roof to help with battery recharging. The F3DM, too, is slated for US sale.

You couldn't ask for better publicity than BYD has gotten

in the United States, thanks largely to the Buffett investment (and the nod from Gates, too). In 2010, *Businessweek* rated BYD the world's 8th most innovative company, and *Fast Company* said it was the 16th most innovative. CEO Wang Chuanfu is pretty colorful, too. He was number one on the 2009 *Forbes* list of the richest Chinese, with an estimated net worth of more than $5.8 billion, but on the 2010 list he'd moved down to number 10 and $4.2 billion.

That drop on the *Forbes* list is an indication that, despite all the hype, all is not well at BYD. The company had a pretty miserable 2010.[6] Its Hong Kong–listed stock lost half its value between April and December of 2010, and car sales failed to meet a shrunken 600,000 target (it had been 800,000). The final tally was 519,806. Although it seemed like a bargain, the F3DM hardly made a dent—only 300 were sold by the end of 2010.

Of course, there are many Western companies that would be very happy with selling more than half a million cars in a year. The huge volumes and growth (BYD sold 100,000 cars a year just five years ago) reflect the amazingly rapid growth in the Chinese auto industry, which topped that in the United States by a wide margin in 2009 (13.6 million compared to 10.4 million) and again in 2010 (16.4 million to 11.5 million). China had 64 million cars and light trucks on the road in 2009, but that's projected to jump to more than 200 million by 2020.

The Chinese market has become a huge opportunity for Western automakers, which have formed many joint ventures there. In the first half of 2010, General Motors sold more cars in China (Buicks are a big hit there)—1.2 million—than it did in the United States, at 1.1 million.

Of course, the Chinese auto industry plays by markedly different rules. BYD's sales jumped at the end of the year because, according to the *People's Daily Online*, Beijing customers rushed to buy cars before the government imposed a strict 240,000-car limit on new car registrations in the capital in 2011.[7] That kind of antipollution measure, while effective, is unlikely to make it through our Congress.

China is investing heavily in electric cars, and subsidizing them, too. Chinese automakers are also building very affordable gas cars that companies such as Coda and Wheego convert to EVs. For a sense of how cheap cars are on the Chinese market (and why the BYD F3DM is considered expensive), consider that the base F3 gas car costs only $8,750. Even after government subsidies that are available in some cities, the plug-in hybrid is still more than twice the price of the standard vehicle.

I finally got a ride in a F3DM at the Detroit auto show in 2011. The situation wasn't ideal—we were on a makeshift track in the basement of Cobo Hall. Still, after a few laps I could tell that it was better than I thought it would be. The car was definitely noisy and not even in the same universe as the Volt, but it accelerated well and handled reasonably if your standards weren't too high. Of course, the interior was retro in a not particularly good way, lacking in nearly all of the Volt's high-tech features, and the styling was very 1986 Toyota Corolla.

BYD's Patrick Duan told me that gas costs as much in China as it does in the United States, but BYD is still struggling to sell F3DMs on the Chinese market. Why? Well, $24,859 is a lot of money on Chinese wages. But how will the car look to American buyers, if the company can manage to bring it in at half the price of the Volt?

AN ELECTRIC PUSH

In mid-2010, the Chinese government announced a trial program of lucrative subsidies for electric and plug-in hybrid buyers, though in five cities only (Shanghai, Changchun, Shenzhen, Hangzhou, and Hefei). Like the proposed US legislation that targets EV deployment communities, the Chinese money helps to create concentrations of the cars in specific areas, with the subsidized charging stations to go with them. Ever the optimist, Better Place's Shai Agassi thinks that by 2020 China could be solely an electric car market, though most observers think it will take far longer.

US buyers get a $7,500 federal tax credit when they buy an electric car (plus a $1,000 credit for installing a charging station). Chinese customers get their bills reduced with payments of $440 per battery kilowatt-hour paid directly to carmakers. For plug-in hybrid buyers, the subsidy is capped at $7,320, and for battery cars the top payment is $8,784. Those are big numbers (awarded to buyers of Chinese-made cars only), and it's doubly helpful to get the money up front like that. US EV advocates want to turn tax credits into subsidies, too.

The Chinese cities in the program are all home to carmakers, of which China has no less than 120, ranging from such relatively small companies as Great Wall and Fudi Auto to big players Geely (which recently purchased Volvo), BYD, SAIC, and Chery. There are more carmakers in China than in the rest of the world combined. And they're thinking electric.

The Chinese government has committed $17 billion to building charging stations and subsidizing EV purchases, which makes it the world leader, and provincial governments are offering subsidies, too. According to *Fortune*, "Beijing has pledged that it will do whatever it takes to help the Chinese car industry take the lead in electric vehicles."[8] HSBC Research has predicted that China will grow its share of the world EV market from just 2.7 percent in 2010 to 35 percent by 2020.

At the 2010 Beijing auto show, some 95 electric car models were shown. The country's biggest automaker, SAIC Motor Corporation, debuted the electric E1 concept and a ready-for-production hybrid Roewe 750. Brilliance offered a Smart-sized electric commuter car with a one-click operating system and a lot of recyclable materials. Beijing Automotive Industry Holding Company brought out the BE701 electric car and announced that it will have the capacity to produce 50,000 EVs a year. FAW Group, another big player with Toyota and Volkswagen joint ventures, said it will be fully geared up to make, market, and service electric cars by 2012.

Given GM's huge success selling cars in China, it's not surprising how many foreign companies operate there in joint ventures. And they're marketing electric cars there, too. The Chevy Volt is for sale in China, though the price is likely to be daunting to local buyers. The Mitsubishi i will be offered in China by 2012, and the Nissan Leaf, too. Nissan delayed putting a date on the launch because of concern about China's not yet having a national charging standard (as the United States does with J1772).

That issue is a big one, and could suggest that Chinese officials are rushing things a bit. Cars without standard plugs or places to plug in won't be of much use, and only a few places in a very big country are getting subsidized. Wan Gang, China's minister of science and technology, predicted that a million electric cars will be produced annually by 2020. I believe that Chinese industry is fully capable of achieving that goal, but it will take a lot of partners working together, including carmakers, utilities, and politicians.

THE EXPORT QUESTION

Look around you. What *isn't* made in China? America may be the number one manufacturing country, outpacing China by 40 percent, but we're specialists, making computer chips and fighter jets but not the myriad inexpensive products that crowd a Walmart store. In 2010, we exported $92 billion worth of goods to China and imported $365 billion, a mammoth trade imbalance.[9] And China is such a manufacturing powerhouse that only about a quarter of its exports go to the United States.

So why aren't we driving Chinese cars the same way we wear Chinese-made clothes and use Chinese-made computers? The answer isn't all that complicated. To put it bluntly, Chinese cars aren't good enough for the world market, though they could get there soon.

When Chinese export toys (from *High School Musical* jewelry to Mattel *Dora the Explorer* backpacks) were found to be contaminated with lead in 2007 and then milk products showed up tainted with the industrial chemical melamine (used to make plastics and fertilizers) in both 2008 and 2010, it led to a lot of concern about Chinese quality control.

But the Chinese response was hardly what we'd expect if it had been a Western country in crisis mode. After the FDA issued a warning about Chinese-made toothpaste containing the anti-freeze solvent diethylene glycol, the Chinese government denied that the chemical presented any danger. Chinese-made products are in fact consistently near the top of the list when it comes to products turned away at the border by the FDA. In 2007, only Mexico and India had more problems.[10]

The process is complicated by the fact that it's often American companies (like Mattel) overseeing the Chinese production. They claim they're monitoring the manufacturing, but obviously a lot gets past them. And the fact that Chinese companies were still using lead paint made it more likely to show up in toys and other products (including pottery and makeup) headed for the United States.

Thomas G. Rawski, an economics professor at the University of Pittsburgh and a regular visitor to Chinese factories, told the *New York Times*, "The mechanisms for preventing this stuff don't leap out of a tree. They have to be built up carefully, and I think it's very clear this process of building is going on in China right now. That means there are lots of things happening that in an ideal world shouldn't be happening, including things that wouldn't happen in Japan or the U.S."[11]

Chinese quality control issues are detailed in *Poorly Made in China*, a 2009 book by Paul Midler, who spent 15 years as a middleman between Chinese manufacturers and American importers. The book chronicles appalling instances of companies skimping on agreed-upon product formulations to increase their own profit margins. Midler told me, "China most certainly does have a quality challenge. Some of the problems there are due to error, and some are due to a lack of education. The factories would like to do a better job, but they are prevented from doing so due to external factors. Unfortunately in China's case, there are also instances of willful misconduct."[12]

According to Midler, intense competition to reduce product prices (the factor that attracts Western companies in the first place) also leads to quality problems. And he points out that China's auto industry, "like so many other sectors, is characterized by intense competition. . . . I'm not sure whether China's automotive ambitions might be hampered more by accidental failures or willful manipulation, but there has already been talk in China of quality issues in the automotive sector."

VOLVO: SAFETY ON THE LINE

There has indeed been talk about Chinese auto quality, and it was stoked when one of China's top companies, Geely, bought Volvo—the global company with probably the world's best safety reputation—for $1.5 billion in 2010.

Geely, unfortunately, can't claim Volvo's quality reputation. A video posted on YouTube in 2007[13] shows what happens when a Geely Otaka compact sedan hits an offset barrier in a Russian crash test using the European New Car Assessment Program standard. The entire front end of the car appears to disintegrate and the front-seat dummies' heads hit the steering wheel and windshield. A 2009 crash test of a similar Geely car looks no better.

Maybe things are improving. The *China Daily* chimed in with a 2011 article on Geely's safety record, claiming that the company's first midsize model, the Emgrand EC7, had managed a five-star safety ranking, "a record high for a Chinese car of this size. . . . The results show that Geely has outperformed other local brands in safety and has grown into a domestic auto industry leader." But the article also admitted that five-star ratings "are mainly found among the high-end foreign brands, which are generally designed to give better protection in a collision." [14]

Results of the 2010 Car Brand Perceptions Survey from *Consumer Reports* put safety as its US readers' most important consideration in buying a new car. It was in the top three for 64 percent of respondents. And safety is a really big reason people buy Volvos. I'll never forget a really effective Volvo ad featuring a concerned father contemplating a stormy night and extending a set of keys to his daughter with the words "Here, take the Volvo."

I've been to Volvo's test track in Gothenburg, Sweden, and been amazed by the company's work with cutting-edge pedestrian safety, lane departure warning, and adaptive cruise control (which can brake your car when it's in danger of hitting the vehicle ahead). The passenger-protection features on the Volvo XC60 crossover, undoubtedly one of the world's safest cars, would fill a whole page. So it was a bit of a shocker when, in January of 2011, Volvo CEO Stefan Jacoby told the *Wall Street Journal* that the company was thinking of building Volvos in China for export to the United States. The *Journal* correctly noted that it would be "a potentially risky move that might harm the brand's Scandinavian identity." [15]

That identity has yet to be tested with electric cars, but Volvo has that base covered. I had seen Jacoby earlier that week at the Detroit auto show sharing the stage with a wrecked Volvo C30 electric car, one of the company's small test fleet (complementing its V60 plug-in hybrid). After a 40-mph front corner offset crash, the poor car was a mess, but its battery pack was largely intact and still functioning, and its occupants would have walked away, had they not been dummies.

"The motor shows are full of shiny electric cars," Jacoby said. "They talk about usability, driving range. Only a few are focused on the safety aspect. The C30 doesn't compromise its safety in the unlikely event of a collision." One way the company keeps the C30 safe is by isolating the battery pack from the car's crumple zones, and protecting the cables, too. Other EU makers take the same precaution.

It was soon after that press conference that Jacoby talked about building Volvos for the US market in China. He didn't address safety, instead pointing out that such an arrangement could help Volvo with its currency exchange issues.

Volvo already builds S40 and S80 cars in China, but for the Chinese market. That makes sense. The factory that makes Volvos is co-owned by Ford and Chongqing Changan Automobile, but the company is likely to build its own production facility—or tie into Geely's.

A coterie of Volvo officials has told me privately that Geely intends to leave the company alone and will be careful to protect its image as a premium, luxury brand. That makes sense, too, but producing export Volvos in China without vigilant quality control could be perilous. Jacoby, who headed Volkswagen in the United States, is a very forceful leader. His challenge will be preserving the brand's safety image, even if that means telling Geely's leadership that China-made cars aren't yet good enough for export to the United States.

Is there opportunity for Volvo in having Chinese owners? You bet, and electric cars are a good example of that. Volvo-branded EVs could be a big hit on the Chinese market, and as Chinese cars with foreign cachet they'll benefit from those government subsidies. Volvo announced even before its acquisition by Geely was complete that it planned to sell the C30 electric in China.[16]

Geely has ambitious plans for Volvo. The company sold 373,525 cars worldwide in 2010, but Geely and Volvo are aiming for 800,000 in 2020. And that includes 300,000 Volvos in China.[17] If the country's electric car strategy bears fruit, a big percentage of those Chinese sales could be cars with plugs. As Shai Agassi put it, "The Chinese government has set a goal to become the number one producer of electric cars by 2012. When China says it will create a new industry, it means exactly that, and the world will take notice. . . . History shows that when China gets into a leadership position in manufacturing an electric device, it tends to hold on to it."[18]

A CODA

Long term, I think we should all get used to the idea of buying and driving Chinese cars. Quality is an issue that the Chinese will address squarely, because like BYD they really do want to sell cars, especially electrics, in the United States and other Western countries. They're working on it. As I've mentioned, both the Wheego LiFe and the Coda electric cars have Chinese underpinnings. Both companies have taken those vehicles through and passed American crash testing. But it wasn't easy—the Chinese cars benefited from a fair amount of postproduction strengthening.

Kevin Czinger, Coda's former CEO and a veteran of Goldman Sachs, said repeatedly that steel chassis reinforcement meant that his electric car was considerably strengthened from its humble origins as a Mitsubishi model built under license in China.[19] In fact, he bristled whenever the Coda (finished at a California factory) was described as "a Chinese car."

I asked Czinger to name his lowest point in bringing the Coda to market, and he recalled the day when he learned his car was not going to survive the new and tougher US side-impact crash tests. But Czinger possesses what *The New Yorker* described as "an intensity that borders on the unnerving," and he was up to the task. He brought in Western specialty companies that work with the major automakers in modeling safety systems, building "a team to get this done."

It wasn't only crash testing. Coda's head of Chinese operations, Mark Atkeson, told me the company had to change gears on its China strategy when it became apparent that, despite their promises, Chinese suppliers could not provide high-quality, off-the-shelf components for electric cars. Czinger adapted quickly to that reality, Atkeson said, lining up established Western manufacturers for electric motors, controllers, and power steering.

Santa Monica, California–based Coda makes an interesting case study, both because of its up-and-down prospects and because of its strong Chinese connections. The Coda is a five-passenger compact car about the size of a Honda Civic, with its dated Chinese styling benefiting from front and rear design upgrades. Its primary asset is a relatively large 33.8-kilowatt-hour lithium-ion battery pack sourced from its joint venture in China with Tianjin Lishen. The Coda offers 120-mile range—more than the Leaf—and thermal management for the battery system, also lacking in the Leaf.

But the Coda also sports a $44,900 price tag, considerably

more than the Leaf for a car with a lot less of the Nissan's razzle-dazzle. And, as much as Czinger hated it, there was that "Chinese car" thing.

The first sign that all was not well with Coda was when Czinger unexpectedly resigned from the company in November of 2010. Czinger, who is fiercely focused and a brilliant talker, was Coda's public face and virtually synonymous with the car. Very little explanation was given, and I watched an awkward press conference at the Los Angeles Auto Show in which Czinger stood by while his successor as interim CEO, Steven "Mac" Heller (also a Goldman Sachs veteran), announced a production delay until the third quarter of 2011. "We're eager to get to the market, but we have to be triple sure that we could deliver the quality our customers expect and deserve," Heller said. "This kind of delay is not unusual for new car introductions."[20]

Coda has an Internet marketing strategy, a deal with several rental car companies, and a plan to sell initially only in the EV mecca of California. Its fortunes will rise and fall with China. New CEO Phil Murtaugh, announced to succeed Heller in early 2011, is a veteran of General Motors' operations in China, and the company plans to sell the Coda there. "The vast majority of Coda's manufacturing will be China-based," Murtaugh said.

It's unclear what the Coda's price will be in China, but if a $24,859 BYD plug-in hybrid is a slow seller there, a $44,900 battery EV would seem to be an even tougher proposition. Perhaps a bare-bones version, with a smaller battery pack and minus the bells and whistles needed for the Western market, could work there.

Whether Coda will succeed as an international carmaker is unclear—there are long odds. It could become more of a battery supplier and grid-storage player than an automaker. But what is clear is that the company's vicissitudes (and those of Wheego, too) dramatize the shortcomings of a Western company sourcing an electric car in China.

Consider Walmart: It has great success selling imported Chinese-made products because it can sell them for considerably less than American-made alternatives. At the right price, people discount the "Made in China" stigma. There would seem to me to be an opportunity at hand, for both Coda and Wheego, if they can sell their electric cars for appreciably less than the Nissan Leaf, Ford Focus Electric, and other major entries. Instead, the Wheego is the same price as the Leaf, and the Coda costs $12,000 *more*. What happened to the Chinese discount?

Coda's pricing strategy became clearer when it announced in the summer of 2011 a strategic alliance with the Chinese automaker Great Wall Motors. One likely result is a new Chinese-American competitor for the Nissan Leaf—presumably much cheaper than the Coda sedan.

I'd take a close look at a $20,000 Wheego LiFe and a $25,000 Coda sedan, in particular because they would get very cheap indeed with federal tax credits. But the reality is that the burn rate in starting a new car company is extraordinary, and EVs add the complicating factor of incredibly expensive battery packs and the electronics to keep them happy. Importing car bodies from far-off China is costly, too. Start-up carmakers can't set aspirational prices and make the payroll, too. Once the development costs are amortized and economies of scale work their magic, the prices can come down. But those same forces benefit the big guys, too.

CHAPTER EIGHT

ICELAND'S FAST TRACK

We are completely on track to bring electric cars to Iceland.

—GÍSLI GÍSLASON

WHICH COUNTRY WILL BE THE FIRST in the world to have an all-electric transportation fleet? Here's a contender that is very unlikely to be on your radar: Iceland. Until 2008, it was known best for whale watching (and whale killing), as well as for geothermal energy and a name that in all fairness should be swapped with Greenland. After 2008, an economic meltdown put it on the map.

But there are other reasons to pay attention to Iceland: It's the perfect country to lead the way with EVs. All the forces align: It's small and compact, geothermal makes electricity almost free, imported gasoline is hugely expensive, and it's got a small, highly educated population with a pervasive green consciousness. If they can't say good-bye to the internal-combustion engine in Iceland, it can't be done anywhere.

There is a glass of red wine in front of me, and I am sitting in front of a roaring fire in the comfortable Reykjavík living room of an Icelandic entrepreneur named Gísli Gíslason. The energetic, red-haired Gíslason told me that his stately 1920s home, just down the street from the American embassy, once belonged to Jon Ásgeir Jóhannesson, a retail tycoon caught up in the 2008 bank collapse.

"We are completely on track to bring electric cars to Iceland," the ever-optimistic Gíslason said. And he dreams big: He ordered 1,000 Tesla Model S cars and another 1,000 Amp electric conversions. He's eyeing battery production and car assembly in Iceland, as well as a plant in Norway, with distribution all over northern Europe. On his side are the lowest electricity (and some of the highest gasoline) prices in the Western world, plus a supportive government and an ultragreen population. The only problem is an economy still reeling from the consequences of a major meltdown.

As you may have heard, the "Icelandic miracle" was based on a hugely successful financial services sector that offered international investors high interest rates and few regulations. The bankers brought unprecedented prosperity to Iceland—they were the country's rock stars, and they spent like rock stars, too, with their institutions amassing liabilities six times larger than Iceland's entire economy.[1] The banks were deregulated in 2000, and in just a few years these strictly local lenders transformed themselves into major financial players on the global stage. They gobbled up foreign assets, mainly in Britain and Scandinavia.

It was a bubble, and not even vaguely sustainable: Iceland is a tiny island of 310,000 souls that has no significant manufacturing sector, and it was briefly one of the richest countries in the world. But when the banks defaulted on their debts, the government was forced to nationalize the three leading players and seek billions in emergency loans from the International

Monetary Fund and others. Iceland's conservative government collapsed in early 2009.

When I first visited the cozy, low-rise city of Reykjavík in 2007, before the crash, the capital glittered, the stores were full of expensive imported goods, and a cup of coffee at a left-wing café (where an international cast discussed Noam Chomsky) cost $10. When I went back for my third visit two years later, my money had doubled in value, the left was in power, and I could now afford the coffee. A young English filmmaker exulted in the difference. "I changed 20 pounds and I got 20,000 million kronur—it was ridiculous," she said.

Green cars brought me to Iceland. I was sharing that glass of wine with Gíslason because he was the latest visionary who wanted to transform the country's transportation sector with a zero-emission strategy. Everyone agrees that Iceland is the ideal candidate to plug into green cars. The island is just a little bit smaller than Kentucky, but two-thirds of the population is concentrated in Greater Reykjavík—and that makes building a new energy infrastructure serving nearly everybody a relative snap.

Just 200 miles south of the Arctic Circle, Iceland sits on the boundary of the North American and Eurasian plates, which are very slowly moving away from each other. Superheated water lies just below the surface, and it's not uncommon to see steam rising from natural vents—no wonder belief in fairies is common there. There are approximately 35 active volcanoes (including the giant underneath the Eyjafjallajökull glacier that disrupted European air traffic in 2010). The word *geysir* is Icelandic in origin, and the Vikings used to hold their annual councils at the restless site where the two continental plates meet.

Iceland's modern geothermal story began when the first district hot water heating was introduced in 1928. These days, nature's gift of geothermal energy heats 85 percent of Icelandic homes. Because there are abundant hydroelectric resources to complement the geothermal, renewable energy provides more than 70 percent of the country's electricity. In fact, it's only the cars, trucks, and fishing boats that await a makeover. But, of course, there are complications.

IT STARTED WITH HYDROGEN

The first time I visited Iceland, the buzz was about hydrogen and fuel-cell cars, not plug-in electrics. The plan to become the world's first hydrogen energy economy dates to 1998 and the formation of Icelandic New Energy. The consortium included a number of Icelandic power companies, the University of Iceland, Daimler, Norsk Hydro, and Shell.

In 2003, the Icelanders opened the world's first commercial hydrogen filling station in Reykjavík. As part of the SMART-H_2 project, a trio of Daimler Citaro hydrogen buses was brought to Iceland and had a successful four-year run in passenger service. In fact, the buses had just been taken out of service when I visited with a General Motors contingent in 2007. A pair of small Mercedes A-Class fuel-cell cars rode the Icelandic roads, and two Fords, too.

The big question was how Iceland could get its hands on more fuel-cell vehicles. With the cars and buses then costing a cool million dollars each, there were few on the ground—and tiny Iceland was hardly in a position to build the cars itself.

Global carmakers had other priorities—usually test programs in California or Europe.

To understand the dilemma Iceland was in, you need to know a bit more about hydrogen cars. The principle of the fuel cell is as old as the storage battery, dating to the early 19th century. The flat cells, grouped together in stacks, generate electricity through a chemical process having hydrogen and oxygen as the raw materials. Water (drinkable!) and heat are by-products, which explains why efficient fuel cells built by General Electric were taken on board NASA's Gemini and Apollo manned space missions in the 1960s and 1970s.

Around the same time, General Motors got interested in building fuel-cell cars and developed the Electrovan in 1966, which used a Union Carbide fuel cell and ran on supercold liquid hydrogen. As a measure of the challenge ahead, the six-seat van's interior was completely filled with a bulky and very heavy chemical factory, leaving barely enough room for two passengers. The van had a range of 150 miles, which was already better than most battery cars would achieve 35 years later.[2]

The Electrovan was a beginning. Fuel-cell research has proceeded steadily since then, with the stack size shrinking and the power output increasing. GM retained its leadership position, but many other companies—Honda, Toyota, Ford—also developed fuel-cell car programs. Opportunities for commercializing the technology have consistently been stymied by the high cost of making not only the fuel cell stacks (which use platinum as a catalyst) but also hydrogen. The element is the most abundant in the universe, but it isn't found in isolation, and the process of separating it (from water using electrolysis or from natural gas with steam reformation) is energy intensive and expensive.

But we're getting close, and Daimler, Hyundai, Honda, and Toyota say they'll have commercial fuel-cell cars on the road as early as 2014. They're talking about tens of thousands of cars. In the meantime, automakers are putting increasingly capable prototypes (all of which I've driven) into test fleets. In February of 2011, I took delivery of one such car, a fuel-cell Toyota Highlander, for a six-month test.

It was an interesting opportunity, made possible by a serendipitous series of events. In 2008, Tom Sullivan, the founder of the national hardwood flooring chain Lumber Liquidators, decided to go online and research what was happening with the next generation of transportation fuels. He found some promising material on fuel cells. "It seemed ridiculous we were spending $1 billion a day on imported oil when we could make our own zero-emission hydrogen," he told me. "If we can make hydrogen from wind or solar, that's as good as it gets."[3]

Most people would leave it at that, but being a man of action, Sullivan plugged "solar-powered hydrogen" into a search engine, and that led him to the Connecticut-based Proton Energy Systems, now called Proton OnSite, a hydrogen producer (through electrolysis of water) that was about to be sold at a bankruptcy auction. Only a few days later, after some quick due diligence, Sullivan was the successful bidder, buying Proton for $10.2 million. And it wasn't long before he hatched a $15 million or $20 million plan, entirely self-funded, to stage hydrogen filling stations up and down the East Coast, from Maine to Florida, approximately 300 miles apart (the range of most fuel-cell cars). It was the "hydrogen highway" that eluded Governor Arnold Schwarzenegger of California.

The first station opened at Proton in Wallingford, Connecticut, in October of 2010. Operating under the SunHydro banner, it is indeed partially powered by solar energy. Toyota said it would base a fleet of 10 fuel-cell Highlanders there, and I was selected to be one of the first five to conduct a long-term test. It's amazing how quickly driving an experimental fuel-cell vehicle became totally normal. The experience is almost exactly the same as driving an electric battery car, because that's essentially what fuel-cell vehicles are—electric cars with fuel cells replacing battery packs. Early fuel-cell cars I drove made all kinds of avant-garde sounds from noisy compressors and unshielded electric motors, but all of that's been dialed out and replaced by an eerie quiet.

Unfortunately, it's easier to get access to fuel-cell cars in Connecticut than it is in Iceland. Things got so desperate in Reykjavík that a fleet of 10 Toyota Priuses converted by Quantum to burn hydrogen was imported. Burning hydrogen in an internal-combustion engine isn't an ideal scenario—at best it's a stopgap measure on the way to fuel cells—but it was the only affordable option available.

I took a ride in one of the hydrogen-burning Priuses (which were available for consumer leases or rental by Hertz) with Jón Björn Skúlason, general manager of Icelandic New Energy and a tireless hydrogen advocate.

Skúlason told me as a barren landscape flashed by that the brief run of the Daimler fuel-cell buses saved 18,000 gallons of diesel fuel and the emission of 300 tons of greenhouse gas. By mid-2009, he said, Iceland hoped to have as many as 40 hydrogen cars on the road, not to mention the first fuel cell on the *Elding*— a 150-passenger whale-watching tourist craft. Alas, the 10- to 15-kilowatt Ballard fuel cell wasn't big enough to replace the ship's diesel engine, just the auxiliary power unit that provides electrical power.[4] "We're hoping to prove that fuel cells can work at sea, since they hate salt," Skúlason said.[5]

A timeline on the wall at the Shell hydrogen station in Reykjavík outlined an orderly procession to Iceland's hydrogen economy—unfortunately, by the time of my 2007 visit it was already running about five years behind. The commercial phase (with vehicles reaching actual paying customers) was scheduled to start in 2010, and it was already clear that this wouldn't happen. Icelandic New Energy's Web site now sees a transition to hydrogen around 2050. But the group admitted it will happen only if "technical, economic and social development becomes aligned toward this goal." A big if.

The Icelanders should be forgiven for thinking that fuel-cell cars would get off the ground sooner. When I wrote my first book, *Forward Drive*, published in 2000, Daimler's Ferdinand Panik, at the time head of the company's Fuel Cell Project, was assuring me that it would have fleets of 100,000 cars on the road by 2006.[6]

The potential to make hydrogen in Iceland was huge. According to Thorsteinn Sigfusson, a hydrogen pioneer and professor of physics at the University of Iceland, thanks to geothermal and hydroelectric, Icelanders' per capita annual carbon dioxide emissions are already half that of Americans, at 12 tons versus 23 tons. Most of the remaining emissions are from transportation, so transforming the car and truck fleet is a big priority. "The use of hydrocarbons will turn out to be a glitch in time," Sigfusson said.

If hydrogen was an export product, Iceland could have a dynamic and much-needed new industry. Unfortunately, like electricity itself, hydrogen is best used when and where it is. It's so light that it wants to escape from pipelines, and moving it in bulk is problematic unless it's either severely compressed or turned into liquid. And both of those options are impractical.

Less than 10 percent of Iceland's geothermal potential has been harnessed, so the country's ability to produce energy in the form of electricity or hydrogen is unlimited. But there's no economically feasible way to get it off the island.

POWERING ALCOA

Instead, Iceland has followed another path. Seventy-five percent of the electricity produced is channeled into producing aluminum for export. The big producers are foreign, including Alcoa, Rio Tinto Alcan, and Century Aluminum. It's hardly a sustainable solution, since the raw material, bauxite, has to be shipped from Australia, Jamaica, Brazil, and other locations halfway around the world.

In the central highlands of Iceland is the new $1 billion plus Kárahnjúkar Hydropower Project, a plant so big it could power the entire country. Instead, its electricity is wholly consumed by a new Alcoa aluminum smelter. Alcoa says its Icelandic aluminum production is the lowest emission of its kind in the world, but that hardly assuages critics such as the pop star Björk Gudmundsdóttir, who called the project "crazy." Björk is the best-known Icelander, so it made headlines when her mother staged a hunger strike over Kárahnjúkar.

Thora Ellen Thorhallsdottir of the Institute of Biology at the University of Iceland points out that if all of the geothermal and hydroelectric plants planned for Iceland were built, they would affect or flood 3 percent of the country's landmass—in some pristine areas. "This is the largest wilderness area in Europe, much of it never inhabited by humans," she said. The reservoir for Kárahnjúkar alone covers 22 square miles and flooded reindeer and bird habitat. The reindeer are descendants of animals imported from Norway and thus nonnative, but still.

"We're putting the majority of our energy into aluminum smelting, and there's no value added in that,"[7] said Pétur Albert Haraldsson, a serial entrepreneur who runs the annual Driving Sustainability conference in Reykjavík and recently started Iceland Energy, a project to promote the switch to 100 percent locally produced power. Since transportation is the only sector *not* running on local energy, that's the group's focus. I've attended the Driving Sustainability conference twice and spoken at it once, and through its filter I see a growing consensus for a transportation regime based not on hydrogen, but on battery electric cars.

THE PLUG-IN PATH

In the first six months of 2010, some 2,500 new cars were sold in Iceland, a number that would be a footnote in any major company's annual accounting. Over the last 17 years, annual sales had averaged 11,000, so it's clear that there's been a big plunge. Many of the major automobile franchises, including Volkswagen and Nissan, were riddled with debt and nationalized at the same time the banks were. One dealer told me that in the immediate aftermath of the crash, car sales dropped 90 percent.

Not the most propitious market for launching a transformative electric car industry, perhaps. "Long-term thinking isn't quite the thing in Iceland now," Haraldsson told me. "Everybody's worried about getting by, and the government is thinking of other things." But the government was focused enough to finally remove sales tax on electric cars, and the president of Iceland is a major booster. I visited His Excellency Ólafur Ragnar Grímsson in the library of the seaside presidential residence, Bessastaðir. If the white-haired Grímsson wasn't the president, he could get hired by Hollywood to play world leaders.

As we talked, he gestured expansively. "Look at our activity and bustling traffic," he said.[8] "Does this look like a country in crisis? A key reason we're able to weather our financial collapse is the low cost of electricity and home heating here. A family pays only a couple hundred dollars per year to heat their home with geothermal energy. Our difficulties would be much worse if we were still heating and creating electricity with imported oil and coal. Clean energy is good for the well-being of individuals and companies—it's a pillar of the economy."

Iceland has extremely cheap electricity, priced as low as 2.5 cents per kilowatt-hour. According to Grímsson, the math for electric cars is extremely favorable, and lucky motorists should be able to drive their plug-in cars for a whole year for what two fill-ups now cost them. "Our greatest stumbling block is getting the EVs actually on the road here and on the world market," he told me. "The car producers are not yet able to meet the growing demand."[9]

Northern Lights Energy (NLE) is trying to do something about the car-supply problem, which is the same one that sank the hydrogen effort. And that's why I was sitting around that fire with Gísli Gíslason, a man with a knack for reinventing himself.

He has been variously a lawyer, the operator of the Re/Max real-estate franchise in Denmark, a film producer (the 2009 horror film *Reykjavík Whale-Watching Massacre*, starring the original Leatherface of *Texas Chainsaw* fame, was his), and, currently, the CEO of NLE.

Despite the terrible economy, NLE is moving fast to bring green cars to Iceland. A bright spot is that the failing economy sent the price of imported gasoline, already among the most expensive in the world, to new heights above $7 a gallon. NLE started out by signing up large businesses, government agencies, and municipalities to host electric car charging stations and buy the cars. The goal is to get 300 major players signed on for a fast-track start to greening the transportation base.

Gíslason, a stylish dresser, has become a familiar figure at the headquarters of major EV producers, order book in hand. He makes a big impression: Among his plans are to journey into space aboard the *Virgin Galactic*, a $200,000 ticket. No wonder Gíslason gets along with rocket pioneer Elon Musk.

An early NLE partner was Reva, the Indian EV maker whose cheap and cheerful $9,000 to $11,000 G-Wiz actually became a bestseller in Britain because it was an affordable way to avoid the daily London congestion tax. I drove one in Reykjavík and found it to be remarkably poor. Gíslason had ordered the supposedly much improved $23,000 NXR model, but delivery was delayed and he looked elsewhere.

Because I thought there might be some synergy there (no money was involved), I introduced Gíslason to the Cincinnati-based Amp Electric Vehicles, which started out converting the Chevy Equinox and a twinned pair of General Motors roadsters, the Pontiac Solstice and Saturn Sky, to electric. Conversions like that aren't cheap—the Equinox conversion is $50,000, including the $25,000 cost of the donor car. But Gíslason wanted vehicles, and Amp was in production and wanted customers. Negotiations began in late 2010, followed by Gíslason's order in November of that year for 1,000 conversions over five years.[10]

More than 1,000 hybrids have been converted to plug-in hybrids since 2004. But conversion of gasoline cars to plug-in, which has the potential to rapidly accelerate a transition to electric cars, has been slow in gaining public support and incentives. Texas entrepreneur T. Boone Pickens has spent $50 million promoting the conversion of gasoline vehicles to run on natural gas.

That was a huge order that made headlines all over the world. "The combination of EVs and Iceland make for a perfect storm," Amp's then-CEO, Steve Burns, said. "Everything is present—a low cost of electricity coupled with the high cost of gasoline, the inherent short commutes of an island community and the desire to reduce dependence on foreign oil."[11]

By late May of 2011, Gíslason had taken delivery of the first two cars, an Equinox and another conversion that should be very Europe friendly, a Mercedes ML350 SUV. The cars were on hand for a ceremony at Reykjavík's new glass-facade opera house, Harpa. Gíslason told the audience, which included the American ambassador, that Northern Lights Energy had gotten a lot of promises from EV companies. "But then we met the guys from Amp," he said. "We made an order, and they shipped us the cars."

Around this same time, Gíslason got more good news: Iceland's Parliament voted unanimously to not only remove the value-added tax (VAT) from electric cars, but import duties as well. That's huge, because the VAT alone amounts to 25.5 percent of the purchase price. Gíslason's Tesla Roadster—reportedly the first one in Europe—was unregistered for months simply because he wanted to avoid paying that crushing VAT.

NLE's vision is multifaceted. In addition to ordering conversions, it has also proposed assembling Amp electric vehicles in Think's assembly plant in Aurskog, Norway, abandoned when Think announced that it was moving expanded operations to Finland in 2009. The move put 85 experienced Norwegian workers out of jobs, and they could form the basis of a NLE/Amp workforce. From Norway, NLE could deliver cars all over Europe.

NLE also issued a letter of intent to order 1,000 Model S cars, over four years, from Tesla Motors. "It is our commitment to purchase the Model S when it becomes available as a production program starting in the first quarter of the 2012 calendar year," Gíslason wrote to Tesla's European operation in September of 2010.[12] Privately, several people at Tesla asked me, "Is Gíslason for real?" My answer was always, "We'll see, won't we?"

Through another suggestion I made, NLE also started talking to Mike McQuary of Wheego. The Wheego LiFe could actually be assembled in Iceland, with the car chassis being shipped from China and the various components delivered from Wheego's suppliers.

NLE's young cofounder and managing director, Sturla Sighvatsson, told me, "Having the cars built by Wheego in California and shipped here to Iceland wouldn't make any sense. We'd want to get the gliders [the cars without drivetrains installed] directly from China."[13] And that would mean the Wheegos could actually be "Icelandic cars," the very first ever made in the country.

"We found out it takes four hours for two men to install the electric components into a Wheego vehicle," Sighvatsson said. "We could do that in Iceland."

Sighvatsson, named after a 13th-century Icelandic chieftain, is a younger version of Gíslason, and he shares his background as a Re/Max broker. But he became a driven real-estate speculator in the go-go period between 2003 and 2008, and he tells a classic rags-to-riches-to-rags story.

"I bought land with rundown buildings on it and sold it to contractors at a profit," Sighvatsson told me. "At one time I was worth $10 million, though I reinvested most of the money I made back in the business for the next deal. I bought a nice BMW, traveled, and at the height, in early 2007, I actually talked about buying a private plane with some other investors. I lost all sense of reality—people thought it would go on forever. Icelandic bankers became like modern Vikings, capturing the banks in Britain."

It didn't go on forever. NLE's efforts still face the hurdle of a cash-poor Iceland. The company is trying to line up financing, because few companies in Iceland have cash to invest up front in electric cars and chargers. General Electric, recognizing that reality (certainly not just in Iceland), is partnering GE Capital with GE Energy to provide financing for its WattStations.

NLE's elaborate plans could turn into castles made of sand, kicked into nothingness by the bullies of limited capital and limited leverage on an island near the Arctic Circle. But Haraldsson put it best when he told me, "It makes no sense to import energy into Iceland. We are the perfect market for electric cars. We're like a little test tube."

CHAPTER NINE

ON THE ROAD

While it appears that the goal [1 million plug-in cars by 2015]
is within reach in terms of production capacity, initial costs
and lack of familiarity with the technology could be barriers.

—US DEPARTMENT OF ENERGY

UNTIL THE VERY END OF 2010, most people experienced electric cars at auto shows, in the pages of magazines, or as image advertising—they weren't *tangible*. All that's changed now: You can actually see electric and plug-in hybrid cars on the street, picking up groceries with early adopters at the wheel, taking the kids to Little League, and—lo and behold—even charging up at public stations.

Until EVs are integrated into the fabric of daily life, we won't really know how they'll be received. Without people plugging in, it's all guesswork. President Obama reiterated his call for 1 million plug-in cars during the State of the Union speech in January of 2011, but is that goal feasible?

Yes, according to a Department of Energy report, which totaled up the announcements of electric and plug-in hybrid production numbers and arrived at 1.2 million by 2015.[1] Of course, some of the numbers in its accounting are both decidedly optimistic and tentative, as well as definitely subject to change. Will GM really produce 120,000 Volts a year by 2015? Will Fisker gear up to producing 75,000 Nina plug-in hybrids annually by 2015? And the DOE did offer a caveat. "While it appears that the goal is within reach in terms of production capacity, initial costs and lack of familiarity with the technology could be barriers."

An expert panel convened by Indiana University, which issued a *Practical Plan for Progress* shortly before the DOE report came out, begs to differ that the goal is in sight. "The production intentions of automakers are currently insufficient to meet the 2015 goal, and even the current plans for production volumes may not be met," the report said. But it added, "Automakers could ramp up [plug-in vehicle] production if consumer demand proves to be larger than expected."[2]

That last sentence is key, because consumer demand is a total wild card. Demand may be so low that carmakers don't even meet the targets they have in place now, or it could be high enough for them to far exceed those numbers. I don't know, and neither do the experts assembled by Indiana University. If I had to bet, I'd say the Obama goal won't be reached, but if gas prices soar out of control, all bets are off. Pain at the pump is a driver for huge electric car sales.

Industry opinions are divided, too. "The DOE report did a good job of showing how we get to 1 million by 2015," said Michael Mahan, leader of General Electric's EV product team. "It's not only desirable, it's likely." But Alex Molinaroli, president of major battery maker Johnson Controls Power Solutions, is much more pessimistic. "I don't see how we're going to get there, knowing how long it takes to ramp up."

In the first two sale months (December 2010 and January

2011), General Motors sold 646 Volts, but that number is completely meaningless—it just represents how many cars the company produced as it ramped up for full production. And there's a long waiting list. "As soon as they hit, they're being sold," Chevrolet spokesman Randy Fox told me.

The Volt and Nissan Leaf were up and down against each other in the early months, and journalists followed the tallies as if it were a horse race—with the Volt often leading. In reality, Leaf availability in the wake of the Japanese earthquake was very limited. But in June of 2011, Nissan and Chevrolet reported on sales for the first six months of the year, and the Leaf was in the lead with 3,875 cars sold, compared to 2,745 Volts. Consider that simply a snapshot in time, as automakers catch up to their reservations.

It took a while to actually start selling electric cars. In the middle of February 2011, Mike McQuary of Wheego finally got the piece of paper he'd been waiting for—an exemption from the federal Department of Transportation that let him sell his car without an advanced passenger-side airbag. It had been a while in coming. "For a couple of months I felt like that guy in that movie, what's his name—Preston Tucker?" McQ said. That movie, which came out in 1988, was called *Tucker: The Man and His Dream*. As you may recall, Tucker claimed to have been hounded out of business in the 1950s (by the government, competitors, or both) as he tried to go into production with the innovative Tucker Torpedo sedan. Maybe, but Tucker also had some rather creative financing ideas, and it's not surprising that the Securities and Exchange Commission got interested.

Wheego was authorized to sell cars 30 days after the exemption was issued, so McQ was anxious to deliver them. His intention was to deliver the first 300 LiFes to waiting customers and use the revenue to produce more at the California plant. With cars in the pipeline, he hoped to get a credit line to order more battery packs and other components. It was a high-wire act with plenty of precedent in the auto start-up business—Preston Tucker had gotten creative (including asking customers to pay for seat covers and radios up front) because he desperately needed cash.

Another hope was that Wheego could go into business with Northern Lights Energy and assemble LiFes in Iceland. Nobody had ever built a car in Iceland, so it was a long shot, but hardly one that McQ could ignore.

Wheego has modest ambitions, and spokeswoman Susan Nicholson says the company will be happy with sales of 100 a month. "We don't ever expect to be selling 1,000 cars a week," she said. "We don't need to sell that many to be successful because we're a very small operation."[3]

By early 2011, cars were finally reaching dealerships, and that meant that people could walk in, kick the tires, and go for test rides. It was an exciting moment. Would they be disappointed by what they found? Could they live with 100 miles of range?

I've spent behind-the-wheel time with all of the electric and plug-in hybrid cars, and I do think that people will like them—especially because they're generally a blast to drive. Unlike gasoline cars, which achieve peak horsepower only at a set engine speed, EVs have "instant on" power. They're not all performance cars, but they're all at least lively.

Here's a brief look from the driver's seat at some of the new

EVs, including some that are likely to be casualties in a ruthless business that doesn't give you points for trying.

CHEVY VOLT: THE EV WITH OPTIONS

I persuaded GM to lend me a Volt soon after they went on sale because I'd taken only short hops in the car. I wanted to have the full experience, which included charging the car in my garage. The Volt makes charging easy, because eight hours of 110 house current will fill up the 16-kilowatt-hour battery pack.

The Volt has electric-only range cited at 25 to 50 miles, and there's a reason it's cited as being variable. I got the car in the middle of winter, and the most I could get out of it was about 28 miles on batteries. The reasons for that are twofold—the batteries aren't as efficient in the cold, and the heater draws a *lot* of power (almost as much as is used to drive the car). The range displayed at the end of a charge is determined by an algorithm that takes into account past driving behavior—so your result might differ from mine.

The Volt actually offers owners the option of extending range by choosing the Eco climate option, which limits use of the electric heater. Instead, occupants are warmed mostly by the seat heaters until the engine kicks in. It's not my preferred method of travel—I would have been half frozen, especially since I mostly ran the Volt on batteries.

The Volt is enormously fun to drive, offering the same kind of spirited performance as its predecessor the EV1, but with three times the range. It's fast off the line, and has the best handling around fast corners that I've experienced in a GM car (including the Corvette, which always felt too heavy to me). The switch from battery to gas mode is practically seamless—if I hadn't seen the dash display, I wouldn't have realized anything had happened. As Jay Leno says, this is the car you'd take on the long trips.

Since it was cold, the gas engine occasionally started to run the heater, but otherwise I rarely engaged it. In 200 miles, I used 3.3 gallons of gasoline and, at least according to the car, achieved 60 mpg. Among my few quibbles: I think I'd prefer an enclosed trunk instead of the open area behind the seats, and the rear-seat legroom could be better (room for five would be nice, too). I liked everything else about the car, and I'd never get tired of the imaginative and informative graphic displays. If I had $41,000 to spend on a car, I'd spend it on the Volt.

The Volt is likely to have a family, including a crossover version that could do very well. Tony Posawatz, the Volt line director, told me he'd "like to see the Volt drivetrain dropped into a Corvette chassis. But let's do the first one right, and then think about what comes next." What came next turned out to be a luxury car built on the Volt platform and sold as the Cadillac ELR (based on the Converj show car of 2009). The Volt will also need a passport, because target markets include Europe and China.

NISSAN LEAF: THE BIG BATTERY GAMBLE

Carlos Ghosn is a gambler. The CEO of both Nissan and Renault really threw the rule book away when he ordered a full-court press on getting the mainstream industry's very first all-original battery car onto the market by the end of 2010.

The Leaf is on a high wire, with only its batteries keeping it aloft. The Volt's Tony Posawatz is constantly taking potshots at the Leaf (its biggest mainstream competitor in the green car sweepstakes). "Now that we're on the market, people are really seeing the difference between extended-range cars like ours and vehicles with limited battery-only range," Posawatz said.

The big question is not only whether people can live with 100 miles of range (on a good day), but whether they're willing to spend $35,200 (before rebates) to pioneer the plug-in. "There's not a good deal of uncertainty about their selling the first 25,000 cars," said Jack Nerad, executive editorial director of Kelley Blue Book. "They'll find that many environmentalists and technology-oriented customers in a country of 300 million. But what about after that? Is this a consumer product with legs, or will the demand dry up?"[4]

I can't answer Nerad's questions because the important factors—the price of oil, the state of the economy—aren't reliably predictable. I want to think it's a beachhead leading to Shai Agassi's vision of all-electric transportation, but there are too many wild cards.

I'd had a variety of short test drives in the Leaf, but I didn't get a chance to live with it until February of 2011, when it had effectively been on the market only a couple of months. The Leaf arrived in a covered trailer, which says something about its limited battery range—the Volt was driven to my door. The sky blue car came with an iPhone in the glove compartment, which was great for testing out the remote features.

The iPhone app for "Blue Unit 0060" was *really* cool, with almost psychedelic colors that gave such details as state of charge and time needed to finish charging. Start charging, and a text or e-mail will tell you when it's done. I tried turning on the preheating feature, and it was a matter of a couple of finger taps.

For our first test ride, my wife and I chose a mixed city and highway route to a seaside restaurant 10 miles and a couple of towns away. We stepped into a preheated toasty warm car. The iPhone said we had 106 miles of range, which proved illusory.

The Leaf was truly a delight to drive—smooth, tight, responsive. It accelerates plenty fast enough for me, though certainly not in the five-second zero-to-60 time frame claimed on the *CBS Evening News*.[5] There was a whooshing noise on fast takeoff that my wife compared to an airplane. The brakes were excellent. Our ride sacrificed nothing—except range certainty. Yes, despite the multiplicity of displays, we found ourselves constantly checking the remaining distance to empty. After our 20-mile up-and-back, the display read 55 miles (though, oddly, 61 miles on the iPhone). We were hemorrhaging range.

As with the Volt, here was proof that cold weather takes its toll on battery range. Many drivers report equaling or exceeding the stated 100-mile range in warm weather. We were cranking both the heater and the satellite radio, and yet another dash display confirmed that the climate control drains a lot of power (the radio is minuscule by comparison). The car informed us that turning off the heat would gain us another 15 miles. But the modern driver is going to use accessories.

Nissan made some predictions about how the Leaf would perform under various weather conditions, and they range from 138 miles at a steady 38 mph at 68°F to just 62 miles when the mercury hits 14°F in stop-and-go traffic with the heater blasting.

And that's not the worst-case scenario—in some non-US "extreme" driving conditions, range would be reduced to just 47 miles. Another factor affecting range is the highway driving. During the in-town stop-and-go, we could plainly see the benefit of regenerative brakes—we actually gained one mile of range.

Wanting to build back some range, we plugged into our 110 garage outlet and then started the charging session with the iPhone. Again, dead easy and a very similar procedure to charging the Volt. We failed to plug the charger in all the way, and the phone informed us of that fact. Refilling the car with the 110 "trickle charge" was going to take 10 hours, the all-knowing phone said. Curious, we checked some of the many energy-related features through the dash display and discovered that the nearest 240-volt charging station was, gulp, 40 miles away, on I-95.

EVs have yet to make much of a dent in my little corner of the world, so it was good to see that the iPhone app offered the option of calling roadside assistance.

The Leaf battery pack lacks active battery management (a pack warmer was added for 2012), but Nissan is reassuring owners with an eight-year/100,000-mile warranty. I loved everything about the Leaf except the range challenges, and I'd probably develop ways around them if I actually owned the car.

TESLA MODEL S: THE GREEN FERRARI

Tesla sent us bloggers a lovely video of some lucky fellow driving the Model S sedan on country roads. It was kind of like watching someone else have sex. The Model S is a huge gamble for Tesla, and it really matters if it lives up to the company's high performance standards (which include zero to 60 in 5.6 seconds). It has to be, for instance, a lot better than the very nice Volt, because it costs $16,500 more.

I started out with a chauffeured ride, this one at Chelsea Piers in New York City in the spring of 2009. I recorded a few impressions.

> ✓ The car is oh-my-god fast, but not quite as big an assault on the senses as the Tesla Roadster. We drove around in a circle in a vast warehouse space, but it was enough to give the impression of supercar acceleration. Although the test car was the only drivable Model S in the world at that time and had been through the mill, it was impressively squeak and rattle free. The seats were comfortable, and vision seemed good all around. After my ride, I stood and watched others going out, and it was like an optical illusion—one moment the Model S was there, and the next it was at the far end of the space.

> ✓ The interior, now subtler than it was then, is beautifully finished. Techies will love the enormous 17-inch infotainment touch screen, which offers 3-D graphics. The display runs on a Nvidia Tegra chip (also used by BMW), which Tesla describes as "power stingy"—a very important consideration for battery cars. Radio and climate controls and almost everything else are virtual features on the 3G-enabled touch screen—forget about buttons. If you don't like the design of the controls, you can change them. According to Franz von Holzhausen, Tesla's chief designer: "I don't understand how I can pay $299 for iPhone and then get in my car and still have to turn knobs."[6] A full

browser is promised, though like a knob-free dash it would be massively distracting if usable when the car is under way. Von Holzhausen says the infotainment offerings are "wrapped up in a very aspirational package."[7]

✓ The two rear-facing Country Squire–type "way back" seats that are supposed to give this relatively compact sedan an impressive seven-seat capacity were not in evidence on the test car. The battery drivetrain means there will be storage both under the hood and in the long but shallow trunk. "More room than a station wagon," Tesla claims.

✓ It's really pretty in person, with swooping Italianate lines that have undergone some minor revisions as the car has gone forward. One nonworking model had incredible iridescent pearl paint that could also boast of being water based and environmentally friendly. Other green features include 100 percent recycled PET carpeting and chrome-free, vegetable-tanned Italian leather (but vegetarians will still object).

The Model S will be offered with three separate battery packages, offering 160, 230, and, gulp, 300 miles of range. The price escalates accordingly for the bigger packs. The battery necessary to give the Model S 300 miles of range is a whopper, estimated by Tesla at 85 to 90 kilowatt-hours. Nobody has put that large a pack in an EV: Even some of the trucks made by Smith Electric Vehicles have smaller ones.

The challenge for Tesla will be making the bigger pack fit the space occupied by the smaller batteries, keeping the cost down, and ensuring that the charge time isn't excessive. When I talked to Peter Rawlinson, the Model S's chief engineer, at the 2011 Detroit auto show, he said that weight reduction is a key to reaching performance goals. Obviously, the lighter the car, the smaller the battery necessary to get it to cover 300 miles. Still, Tesla is confident enough about its long-distance battery to say it will be offered on the first 1,000 cars.

Elon Musk claims that leasing the Model S is similar in cost to a $35,000 gasoline car, with likely $4 a gallon gas factored in. Tesla likes to cite the price as $49,900, but that's with the $7,500 tax credit subtracted. All the automakers support turning the credit into a rebate paid at the time of purchase, for obvious reasons.

THINK CITY: A NORDIC JOURNEY

I'd driven the tiny, two-seat Think City in Detroit and in Indiana, too, but it was in Turku, Finland, that I was really able to take its measure.

The Think City, with 100 miles of range, is built in Finland, but it actually isn't Finnish—it is proudly Norwegian (with a bit of an American accent). Founded in Oslo in 1991 as Personal Independent Vehicle Company (PIVCO), the company initially made a very cute plastic-bodied electric car called the City Bee that took part in some US-based test programs. That may be what put it on Ford's radar, because PIVCO was snatched up in 1999, when the Big Three were facing some daunting electric car mandates in California. Ford invested $150 million in what became known as the Th!NK division. (There was also a little golf-cart-like local transporter called the TH!NK Neighbor.)

Ford, sensing that California was easing up its battery-car

requirements, jettisoned what became simply Think in 2003, and 300 unsold cars were shipped back to Norway. Think became Europe focused, and it managed to sell 1,000 of its older models and 500 of a revamped new version of the Think City before it effectively went bankrupt at the end of 2008. An emergency infusion of $47 million, led by Charles Gassenheimer of the US-based Ener1 battery company, reenergized Think and helped fuel the company's US sales hopes.

Ener1, based in Indiana, then owned more than 30 percent of Think. The EV maker became fairly well established in Europe, with sales in Norway (the best customer), Spain, Sweden, Switzerland, and France. More than 2,000 had been purchased by the end of 2010. Think soon said it would also build a base in Indiana and make cars in hard-hit Elkhart, once known as the RV Capital of the World. Elkhart became a poster city for job loss (President Obama visited three times), so it wasn't hard to find a vacant and affordable 200,000-square-foot factory that once made RV windows. The city of Elkhart offered a $2.7 million tax abatement, and the state of Indiana provided $3 million. I visited Elkhart in early 2011 and found it heartening to see more than 200 electric cars together in one place. The factory, which in the early stages was assembling partially built cars from Finland, was eerily quiet. Even the cars whizzing around the huge space (part of a final test procedure) were virtually silent.

It was snowing, but that didn't stop Think from offering a test drive around the suburbs of Elkhart. The Think City is not the Leaf—the US model is strictly for two passengers, though there is a 2+2 version that incorporates child-sized rear seats. The interior is functional rather than luxurious, and space is a little tight. The City also lacks the sophisticated electronic displays of the Volt and Leaf. But it's a decent performer on wet roads—I was able to goose it along without losing grip. All in all, the car is a midlevel performer—think the Honda Civic. It's cute, with a no-paint plastic skin resembling the outside of an old thermos bottle, and it seems solidly built. It would do fine as a commuter car or local transport for empty nesters, and it would do well on official government business. But it isn't likely to get American youth excited with a featured spot on the cover of *Road & Track*.

The sense I got of a company ramping up in Indiana proved deceptive. Think actually started relatively well in the United States, but then it stalled. The first few hundred cars were supposedly spoken for—15 were bought by the Indiana Department of Natural Resources to patrol the state parks, and another 17 were bought by utilities. But the fleet price was really high at about $41,000, the same as the Volt and more than the Leaf. No groundswell of demand appeared and the Norwegian parent company declared bankruptcy—once again—in June of 2011, leaving the dependent US operation in limbo. Battery maker Ener1 promptly wrote off its entire investment in the company. Think had survived other near-death experiences, and once again a last-minute savior appeared—this time a Russian timber magnate. The safest thing to say about Think is that its future is unclear.

APTERA 2E: THE CAR THAT THINKS IT'S A PLANE

I was the first journalist to drive the 2e, which is definitely the most physically striking battery-electric car. Since it looks like a three-wheeled Piper Cub without wings, it's not surprising that it was an extra in a *Star Trek* remake. But California-based Aptera wants to do more than build movie props—it genuinely thinks its cockpit-oriented styling, originally drawn on a cocktail napkin, is the wave of the future.

It was early 2009 when I first met the Aptera in Lower Manhattan, where it was sharing showroom space with some supercar exotics that looked tame by comparison. CEO Paul Wilbur was there, and he told me that the three-wheel setup and sculpted look were all about efficiency and aerodynamics. The early version of the car, made of foam core composite, weighed just 1,700 pounds and had a 0.15 coefficient of drag, "which is less than Lance Armstrong riding his bicycle," Wilbur said.

My daughter and I got a ride, but Wilbur wouldn't let us drive. I rode shotgun for enough miles to form an opinion, though. The potholes and cobblestones set off some rattles, and the dramatic gullwing doors didn't seem very well aligned. The trunk wasn't in place yet. But the car was comfortable and felt relatively stable on its three wheels.

A year and a half later, I finally got to drive the Aptera 2e at an event hosted by Aptera investor NRG Energy in Princeton, New Jersey. The weight had crept up to 2,000 pounds, but the car was now much more finished looking. The 2e, which is supposed to have a hybrid sister car down the road, offers just 110 horsepower from its electric motor, connected to a 20-kilowatt-hour A123 battery pack. Range is supposed to be 100 to 120 miles.

Driving it was an experience: I reached the maximum 65 mph cruising speed allowed during the test, but it was somewhat fraught. The handling was very good, but Aptera clearly still had work to do. The steering effort was considerable, and the brakes very weak. It would all be fixed in the production car, said Tom Reichenbach, Aptera's chief engineer, who rode with me in the passenger seat.

The option of fixing problems down the road assumes there *is* a production car. Aptera's fortunes weren't looking much better than Think's when this book went to press, and several on-sale deadlines had come and gone, and deposits were returned. Like many other carmakers, including Think, Aptera was staking its fortunes on the kind of Department of Energy loan that lifted the fortunes of Tesla and Fisker. With the loan, it would take a year to get to market, spokesman Marques McCammon told me. Without the loan, there's a fallback plan, but it would take "longer," he said.

TOYOTA HIGHLANDER FCHV-ADV FUEL-CELL CAR: A STEADY STATE REVOLUTION

People who expect green cars to be a totally new driving experience might be disappointed—for the most part, they were designed to make the transition from customers' experience as seamless as possible. For that reason, instruments and controls are where you'd expect them to be, and driving isn't too different, either—when you lift your foot off the brake at a stoplight, the cars "creep" forward, just as conventional ones do. That has to be dialed in by the engineers.

So the Toyota FCHV is not some moon-shot exotic. First of all, it's a Toyota Highlander, with all of that small SUV's utility (except four-wheel drive). After several hundred miles of driving, it's easy to forget that there's anything unusual about the car. It's super-quiet but punchy, with plenty of the instant torque that comes as a bonus with electric motors.

When I told people I was testing a fuel-cell vehicle, they often referenced the 1937 *Hindenburg* crash, which killed 35. But one way to look at it is that memories of that airship disaster have ensured redundant safety systems on cars like the FCHV. In the event of even a tiny hydrogen leak, the car shuts down. I certainly didn't drive around obsessing about the highly flammable pressurized hydrogen on board with my kids and me.

Two things stood out as departures from the standard driving routine: The refueling process and the cold-weather performance. Like battery cars, fuel-cell vehicles are challenged by the cold. The danger is that the water produced as part of electricity production can freeze in the cells, causing damage. For that reason, when you push the cold-weather button on the dashboard (as I did), it purges water from the cells after the car is shut down, increases water storage capacity, and raises the stack temperature quicker. All that takes energy, so the car loses range.[8]

Toyota has cold-started the FCHV in −37°F, and it achieved more than 400 miles of range in Los Angeles rush-hour traffic. But I estimated that with the cold-weather button pushed, range dropped to 225 miles. That was a bit of an issue for me as an FCHV user, because the Wallingford station is 40 miles away. I had to carefully husband the miles so I didn't make the trek upstate too often.

Refueling was fun, though. The solar-powered SunHydro station can deliver hydrogen at either 5,000 or 10,000 pounds per square inch. The FCHV accepts the latter, which is why it has more range. I attached the heavy cable (not unlike an EV charger) to the hydrogen port, punched in some codes, including a long ID number and an odometer reading, and the hydrogen started flowing with a high-pitched hiss. It was done in five minutes.

That quick refueling is a major advantage of hydrogen

vehicles—it's very like the current gas station experience, and takes no longer. But the drawback is the station cost. The SunHydro stations are between $1 million and $2 million each, compared to less than $10,000 installed for a 240-volt electric car charge station.

The cars are still very expensive, too, but projected prices are coming down rapidly. Takeshi Uchiyamada, a Toyota research vice president, told Bloomberg that the cost of producing a car like the FCHV had dropped below $100,000 by the end of 2010, and the company is confident of halving that to $50,000 by 2015 (or maybe even 2014), when it intends to commercialize the technology.[9] That's still not cheap, but it finally gets fuel cells in range of the current auto market.

According to Toyota, the well-to-wheel efficiency of the FCHV is 40 percent, compared to 33 percent for battery EVs, 34 percent for hybrids like the Toyota Prius, and just 19 percent for gasoline cars. But efficiency results may depend on how you make the hydrogen—it can be produced from water through electrolysis, from fossil fuels through steam reforming, or from renewables, and the well-to-wheel results will vary in each case. And efficiency alone isn't going to win the day—nice guys finish last sometimes. Fuel cells need fueling stations, and it still isn't clear who will build them.

That infrastructure issue, plus the high cost of producing the hydrogen, led the Obama Department of Energy to declare that hydrogen is a technology for tomorrow—and to twice try to defund it, in 2009 and 2011 (but Congress, which has caucuses of pro-hydrogen members, fought back).

There are, inevitably, going to be also-ran and did-not-finish companies in the race to get electric cars on the market. That's to be expected, because the last time we had so many new start-ups (eek, could it have been the 1910s and 1920s?), huge numbers didn't survive the Depression. Of 60 American carmakers in production circa 1930, only 18 made it to the end of the decade. Good-bye, Essex, Stutz, Reo, Franklin, Pierce-Arrow, and Duesenberg.[10]

In the summer of 2010, I talked to a fairly bitter Barry Bernsten, a Philadelphia-based steel wholesaler who had just closed his BG ("Be Green") Automotive Group. Launched in 2008, the enterprise intended to produce the BG-C100, an electric car based (like the Wheego LiFe and the Coda sedan) on a Chinese body and chassis. "I visited six plants [in China], and though I saw some where the cars had paint peeling off the plastic bumpers, and the wheels and hub-caps were rusting, one of them made high-quality automobiles. In fact, its cars were better built than many US and Japanese cars on the market now."[11]

But the BG-C100 was not to be. Bernsten applied for Department of Energy funds and didn't get them. He was daunted by what he said was the DOE's demand for "performance tests that cost many millions,"[12] and he also said he lacked the necessary connections. "The well-connected guys with the lobbying teams got the loan guarantees," he told me. "I'm frustrated that we couldn't even get partial funding. . . . I'm going back to selling steel."

BG won't be the last to fail, but there will be winners, too. No mainstream carmaker has been successfully launched since Chrysler in the 1920s, but that doesn't mean it won't happen now. In fact, I'd bet on it. Electric cars are better than most people think, and the electrification of the automobile is inevitable.

CHAPTER TEN

EDEN ATTAINED?

*Any time someone has a game-changing technology or
invention, people need to learn about it,
get comfortable with it.*

—GEORGE BLANKENSHIP, FROM APPLE TO TESLA

WHAT WILL THE FUTURE OF commuting look like? I have an educated guess that ramps up some of the technology that's already quite feasible today. Try this vision on for size:

It is a warm morning in the summer of 2030, and you're running late to work at the cloud-computing server center in San Francisco. You step outside the condo and press a button on your half-dollar-sized cell phone. That awakens your 10G-connected and partially folded electric car in its storage space under the house and sends it, now fully reconstituted (*The Jetsons* got one aspect of the future right—folding cars), out to the curb via the auto-drive feature. No need to unplug anything, because your 2029 Nissan Charger electric car connected wirelessly, using a version of Evatran technology[1] first demonstrated in 2011.

You pilot the car out into the traffic stream, and then reengage auto-drive via the touch screen. Although the car is fully charged, it doesn't have to expend energy on the main highway because the road has embedded inductive charging strips that transfer power magnetically.[2] Freed from driving responsibility, you check your 3-D video texts and surf the ultra-Web through the car's browser. Connecting to a cloud project, you settle in for an hour of work in the virtual office. You note the car behind (only an inch from your rear bumper), moving, like you, at 130 miles per hour,[3] and muse that your ancestors would have found the experience upsetting.

The car exits the highway and flashes a message that manual control will resume in two minutes. You click off the computer and grab the steering pod. A minute later you're in front of your office building and heading for the human transporter while the car parks itself, refolding for easy storage.

After a long day spent fighting the competition from the new economic monolith of Mongolia, you're back in your car, popping up a video image of your wife, who's similarly en route from the office. Her day was harder than yours, so you take the initiative and use the car's 10G connection to start dinner cooking at home, picking from a downloaded menu stored in the wired kitchen. Since the car is in control, there's no reason not to have a cocktail from the Charger's discreet minibar. One drink won't hurt, especially since the onboard breath tester is keeping tabs on your alcohol intake.[4]

The only part of this scenario that's far-fetched is the folding cars (well, maybe the inductive charging strips and the automated driving, too, since General Motors' experiments with driver-free Buicks in the mid-1990s showed that the technology worked fine, but there were troubling human error factors).[5] Future scenarios are certainly wrong all the time, but this one isn't completely over the top. And GM did say it would produce a line of hands-free-capable electric city cars by 2020.

Alternate realities are also possible. In one, battery-only electric cars flop because of high cost, range issues, relatively low fuel prices, and a scarcity of federal incentives. That scenario doesn't preclude modest success for plug-in hybrids, and indeed, a growing market for hybrid cars of all types. Taking range out of the equation makes a strong argument for the sterling economy of combined gas and electric drivetrains. "Hybrids will be adopted a lot faster than electric vehicles, because they'll pay for themselves quicker," Alex Molinaroli of Johnson Controls Power Solutions told me. "The electric car isn't yet economically viable, though in the long term we believe this technology will be adopted."

In another scenario, both electric vehicles and plug-in hybrids are resoundingly rejected in the marketplace, resulting in a debacle similar to the failure of the General Motors EV1, Toyota RAV4 EV, and Honda EVPlus in the late 1990s and early 2000s. If that happens, all the evolutionary technology I described above will probably never happen (the same way it stopped dead after electric cars lost momentum in the 1920s).

Finally, there's a scenario in which climate change, peak oil, and other strategic considerations lead to an international push for electrifying transportation, with the United States working as a leader in the accelerated race.

A look back at the most recent wave of EV introductions is instructive here. The RAV4 probably did the best, with more than 1,400 leased between 1997 and 2003 and enough sold to ensure that (unlike the ill-fated EV1) more than 700 remain in service.

Celebrities pilot them, including Hollywood's number one booster of electric transportation, Ed Begley Jr., and Tom Hanks. Begley was nice enough to take me into his garage and demonstrate how he still plugs in his faithful RAV4, after all these years. But Toyota still had a tiny program, unfolding over six years.

Only 1,100 EV1s were produced, and most were crushed. That chilling reality was documented by Chris Paine's 2006 hit documentary *Who Killed the Electric Car?* Viewers shared Paine's outrage over the cars' destruction, though the public didn't exactly flock to lease the cars.

Paine is much more optimistic that the electric car is now on a glide path to consumer acceptance. The successor to *Who Killed* is *Revenge of the Electric Car* (2011), which paints an encouraging picture of a high-stakes race to market with cool technology.

Paine was still editing the film when I talked to him in December of 2010. (It premiered on Earth Day 2011.) "I think 2011 and 2012 are critical years for the electric car," he said. "The game is on, and I'd like to see the new film help get us off oil and build momentum for the new generation of cars."[6]

Paine was an early Tesla customer and loves his Roadster, but he also says "both the Leaf and Volt are pretty strong entries. There's no way that anyone is making money on these first cars, but they didn't make anything on the first Priuses, either."

I agree: Carmakers, whether old pros or start-ups, won't make money on the EVs they're selling to early adopters. The high cost of tooling up for production; paying for expensive batteries; branding, advertising, and promoting; setting up dealerships; and more ensures that. But I do think electric cars will make inroads into the market, slowly at first but gradually building momentum, and that profit will eventually happen.

As Paine points out, the story of the Toyota Prius hybrid is instructive. The Prius debuted in 1997 in Japan and 2000 in the United States. It was viewed as Toyota's folly at the time, because the company was losing money on every car sold. I remember debating the editor of *Car and Driver* about hybrids on NPR's *Diane Rehm Show* in 2000, and he was emphatic that Americans would never buy them in any numbers—they were too expensive with two drivetrains, plus they couldn't tow anything.

Let's flash forward about a decade, with the Prius reigning as the best-selling car in Japan for 20 months in a row and unbeatable as the best-selling hybrid in the United States by a huge margin. Granted, hybrids aren't a huge percentage of the market, but they're a successful and growing one.

According to a 2009 Japanese Nikkei report,[7] with the hybrid cost margin coming down, both Toyota and Honda were making approximately $3,100 on every hybrid sold, about the same profit as on small gas cars. In 2008, the report said, Toyota made gross profits of $1 billion on sales of the second-generation Prius. Don't worry about Toyota betting on green: Despite the strong yen and sudden-acceleration problems in the United States, it became still the world's biggest carmaker in 2009. (GM soon took the title back—the earthquake and tsunami really impacted Toyota.)

Eventually, nearly all manufacturers started making hybrids, even the somewhat reluctant Germans (who generally prefer clean diesels). But Toyota had such a head start that by 2009 it had a nearly 75 percent share of the hybrid market in the United States (when Lexus was added to the mix).[8] Sales of Toyota hybrids reached a total of 2 million worldwide in 2010.

Ford is the hybrid leader among the Big Three, and that's in part because it got in relatively early (2004) with the gas-electric Escape. GM and Chrysler have never been successful with hybrids, which is why the Volt is a game changer.

Many of the things that GM did wrong with the EV1 (making it a two-seater, emphasizing performance over range) it has since corrected on the Volt. I think the Volt will do very well—in the first few months its sales exceeded the sum total of EV1 leases over something like six years. There's an advantage to being a first mover, but you have to get the details right.

MAKING IT WORK

Nobody has to explain what stands behind's Ford's blue oval— the very sight of it conjures, for most people, the more-than-hundred-year history of the Ford Motor Company, the flinty gentleman who pioneered the assembly line, and the long line of cars either they owned or their parents did. "Ford" has legs, but it still advertises a lot.

It's harder when your name is Wheego, Coda, Aptera, Fisker, or Tesla—they still have very low profiles in the American consciousness and lack enormous marketing budgets. Tesla, which benefited in the early years from torrents of good publicity (thanks to the double whammy of billionaire Elon Musk and a sexy sports car), is undoubtedly the best known.

Since the Roadster is very Euro in concept, I thought it would be a no-brainer for sales in Europe. But Cristiano Carlutti, who heads European sales for the brand, told me otherwise in the fall of 2010. "Tesla's image is a positive one, but the car is not well known in many European countries," he said. "And getting the message out about the Tesla Roadster is complicated by multiple languages and very dispersed media markets." The company had sold 300 Roadsters in Europe (and 1,300 worldwide) at that point.[9]

Tesla has been building brand identity, in part, with stylish stores (it doesn't like the word "dealership") that sell the car as part of a hip, green lifestyle. In the summer of 2010, the company hired Gap and Apple veteran George Blankenship as vice president of design and store development, and among his first projects was to open outlets in Tokyo, Toronto, Copenhagen, Paris, and Washington, DC, making it 28 worldwide by the summer of 2011. He said his goal was to "create a retail experience that is as thrilling as my first drive of the Tesla Roadster."[10]

Since Blankenship came from Apple, it's not surprising that he invokes the iPod when talking about how to market Tesla with show-and-tell stores. "Anytime someone has a game-changing technology or invention, people need to learn about it, get comfortable with it. . . . When you have Apple stores that have natural traffic through them on a day in, day out basis, and you show them this thing called an iPod and a thousand songs in your pocket, people got interested. If there wasn't someone there who could show what it could do, and that it wasn't just another music player that was two to four times more expensive, it might not have become a game changer."[11] The mission, he said, is to turn one-time customers into "evangelists."

Tesla owners, including the very enthusiastic Lukasz Strozek, are definitely evangelists, and when their day-to-day colleagues are hedge fund managers, they can be a huge strategic benefit.

Tesla has thought more about its image and how to draw in the right customer than many of the other new automakers.

But Fisker is right behind. And it's going with sexy. Henrik Fisker told me the brand expects a significant share of its sales to be in Europe, so before the launch it created the Pure Driving Passion campaign for the Paris Motor Show, featuring photos of the car (which nobody had driven at that point) posed with skimpily clad models.[12] In one, a woman in what appears to be a shiny leather or plastic bikini plugs the car in. A short film, *Melting Ice*, adds the concept that the car is "designed to get you hot, not the planet." According to Marti Eulberg, vice president of global sales and marketing, "We wanted people to feel the emotion and sensuality of the Karma through the imagery."

The imagery is probably effective with a certain demographic, but it's unlikely that Fisker, even with its millions from the Department of Energy, can afford to show *Melting Ice* during the Super Bowl. Some 3,400 views on two separate YouTube postings probably won't give you the same boost. Marketing clout is what gives a big advantage to both Nissan (which launched the Leaf with a memorable ad featuring a hugging polar bear) and General Motors (which stuck it to the Leaf with an ad about Americans being "wayfarers" and "nomads," thus needing more than 100 miles of range).

There's still a distance to travel before electric cars have a big public profile. A Maritz Research poll of 1,200 American drivers in the fall of 2010 found that only 16 percent (up from 8 percent in 2006) were "very familiar" with battery electrics.[13] Only 22 percent of respondents said they were very familiar with even gasoline-electric hybrids (it was 15 percent in 2006).

In the same poll, 4 of 10 (39 percent) were familiar with the Chevy Volt, and 17 percent with the Leaf. Obviously, the smaller brands not in the poll would have much less public awareness. Those results contrasted with 75 percent familiarity with the Toyota Prius (but only 57 percent knew it doesn't have to be plugged in). The Prius is now enough of an icon to get lampooned as unmanly police transport in a Will Ferrell comedy[14] (and as the "Pious" on *South Park*).

"The data indicates that consumers are still confused about these new technologies," said Dave Fish, vice president of Maritz. But there were positive signs, too—only 25 percent of respondents said that electric cars were a "fad" they wouldn't consider buying into. It will be up to the new car companies to get their brands— and their messages—in front of the public. Given financial realities, guerrilla marketing (from YouTube videos and sexy photo campaigns to strategic press conferences) may be the order of the day.

LOOKING FORWARD: PRESSURE POINTS

There are some good, compelling reasons to see electric cars finally breaking through this time, after the misfires of the past. I think that in the early years, a fairly small percentage of people will buy electric and plug-in cars solely because they expect to save money on them. They're more likely to be motivated by environmental concern, and especially by the goal of freeing the United States from foreign oil dependence. Unlike concern about climate change, that concept has bipartisan support.

A nationwide 2010 *Consumer Reports* poll[15] found 80 percent of the 1,700 respondents saying they would "strongly support" or "somewhat support" a national goal of reducing oil consumption (though they balk at gas taxes). And more than 70 percent back increasing government funding to achieve that goal. People also say that their next car will have better fuel economy, but a big majority aren't going to pay steep premiums to buy green.

But auto fleets definitely *will* get cleaner, because of state and Obama administration mandates. A major driver is the federal standard, supported by the auto industry, that requires cars to reach 35.5 mpg by 2016. Those rules, which address both fuel economy and climate change, will get even tighter after that. Automakers are deeply skeptical of being able to reach environmentalists' stated goal of 60 mpg by 2025, but they are resigned to tougher national laws.

Although it's the product of a state agency, the California Air Resources Board program of zero-emission vehicle (ZEV) credits has a disproportionate effect on automakers worldwide. The program has had a long and varying history, but by late 2010 it had brought into the pollution-challenged state some 1.7 million cleaner cars, including 300,000 hybrids, 5,100 battery electrics, 300 fuel-cell vehicles, and 28,500 low-speed neighborhood electric vehicles. And the program gets a lot tougher in 2012, when rules kick in requiring the biggest carmakers (those with California sales above 10,000 annually) to produce a combined total of 7,500 zero-emission vehicles by 2014. The number goes up to 25,000 for 2015 to 2017.[16]

California's system has a "cap and trade" element to it, since automakers that don't produce enough battery cars can purchase ZEV credits from other companies or get partial credits from selling either hybrids or low-emission gasoline cars. "Pure" ZEV cars are battery-only vehicles like the Nissan Leaf—even the Volt doesn't qualify, because of its gas engine. Battery booster Tesla made $13.8 million selling ZEV credits to Honda in 2008 and 2009, *Car and Driver* reports, and Nissan could earn a fair amount from its Leaf-related credits.

And then there's the question of oil prices, probably the biggest factor (and unknown) in the swing to cleaner cars. Whether or not you believe in the rapid approach of peak oil (I do), it's quite likely that prices at the gas pump will grow because of increasing world demand (especially from rapidly motorizing China). The gas price surge in 2008 led to a big shift away from SUVs and other gas-guzzlers, though easing of those prices caused some shifting back.

Rising oil demand rubbing up against an increasingly finite supply will send prices up, and demand is in part dictated by the size of the global auto fleet. There's huge room for auto growth in China, where oil demand could double by 2030. As recently as 2008, China had a very light car population of 40 per 1,000 people—compared to 800 per 1,000 in the United States. But the Chinese auto industry grew nearly 50 percent in 2009 alone. Sales of private vehicles in China could top 18 million by 2015, according to a Roland Berger analysis.[17]

It isn't necessary to check in with conspiracy theorists to understand that worldwide oil reserves are under pressure. The US Energy Information Administration projects a 45 percent increase in global transportation-related liquid fuel demand, 1.3 percent a year, between 2007 and 2035.[18] To meet that demand, mainly from outside the Organisation for Economic Co-operation and Development (OECD) member countries, the world will need an additional 26 million barrels of fuel daily by the end of that period. This very conservative projection estimates that oil will cost $99 per barrel at the end of 2012, and $133 in 2035 (the approximate level it reached in 2008). Gasoline hit $4 a gallon in the United States back then. Since it had gotten up near there again in early 2011, it's quite likely to go much higher in the coming decades.

The global demand for oil grew by 2.7 million barrels a day in 2010,[19] according to the International Energy Agency (IEA), at approximately the same time that the agency estimates standard crude oil production reached a "plateau." Growth after that point has to come from natural gas liquids and unconventional oil (including oil shale and tar sands).

"The age of cheap oil is over," said the IEA's *World Energy Outlook 2010.*[20] Despite that, the IEA sees the world's automotive population effectively doubling between 2008 and 2035. Much of that growth will be in China, the IEA said, and the country could add 8.5 million electric and plug-in hybrids by 2035.

No credible observers see fuel prices dropping significantly in the long term. The price for a barrel of international benchmark Brent Crude oil is near $100 as I type this, and the IEA offers the hope that "for the avoidance of collateral economic damage" the price will stay below three figures.[21]

Climate change is another major factor. Even in the face of a cheap oil glut, we'd have the world's most eminent scientists telling us to draw the brakes on fossil fuels. The synthesis report of the 2007 Intergovernmental Panel on Climate Change assessment points to a pattern of record-temperature years, rising sea levels, drought, and melting glaciers and sea ice. "Average Northern Hemisphere temperatures during the second half of the 20th century were *very likely* higher than during any other 50-year period in the last 500 years and *likely* the highest in at least the past 1300 years," the report said (emphasis in the original).[22]Internationally known climate scientist James Hansen, who heads the NASA Goddard Institute for Space Studies, points out that it's hard to limit fossil fuels because they offer the cheapest form of energy. He writes in his book *Storms of My Grandchildren* that a truly effective way to impact their use is with what he calls a "fee and dividend" plan.[23] All fossil fuels would be taxed on the basis of the amount of carbon dioxide they produced, with the revenue being redistributed to the public. The people with the lowest carbon footprints would get back in dividends more than they pay in increased energy prices. Electric cars and other renewable energy solutions would lose their crippling price disadvantage, and eventually fossil fuel use would dwindle.

If we don't drastically cut back fossil fuel use globally, Hansen predicts that by the end of the 21st century we will have to endure "droughts, heat waves and forest fires of unprecedented ferocity," plus "storms with hurricane-like winds" that will "devastate thousands of coastal cities," and the loss or impending extinction of 20 percent of Earth's species.[24]

Such warnings have gone unheeded in the past, and a lack of public enthusiasm for new energy taxes as measured by *Consumer Reports* means that, despite the dire warnings, Hansen's plan has little chance of passage. By early 2011 there was political momentum away from passing climate legislation, as well as considerable skepticism about global warming science. But poll results vary. A Stanford University poll conducted in June of 2010 found that three of four Americans believe climate change is real and man-made and want the government to intervene, but the 74 percent support for that view was down from 84 percent in 2007.[25]

The results of a yearlong Yale and George Mason University poll released at about the same time said that the 61 percent of Americans who believe climate change is real was actually up four points since the start of 2010. But all the polls show a substantial percentage who think global warming is either an unproven theory or not a major problem.

WHERE WE'RE GOING: PREDICTING THE WINNERS

I could cite poll results and predictions endlessly. EV consultant Chelsea Sexton thinks that electric cars will have to weather "a couple of rough years," getting through "deployment missteps, changes in policy and negative media stories, whether earned or not."[26] She worries about complacency. Now that the cars are actually out and the sexy part is over, will EV activists simply declare victory and move on, when a lot of the tough work of ensuring their acceptance in the marketplace is still ahead? As she points out, if the marketplace isn't ready, then the next film will be called *We Killed the Electric Car*.

There are many external factors that affect auto sales, as any experienced salesman could tell you. Consider the fate of the entrepreneurs who launched Hummer dealerships in early 2008, just before gas prices spiked. But it's the marketplace that's going to pass the ultimate verdict on the new green cars. The evidence is clear that consumers want to do the right thing and drive the cleanest cars they can afford. But they also have some unreasonable expectations about what the auto industry can deliver—in the foreseeable future, we won't see 300-mile-per-charge electric cars at the same prices people are accustomed to paying.

Rather predictably, the first people to take delivery of the cars said they liked them a lot, but those buyers were a self-selected group of environmentalists and alternative technology lovers. There are a lot of them out there, but not enough to make all of these cars marketplace successes.

I predict that both the Chevy Volt and the Nissan Leaf will sell in sufficient numbers to make them, if not runaway hits, at least modest successes. The Fisker Karma and the Tesla Model S are also likely to do well, though both will need to meet high quality and performance standards to stay afloat. Two other cars I'm bullish on are the Ford Focus electric (which will benefit from the company's strong reputation and marketing clout) and the BMW i3 Megacity Vehicle (for the same reasons). Audi could do well with limited numbers of high-end performance-oriented electric and plug-in hybrid cars, as could Porsche. I especially like Daimler's A-Class battery car, though it may not appear in the United States or become a regular commercial entry.

A number of other cars face a tougher time in the market. The Smart car has had a troubled run in the American marketplace, and its "electric drive" version hit the showrooms with a high lease price. Like Smart, Think has an inherent two-seater limitation, plus a relatively high price. Europe may remain its biggest market, and an initial fleet strategy is a good idea for the United States.

Coda has many hurdles, from a high price to plain-Jane styling and high-profile departures that affect the company's embryonic, Internet-based marketing plan (sales and marketing chief Michael Jackson resigned just before CEO Kevin Czinger did). Wheego's ace in the hole is Mike McQuary's can-do attitude and very low overhead, so it could make it with sales of a few thousand cars a year. But even that will be a challenge.

BYD has a good chance of making it in the United States if it keeps prices low and brings quality, design, and safety up to Western standards (big ifs). Aptera, well, that one requires a leap of faith.

So here's my Ten Most Likely to Succeed list of new electric and plug-in hybrid cars, in descending order of optimism.

1. Chevy Volt

2. Toyota Prius plug-in hybrid

3. Nissan Leaf

4. Tesla Model S

5. Ford C-Max Energi plug-in hybrid

6. Ford Focus electric/Toyota RAV4 electric (tie)

7. Fisker Karma

8. Honda Fit/Toyota iQ city electrics (tie)

9. BMW i3 Megacity (and the whole i sub-brand)

10. Porsche 918 Spyder plug-in hybrid

That last one adds some luster to Porsche just by existing, and the $845,000 price means that it will be a "success" with just a few sold. Bubbling just under the top 10 is the Fiat 500 electric, because the company has good marketing resources—plus it's extremely cute. Don't expect large numbers of electric 500s, but they will burnish Fiat's image in the United States. And conversion companies such as Amp Electric Vehicles could have a business, if they make enough of the right connections. I didn't include trucks, but I like the chances of both Bright Automotive (which makes its own lightweight Idea plug-in hybrid panel van, with General Motors investment) and Smith Electric Vehicles, which has willing customers in both the United States and Europe for its high-quality electric box trucks.

Keep in mind that I'm not predicting that any of these cars will make money. I *know* my number one car, the Chevy Volt, won't do so in the early years because its selling price is only slightly higher than its build price. Success in at least some of these programs is relative, based on a burnishing of corporate green image and buzz for the brand. The start-ups generally don't have much of a cushion—if they don't sell, they're dead.

It's been a wild experience covering the emergence of the new green cars. Like full batteries, all of these companies started out bright and charged up and headed for glory. But inevitably, some will cross the finish line and others will run out of juice along the way. There's no dishonor in that: It's a tough business, as they're wont to tell you, and it doesn't get any easier just because these cars are out to save the world.

NOTES

INTRODUCTION

1. James Brazell talks about his new Chevy Volt in a February 28, 2011, video posted on YouTube at www.youtube.com/watch?v=Ja_sSJLOWCg. I wrote about his peak oil concern for National Public Radio's *Car Talk* on March 4, 2011, at http://cartalk.com/blogs/jim-motavalli/?p=750.

2. "Rock the Vote Polling Data Reveals Young Voters Remain Engaged, While Battling Feelings of Cynicism." These preelection poll results were reported in a September 15, 2010, press release and are available at www.rockthevote.com/about/press-room/press-releases/2010rockthevotepoll.html.

3. The Rasmussen poll expressing concern about foreign oil dependence is referenced in a June 21, 2010, *AutoBlog Green* story at http://green.autoblog.com/2010/06/21/poll-73-of-americans-believe-that-reducing-dependency-on-fossi.

4. Union of Concerned Scientists, "Cars, Trucks, and Air Pollution," April 4, 2008, www.ucsusa.org/clean_vehicles/vehicle_impacts/cars_pickups_and_suvs/cars-trucks-air-pollution.html.

5. In 1900, the Electric Vehicle Company had hundreds of electric "Hansom" taxicabs on the streets of New York City. That and other pertinent facts of early automobiling were related by the American Oil and Gas Historical Society in the March 2008 issue of its *Petroleum Age* newsletter, available at http://sites.google.com/site/petroleumhistoryresources/Home/cantankerous-combustion.

6. *Petroleum Age*, March 2008.

7. Virginia Scharff's book *Taking the Wheel: Women and the Coming of the Motor Age* (Albuquerque, NM: University of New Mexico Press, 1992) details this phenomenon.

8. My first book, *Forward Drive: The Race to Build "Clean" Cars for the Future*, was published by Sierra Club Books in 2000.

9. *Time*'s capsule summary of the GM EV1 can be found here: www.time.com/time/specials/2007/article/0,28804,1669723_1669725_1669741,00.html. Author Bryan Walsh concluded that "the car itself was wildly expensive to build and the battery only functioned well in warm weather, finally prompting GM to end the EV1 in 2003, bitterly disappointing its legions—ok, large circle—of fans."

10. *Automotive Landscape 2025: In the Coming 15 Years the Global Automotive Industry Will Undergo the Greatest Transformation It Has Experienced in Its History*, Roland Berger Strategy Consultants, February 28, 2011. The analysis is at www.rolandberger.com/company/press/releases/Automotive-landscape-2025.html.

11. I wrote about the IBM Institute for Business Value study for Hearst's *The Daily Green,* and the details are here: www.thedailygreen.com/living-green/ blogs/cars-transportation/research-on-electric-cars-ibm. Thirty percent of those surveyed said they'd be willing to live with an EV that delivered less than 100 miles of range.

12. Nissan CEO Carlos Ghosn was quoted on Nissan's Leaf blog at http://nissan-leaf.net/2010/11/22/nissan-ceo-carlos-ghosn-talks-up-leaf-takes-test-drive-and-discusses-chevrolet-volt.

13. I wrote about the optimistic projections for micro-hybrids at CBS Interactive's BNET Auto, www.bnet.com/blog/electric-cars/us-could-sell-46-million-start-stop-micro-hybrids-by-2015-lux-says/2620.

14. *Overhaul: An Insider's Account of the Obama Administration's Emergency Rescue of the Auto Industry,* by Steven Rattner (Boston: Houghton Mifflin Harcourt, 2010), p. 97.

15. Rattner's interview with me, and Volt spokesman Rob Peterson's quote, can be found on the *New York Times Wheels* blog at http://wheels.blogs.nytimes.com/2010/11/23/steven-rattner-dishes-on-the-chevrolet-volt. Rattner settled his case with New York State just before Attorney General Andrew Cuomo left to take office as governor.

CHAPTER ONE: RACING FOR THE GOAL

1. Tesla's $465 million loan was described in a Department of Energy press release January 21, 2010. The release can be found at www.energy.gov/ news/8538.htm.

2. The *Wall Street Journal* referred to Fisker as a "Gore-backed" firm in a story on the awarding of the loan posted on September 25, 2009: http://online.wsj.com/article/SB125383160812639013.html. Additional details on the loan deal are in a piece posted at CNET News: http://news.cnet.com/8301-11128_3-10383851-54.html.

3. A video of the Danish crown prince arriving for the climate talks in a Fisker Karma is posted on YouTube at www.youtube.com/watch?v=rM093ZkYdCY. He appears to have been riding in the back.

4. My story about the Fisker Karma's weight was published in the *New York Times Wheels* blog on November 15, 2010: http://wheels.blogs.nytimes.com/2010/11/15/fisker-karma-to-weigh-more-than-5000-pounds.

5. Musk's comments about the difficulty of launching a new car business are from a May 13, 2009, story for *Knowledge@Wharton*: http://knowledge.wharton.upenn.edu/article.cfm?articleid=2240. Musk is a graduate of the Wharton School at the University of Pennsylvania.

6. Musk detailed his roundabout route to Tesla Motors and SpaceX in a second story for *Knowledge@Wharton*: http://knowledge.wharton.upenn.edu/article.cfm?articleid=2245.

7. Stanford University's Entrepreneurship Corner posted a fascinating multipart interview with Musk about SpaceX and beyond that can be found at http://ecorner.stanford.edu/authorMaterialInfo.html?mid=386.

8. Musk's quote about expanding human life beyond Earth is from the British *Telegraph,* December 8, 2010, www.telegraph.co.uk/science/space/8187193/ SpaceX-aims-to-make-history-in-commercial-space-race.html.

9. My interview with Tom Gage, which includes a video concerning his latest electrification project, a Taiwan-sourced minivan, is online at Mother Nature Network: www.mnn.com/green-tech/transportation/blogs/meet-tom-gage-the-man-who-could-have-founded-tesla-but-had-other-ide.

10. Dan Neil's Tesla Roadster article from the *Los Angeles Times,* February 6, 2009, is available here: http://articles.latimes.com/2009/feb/06/business/fi-neil6.

11. My daughter promptly posted the video we shot of our test drive on Facebook. My account of our brief but memorable time behind the wheel was posted for Mother Nature Network on February 27, 2009, at www.mnn.com/green-tech/transportation/blogs/the-tesla-roadster-an-electric-bat-out-of-hell.

12. I wrote about the conflict for Mother Nature Network June 12, 2009, and it can be found here: www.mnn.com/green-tech/transportation/blogs/tesla-vigorously-defends-cofounders-lawsuit.

13. The *Newsweek* article about Musk's dispute with Martin Eberhard was posted November 15, 2008, at www.newsweek.com/2008/11/14/an-electric-car-loses-its-juice.html.

14. "At Tesla, Musk and Eberhard Are Suddenly Such Good Friends," by Andrew S. Ross, SFGate.com, September 21, 2009, www.sfgate.com/cgi-bin/blogs/bottomline/ detail?entry_id=48028. And Eberhard also said of Musk, "As a co-founder of the company, Elon's contributions to Tesla have been extraordinary."

15. "Electric Connection: Tesla, Daimler," by Christopher Palmeri and John Carey, *Businessweek,* May 19, 2009, www.businessweek.com/bwdaily/dnflash/content/ may2009/db20090519_566476.htm. Zetsche also said, "This industry is going through a kind of paradigm shift, and has to reinvent itself ultimately to be independent of petroleum and without CO_2 emissions. We need fast technology change."

16. I videotaped my interview with Naoto Noguchi of Panasonic and posted it on YouTube October 7, 2010. You can find it here: www.youtube.com/ watch?v=Ra3j8MjEpKI.

17. Amendment #4 to Tesla's Form S-1 disclosure statement is at http://sec.gov/ Archives/edgar/data/1318605/000095013010002906/ds1a.htm.

18. "Tesla's Elon Musk: 'I Ran Out of Cash,'" by Owen Thomas, Business Insider, May 28, 2010, www.businessinsider.com/teslas-elon-musk-i-ran-out-of-cash-2010-5-2.

19. "Golddigger," the May 8, 2010, entry on *Minx*, Justine Musk's blog, available at http://moschus.livejournal.com/140610.html?thread=1114690.

20. "Correcting the Record about My Divorce" appeared on the *Huffington Post,* July 8, 2010, www.huffingtonpost.com/elon-musk/correcting-the-record-abo_b_639625.html.

21. "Entrepreneur Elon Musk: Why It's Important to Pinch Pennies on the Road to Riches," *Knowledge@Wharton,* May 27, 2009. In this Q&A interview with his alma mater, the Wharton School at the University of Pennsylvania, Musk also says that he learned an early lesson: "If you make something that people want, they'll pay you for it."

22. "Supercharged: How Elon Musk Turned Tesla into the Car Company of the Future," by Joshua Davis, was published in the October 2010 issue of *Wired*, and it's online at www.wired.com/magazine/2010/09/ff_tesla/all/1.

23. "Tesla Model S: One Whopper of a Battery Pack" by Jim Motavalli, *New York Times Wheels* blog, August 25, 2009, http://wheels.blogs.nytimes .com/2009/08/25/tesla-model-s-one-whopper-of-a-battery-pack.

24. "As the Twig Is Bent: Henrik Fisker Has Always Been Inclined Toward Car Design," *AutoWeek*, January 12, 2009. A portion is online at www.highbeam .com/doc/1G1-192108894.html.

25. "Auto Biography," *Design Week*, September 27, 2001. It's online at www .mad.co.uk/Main/News/Sectors/Consumer-Goods/Articles/73a18e3796534acc9 3c45580598e7ea9/Auto-biography.html.

26. PBS's *MotorWeek* interview with Henrik Fisker was posted on YouTube May 5, 2009, and it appears at www.youtube.com/watch?v=SZwnrvhPPGs&feature =player_embedded.

27. The arbitration decision and award, written by retired judge the Honorable William F. McDonald, was announced November 24, 2008, and is online at www .newmeyeranddillion.com/pdf/Tesla_v._Fisker_Corrected_Final_Award_.PDF.

28. "Tesla Motors Files Suit Against Competitor Over Design Ideas," by John Markoff, *New York Times*, April 15, 2008: www.nytimes.com/2008/04/15/ technology/15tesla.html. Musk said the conflict with Fisker had resulted in a "slight delay" in the sedan project, which was eventually designed in-house.

29. Ricardo Reyes e-mailed me January 2, 2011.

30. PBS *MotorWeek* interview with Henrik Fisker.

31. "2009 Fisker Karma to Appear at Detroit Auto Show," December 3, 2008, http://usnews.rankingsandreviews.com/cars-trucks/daily-news/081203-2009- Fisker-Karma-to-Appear-at-Detroit-Auto-Show.

32. My Mother Nature Network interview with Henrik Fisker, posted January 13, 2009, is on YouTube at www.youtube.com/watch?v=bNqvvFFk4KU.

33. I wrote about Mike Sullivan's dealership in "Hollywood's Hybrid Dealer Gears Up for the Fisker Karma," CBS Interactive's BNET Auto, posted July 8, 2010 at www.bnet.com/blog/electric-cars/hollywood-8217s-hybrid-dealer-gears- up-for-the-fisker-karma/1865.

34. My story on Fisker's loan appeared in the *New York Times Wheels* blog, http:// wheels.blogs.nytimes.com/2009/09/24/fisker-to-receive-5287-million-federal-loan.

35. "Vice President Biden Announces Reopening of Former GM Boxwood Plant," US Department of Energy press release, October 27, 2009, www.energy .gov/news/8222.htm.

36. Vice President Joe Biden was quoted in a *Green Car Reports* post by John Voelcker on October 28, 2009: www.greencarreports.com/blog/1037309_biden- blurts-out-fisker-nina-plug-in-hybrid-line-sedan-coupe-crossover.

37. I wrote about the media storm over Fisker's loan for *The Daily Green*, www .thedailygreen.com/living-green/blogs/cars-transportation/fisker-cars-loan-461009. Fisker told me he would have preferred to build the Karma in the United States, but could not find a partner able to handle the low volumes.

38. I spoke with Michael Brylawski in connection with the revelation that the Fisker Karma weighed more than 5,000 pounds: http://wheels.blogs.nytimes .com/2010/11/15/fisker-karma-to-weigh-more-than-5000-pounds.

39. Russell Datz spoke to me about the Karma dealer tour for my CBS Interactive BNET blog: www.bnet.com/blog/electric-cars/fisker-karma-ev-goes-on-tour-8212-but-still-nobody-8217s-driving-it/1597.

40. My frustrating visit to Fisker HQ in Irvine is detailed on my CBS Interactive BNET blog, "Plugged In," at www.bnet.com/blog/electric-cars/fisker-8217s-high-performance-karma-hybrid-is-still-behind-the-curtain/2078.

41. Henrik Fisker's Q&A interview with *Wired*, published June 22, 2010, is at www.wired.com/magazine/2010/06/ff_qa_fisker_karma.

42. *MotorWeek* interview with Henrik Fisker.

43. I spoke to Britta Gross of GM for a story posted to Mother Nature Network, February 12, 2010, www.mnn.com/green-tech/transportation/blogs/nissan-leaf-and-chevrolet-volt-electric-cars-hit-the-mean-streets-of.

44. I interviewed Fisker spokesman Roger Ormisher for a piece posted at CBS Interactive's BNET Auto, April 14, 2011, www.bnet.com/blog/electric-cars/fisker-raises-1-billion-now-its-car-better-be-good/3881.

CHAPTER TWO:
BUILDING THE BATTERIES

1. The $9,500 estimate (£6,000) is from the *Times* of London, "The Leaf Out of the Green Book," by John Arlidge, April 4, 2010, http://business.timesonline .co.uk/tol/business/industry_sectors/transport/article7086781.ece.

2. The $18,000 estimate for the Leaf battery is from "Nissan Says Leaf Electric Will Be Profitable with U.S. Plant," by Mike Ramsey, *Wall Street Journal,* May 13, 2010, http://online.wsj.com/article/SB1000142405274870463520457524238 2820806878.html?mod=WSJ_auto_IndustryCollection.

3. "Nissan Says Leaf Electric Will Be Profitable with U.S. Plant," by Mike Ramsey, *Wall Street Journal,* May 13, 2010, http://online.wsj.com/article/SB1 000142405274870463520457524238820806878.html?m%20od=WSJ_auto_IndustryCollection.

4. "Nissan Says Leaf Electric Will Be Profitable."

5. "The Cost of Vehicle Electrification: A Literature Review," by Lynette Chea and John Heywood of Sloan Automotive Laboratory at the Massachusetts Institute of Technology, is online at http://web.mit.edu/sloan-auto-lab/research/beforeh2/files/PHEV%20costs.pdf.

6. "Nissan Leaf Battery Pack Costs Only £6,000 ($9,000) or $375/kWh!" by Sam Abuelsamid, Autoblog Green, May 5, 2010, http://green.autoblog .com/2010/05/05/report-nissan-leaf-battery-pack-costs-only-6-000-9-000-or.

7. "Secondary Use of PHEV and EV Batteries: Opportunities and Challenges," a PowerPoint presentation at the 10th Advanced Automotive Battery Conference in Orlando, Florida, May 19–21, 2010. It's online at www.nrel.gov/docs/fy10osti/48872.pdf.

8. Some of these details are from "The Lady and the Li-Ion" by Tekla S. Perry, *IEEE Spectrum*, March 2008. It's online at http://spectrum.ieee.org/energy/renewables/the-lady-and-the-liion.

9. My story for the *New York Times Wheels* blog about Saab's visit is at http://wheels.blogs.nytimes.com/2010/08/06/saabs-owners-offers-a-peek-into-its-future.

10. The affable James Boncek is profiled in a piece on do-it-yourselfers, also for Mother Nature Network, at www.mnn.com/green-tech/transportation/blogs/build-your-own-cheap-electric-car-these-guys-did.

11. I wrote about Bryce Nash and his low-budget hybrid for the *New York Times Wheels* blog at http://wheels.blogs.nytimes.com/2009/11/04/a-pontiac-fiero-hybrid-for-1600.

12. The Web site Bipolar-lives.com has the history of lithium's use in treating mental disorders.

13. The US Consumer Products Safety Commission issued a press release about the Sony battery recall October 23, 2006. It's at www.cpsc.gov/cpscpub/prerel/prhtml07/07011.html.

14. Hybridcars.com summed up the then-emergent world of Li-ion in a post published April 3, 2006, at www.hybridcars.com/technology-stories/lithium-ion-batteries.html.

15. My *New York Times* "Green Tech" story on the Sprinter, "Hybrids with a Power Cord: Plug-In Vans Put to the Test," was published October 1, 2006. It's at www.nytimes.com/2006/10/01/automobiles/01PLUG.html.

16. The University of Dayton posted its "Battery Breakthrough!" press release November 16, 2009. It's at www.udri.udayton.edu/News/2009/Pages/BatteryBreakthrough!.aspx.

17. *ScienceDaily* offered an upbeat assessment on the prospects for lithium-air batteries, "Lithium-Air Batteries Could Displace Gasoline in Future Cars," on December 31, 2009. But the story made it clear that lithium-air will need a lot of development work before it can be commercialized. It's online at www.sciencedaily.com/releases/2009/12/091230024401.htm.

18. *Bottled Lightning: Superbatteries, Electric Cars, and the New Lithium Economy*, by Seth Fletcher. New York: Hill and Wang, 2011, p. 201.

19. My interview with Ann Marie Sastry appeared on the *New York Times Wheels* blog September 9, 2010. It's at http://wheels.blogs.nytimes.com/2010/09/09/g-m-ventures-invests-3-2-million-in-battery-company.

CHAPTER THREE:
FROM COMPUTERS TO CARS

1. "High Tech Investors Race to Build Electric Cars," by Terence Chea for the Associated Press was updated June 27, 2006. It's online at www.msnbc.msn.com/id/13550669/ns/us_news-environment.

2. Martin Eberhard's blog post is entitled "Lotus Position," and it appeared on July 25, 2006, at www.teslamotors.com/blog/lotus-position. In the piece, Eberhard argues forcefully that although Tesla licensed the chassis of the Lotus Elise,

it made many important changes. "The Tesla Roadster does indeed carry some Elise DNA," he wrote. "But it is a very different car, designed to meet different goals and deliver a different experience."

3. Chea, "High Tech Investors Race."

4. "Reporter's Notes—Silicon Valley: The New Detroit?" by Andrea Kissack, October 8, 2010. It's online at KQED's blog page, www.kqed.org/quest/blog/2010/10/08/silicon-valley-the-new-detroit.

5. I interviewed Shai Agassi for the video "Shai Agassi on Better Place in Tokyo," which was posted to YouTube on April 27, 2010, and is available at www.youtube.com/watch?v=l1KhoKkSt_I&feature=related.

6. "Google's Biggest Clean Energy Investment Ever Is Going to Put Solar on Your Rooftop," by Ariel Schwartz, *Fast Company*, June 14, 2011, posted at www.fastcompany.com/1759679/why-googles-biggest-clean-energy-investment-ever-is-in-putting-solar-on-your-rooftop.

7. I wrote about V2G for the *New York Times* "Automobiles" section in "Power to the People: Run Your House on a Prius," September 2, 2007. It's online at www.nytimes.com/2007/09/02/automobiles/02POWER.html.

8. "Power to the People."

9. Stephen W. Sears, *The American Heritage History of the Automobile in America* (New York: American Heritage, 1977), p. 39.

10. "Why Remaking the Auto Industry Makes No Sense," by Maryann N. Keller, *Businessweek*, September 29, 2009, www.businessweek.com/lifestyle/content/sep2009/bw20090929_277702.htm.

11. "Why Silicon Valley Won't Be Detroit for Green Carmakers" by John Voelcker, GreenCarReports.com, April 13, 2011, www.greencarreports.com/blog/1047984_why-silicon-valley-wont-be-detroit-for-green-carmakers.

12. Telephone interview with John Voelcker, January 24, 2011.

13. I wrote about California's EV lead in "Why California Is Leading the EV Race," BNET Auto, July 9, 2010, www.bnet.com/blog/electric-cars/why-california-is-winning-the-electric-car-race/1872.

14. Felix Kramer, telephone interview, January 24, 2011.

15. "This Car Runs on Code," by Robert N. Charette, *IEEE Spectrum*, February 2009. Posted at http://spectrum.ieee.org/green-tech/advanced-cars/this-car-runs-on-code.

16. Farhad Manjoo's article "I'm Sorry, Dave, I'm Afraid I Can't Make a U-Turn" was published by *Slate* on February 16, 2010, and it's at www.slate.com/id/2244887.

17. Keller, "Why Remaking the Auto Industry."

18. The account of the trial's outcome is from an Australian Web site: "Greek Court Rules Against Daimler on Chinese Smart Fortwo Imitator," *The Motor Report*, www.themotorreport.com.au/31935/greek-court-rules-against-daimler-on-chinese-smart-fortwo-imitator.

19. I wrote about the federal plan for the *New York Times Wheels* blog. "Federal Government to Add 100 Electric Cars" is at http://wheels.blogs.nytimes.com/2010/10/06/federal-government-to-add-100-electric-cars.

CHAPTER FOUR: *THE BIG PLAYERS*

1. Chalouhi took delivery of his Leaf at North Bay Nissan in Petaluma, California, on December 11, 2010. Further details are in the Nissan press release posted at www.nissanusa.com/leaf-electric-car/index#/leaf-electric-car/news/press-releases/nissan_to_make_history_with_delivery_of_worlds_first_electric_nissan_leaf.

2. I interviewed Carlos Tavares in Los Angeles and the video was posted to You Tube November 17, 2009. It's available at www.youtube.com/watch?v=oSb2bnpuNEM&feature=player_embedded.

3. Jung was interviewed in a Nissan Leaf in transit to San Francisco on December 11, 2010.

4. Eric Evarts of *Consumer Reports* blogged about its survey November 15, 2010. "Survey: Americans Want Better Fuel Efficiency—But Don't Want to Pay Extra for It" is at http://blogs.consumerreports.org/cars/2010/11/green-car-survey-americans-want-better-mpg-fuel-efficiency-but-dont-want-to-pay-extra-for-it.html.

5. I interviewed Eric Evarts of *Consumer Reports* for "Americans' Expectations for Electric Cars Are on a Collision Course with Reality," posted at *The Daily Green* on December 8, 2010, www.thedailygreen.com/living-green/blogs/cars-transportation/electric-car-facts-461210.

6. "First Full Range Test of Nissan Leaf Yields 116.1 Miles" by Nick Chambers, posted at PlugInCars.com October 21, 2010, www.plugincars.com/nissan-leaf-116-mile-range.html.

7. I videotaped Tavares's speech, and it's online in a December 13, 2010, post at CBS Interactive's BNET Auto, www.bnet.com/blog/electric-cars/nissan-launches-the-leaf-now-electric-cars-have-to-make-their-mark-on-the-sales-floor/2814.

8. Brad Berman interviewed second Leaf customer Tom Franklin for PluginCars.com and posted it at www.plugincars.com/nissan-delivers-worlds-second-nissan-leaf-owner-and-so-106559.html.

9. I interviewed polar bear scientist Steve Amstrup for "Six Things I Learned About the Nissan Leaf," Mother Nature Network, December 13, 2010. It's at www.mnn.com/green-tech/transportation/blogs/6-things-i-learned-about-the-nissan-leaf.

10. Telephone interview with Olivier Chalouhi, January 27, 2011.

11. I wrote about "Test Driving the Chevrolet Volt" for *Forbes* on April 1, 2010. The story, no April Fool's joke, is at www.forbes.com/2010/04/01/electric-vehicle-gm-technology-ecotech-chevy-volt.html.

12. I wrote about the Volt's charging expectations in an October 12, 2010, story, "Bringing Home Baby, Your Electric Car," for the *New York Times* special "Cars" section. It's online at www.nytimes.com/2010/10/14/automobiles/autospecial2/14CHARGE.html.

13. My blog post for *The Daily Green* on December 22, 2010, was "Jay Leno Loves His New Chevrolet Volt," www.thedailygreen.com/living-green/blogs/cars-transportation/jay-leno-chevrolet-volt-review-461210.

14. My story "Jay Leno on EVs: Hurray for No-Compromise Chevy Volts and Porsche Spyders," which appeared on NPR's *Car Talk* blog October 1, 2010, is posted at http://cartalk.com/blogs/jim-motavalli/?p=435. It was distilled from an hour-long conversation that ranged across the car spectrum.

15. Britta Gross was interviewed by Andrew Nusca of SmartPlanet.com on June 25, 2010. The story is at www.smartplanet.com/business/blog/smart-takes/gms-britta-gross-8-ways-cities-can-encourage-electric-vehicles/8047.

16. Telephone interview with Roland Hwang of the Natural Resources Defense Council, January 27, 2011.

17. The highlights of the Mini E study are available from the UC Davis Plug-In Hybrid and Electric Vehicle Research Center at http://phev.ucdavis.edu.

18. I wrote about the range issue in relation to the Volt in an October 5, 2010, post for CBS Interactive's BNET Auto, www.bnet.com/blog/electric-cars/fear-factor-chevy-volt-8217s-range-advantage-matters-now-but-it-could-fade/2435.

19. "Obama Kills Fun Cars, Unveils 35.5 mpg Fuel Economy Plan by 2016" was a *Jalopnik* post May 19, 2009. The unidentified author wrote, "There's no room for a Corvette ZR1 or rear-wheel-drive power wagon. Nope, it's all going to be Priuses and Fusion hybrids from here on out. We'd move to Canada except we're assuming it'd be worse up there."

20. The 60-mpg standard has been endorsed by the Consumer Federation of America and the Natural Resources Defense Council, among others. I wrote about it on September 7, 2010, for CBS Interactive's BNET Auto at www.bnet.com/blog/electric-cars/consumer-groups-says-cars-should-be-60-mpg-by-2025-that-8217s-a-stretch/2231. Charles Territo, a spokesman for the Alliance of Automobile Manufacturers, said then that automakers were struggling to meet the 34-mpg 2016 standard in the face of declining hybrid sales in 2010.

21. I wrote about the Fiat eco-driving software for the *New York Times Wheels* blog November 29, 2010. "Eco-Driving? The Europeans Have Some Lessons to Learn" is at http://wheels.blogs.nytimes.com/2010/11/29/eco-driving-the-europeans-have-some-lessons-to-learn.

22. I interviewed Ulrich Kranz at the 2010 Detroit auto show, and the January 14, 2010, story appeared on the *New York Times Wheels* blog at http://wheels.blogs.nytimes.com/2010/01/14/bmw-concept-activee-only-a-test-for-true-megacity-car.

23. The *McKinsey Quarterly* report, "The Fast Lane to the Adoption of Electric Cars," was posted February 2011, and is available at https://www.mckinseyquarterly.com/Automotive/Strategy_Analysis/The_fast_lane_to_the_adoption_of_electric_cars_2738.

24. Kawanabe was quoted by Bloomberg in "Honda Questions Demand for Electric Cars, Eyes Fuel Cells," which can be found at www.bloomberg.com/news/2010-05-18/honda-lacks-confidence-in-electric-cars-considers-u-s-built-hybrids.html.

25. Reuters reported Ito's comments November 2, 2010, in "Honda CEO Sees Potential in Electric Car Market," available at www.reuters.com/article/2010/11/02/honda-electric-cars-idUSTOE6A106V20101102.

26. I saw the electric Honda Fit unveiled at the Los Angeles Auto Show. My story, "Honda Electrifies the Versatile Fit, Already a Hybrid," appeared November 19,

2010, at CBS Interactive's BNET Auto and is posted at www.bnet.com/blog/electric-cars/honda-electrifies-the-versatile-fit-already-a-hybrid/2686.

27. I wrote "Toyota and Tesla Plan an Electric RAV4" for the *New York Times Wheels* blog July 16, 2010, and it's posted at http://wheels.blogs.nytimes.com/2010/07/16/toyota-and-tesla-plan-an-electric-rav4.

28. "VW Goes Electric, but with an Eye On the U.S. Bottom Line" is a post I wrote for CBS Interactive's BNET Auto November 19, 2010, and it's posted at www.bnet.com/blog/electric-cars/vw-goes-electric-but-with-an-eye-on-the-us-bottom-line/2679.

CHAPTER FIVE: *CHARGING AHEAD*

1. I sat down with Shai Agassi for a video interview in Tokyo, and the relevant section was posted on YouTube April 27, 2010. It's here: www.youtube.com/watch?v=l1KhoKkSt_I&feature=player_embedded. The story I did for *The Daily Green* on the battery-swapping phenomenon, "Battle for Electric Cars Heats Up with Ambitious Battery Swapping Project," was posted the next day at www.thedailygreen.com/living-green/blogs/cars-transportation/better-place-battery-swapping-460410.

2. "All About Yves," by Linda Tischler, *Fast Company*, October 1, 2007, posted at www.fastcompany.com/magazine/119/all-about-yves.html.

3. I wrote about Béhar for Mother Nature Network on February 26, 2010, in a blog post called "From the Man Who Brought You the $100 Laptop, an Electric Vehicle for the Developing World," available at www.mnn.com/green-tech/transportation/blogs/from-the-man-who-brought-you-the-100-laptop-an-electric-vehicle-for-.

4. My story about the debut of Béhar's WattStation, "An Electric Car Charger with a Designer Touch," appeared on the *New York Times Wheels* blog on July 13, 2010. It's at http://wheels.blogs.nytimes.com/2010/07/13/ges-ev-charger-has-that-designer-touch.

5. My story "G.E. and Better Place to Partner on E.V. Charging" appeared on the *New York Times Wheels* blog September 24, 2010, at http://wheels.blogs.nytimes.com/2010/09/24/g-e-and-better-place-to-partner-on-e-v-charging.

6. Jeffrey Immelt's statement, released on November 11, 2010, is posted at GE's Ecomagination site, www.ecomagination.com/topics/ev-electric-vehicles.

7. Vice President Joe Biden's plan is outlined at http://energy.gov/news/10034.htm.

8. Robbie Diamond's comments were in an Electrification Coalition news release entitled "WH Addition of Deployment Communities in Budget Adds to Bipartisan Momentum on Energy Security," January 26, 2011, posted at www.electrificationcoalition.org/media/releases/wh-addition-deployment-communities-budget-adds-bipartisan-momentum-energy-security.

9. I wrote about Chelsea Sexton's charger installation woes for CBS Interactive's BNET Auto October 21, 2010. "Chelsea Sexton's Volt Charger Woes Don't Bode Well for You and Me" is posted at www.bnet.com/blog/electric-cars/chelsea-sexton-8217s-volt-charger-woes-don-8217t-bode-well-for-you-and-me/2514.

10. My account of the Columbia University forum, "A High-Minded Look at Electric Cars," was published as the *New York Times Wheels* blog April 23, 2010, and it appears at http://wheels.blogs.nytimes.com/2010/04/23/a-highminded-look-at-electric-cars.

11. I wrote about $3.50 an hour public EV charging for CBS Interactive's BNET Auto on December 8, 2010. It's posted at www.bnet.com/blog/electric-cars/public-ev-charging-expect-to-pay-350-an-hour-for-the-convenience/2779.

12. The rates quoted were obtained from a Con Edison spokesperson during the course of my research. The amount New York City customers pay for electricity fluctuates, of course, and a table of historic per-kilowatt rates between 2008 and 2010 is posted here: http://w303.com/186/new-york-city-electricity-con-edison-kwh-charge-history.

13. I wrote about the pricing model again in another BNET Auto post on August 27, 2010, available at www.bnet.com/blog/electric-cars/a-first-shot-at-pricing-ev-charging-50-cents-a-kilowatt-hour/2173.

14. I wrote about AeroVironment's partnership with Nissan for CBS Interactive's BNET Auto on January 15, 2010. It's posted at www.bnet.com/blog/electric-cars/detroit-auto-show-nissan-details-8220smart-8221-home-charging-for-the-leaf-ev/1244.

15. My story "Killer App for E.V.'s: 30-Minute Recharges," appeared in the *New York Times* August 6, 2010. It's at www.nytimes.com/2010/08/08/automobiles/08CHARGE.html.

16. I wrote about Best Buy's plan to offer EV charging at CBS Interactive's BNET Auto on July 19, 2010. "Best Buy to Plug In Customers' EVs" is at www.bnet.com/blog/electric-cars/best-buy-to-plug-in-customers-8217-evs-exclusive/1909.

17. "Aside from Best Buy, Big-Box Stores Are in No Hurry on EV Charging," July 22, 2010, CBS Interactive's BNET Auto, www.bnet.com/blog/electric-cars/aside-from-best-buy-big-box-stores-are-in-no-hurry-on-ev-charging/1923.

18. "Fast 30-Minute EV Charging May Not Be DIY," CBS Interactive's BNET Auto, July 22, 2010, www.bnet.com/blog/electric-cars/fast-30-minute-ev-charging-may-not-be-diy/1928.

19. I wrote about high-voltage-charging compatibility issues for the *New York Times Wheels* blog January 12, 2011. It's posted at http://wheels.blogs.nytimes.com/2011/01/12/compatability-questions-loom-for-high-voltage-e-v-charging.

20. The EV Plug Alliance is at www.evplugalliance.org.

21. "Car Charging Group and City of Norwalk Parking Authority Open First EV Charging Station in Fairfield County, CT," January 31, 2011. http://ir.stockpr.com/carcharging/company-news/detail/353/car-charging-group-and-city-of-norwalk-parking-authority-open-first-ev-charging-station-in-fairfield-county-ct. The company said that some of its Manhattan stations are seeing four to eight hours of daily use.

22. I interviewed Michael Farkas and Brian Golomb of the Car Charging Group for "Public EV Charging: Expect to Pay $3.50 an Hour for the Convenience," CBS Interactive's BNET Auto, December 8, 2010, posted at www.bnet.com/blog/electric-cars/public-ev-charging-expect-to-pay-350-an-hour-for-the-convenience/2779.

23. 350Green can be found at http://350green.com. Its San Francisco work was funded in part by a grant from the Bay Area Air Quality Management District as part of its Spare the Air program. Other recipients of BAAQMD funding include ECOtality ($2.2 million, plus $614,800 for fast chargers), Coulomb ($350,000), AeroVironment ($350,000, plus $150,000 for fast chargers), and Clipper Creek ($175,000).

CHAPTER SIX: *THE SMART GRID*

1. I wrote about the Panasonic Eco Ideas House and the CEATEC show for Mother Nature Network October 5, 2010, and the story is at www.mnn.com/green-tech/transportation/blogs/green-tech-plugs-in-at-japanese-electronics-show.

2. "Toyota's Smart Grid Village Launches," by Anita Lienert, September 16, 2010, www.insideline.com/toyota/toyotas-smart-grid-village-launches.html. Lienert wrote, "The concept is reminiscent of Walt Disney's Experimental Prototype Community of Tomorrow, the genesis of EPCOT, the Orlando, Florida, resort designed to generate new ideas for urban living using new technologies."

3. "Mileage from Megawatts," a news release by Anne Haas of the Pacific Northwest National Laboratory, described the study findings on December 11, 2006. Read it at www.pnl.gov/news/release.aspx?id=204. "We were very conservative in looking at the idle capacity of power generation assets," said Pacific Northwest National Labs scientist Michael Kintner-Meyer.

4. The full title of the study is *Assessment of Plug-In Electric Vehicle Integration with ISO/RTO Systems*. ISOs are independent service operators, and RTOs are the regional transmission organizations. The ISO/RTO Council report is highly technical, but if you want to wade through it: www.isorto.org/atf/cf/%7B5B4E85C6-7EAC-40A0-8DC3-003829518EBD%7D/IRC_Report_Assessment_of_Plug-in_Electric_Vehicle_Integration_with_ISO-RTO_Systems_03232010.pdf.

5. "This Is Important: What Would One Million Electric Cars Do to the Grid?" by Michael Graham Richard, Treehugger, March 25, 2010. Posted at www.treehugger.com/files/2010/03/what-would-1-million-electric-cars-do-to-power-grid.php.

6. An account of the JD Power survey is "Hybrid and EV Cars Will Be 3.5 percent of Sales by 2015," by Bill DiBenedetto, June 21, 2010, posted at www.triplepundit.com/2010/06/j-d-power-hybrid-and-ev-cars-will-be-3-5-of-sales-by-2015.

7. I wrote about EVs and the grid for *The Daily Green* on June 11, 2010. "Can You Charge an Electric Car with an iPhone? (Yes)" is posted at www.thedailygreen.com/living-green/blogs/cars-transportation/iphone-app-electric-car-0611.

8. *Livestock's Long Shadow: Environmental Issues and Options* from the Food and Agriculture Organization of the United Nations was posted in 2006 at www.fao.org/docrep/010/a0701e/a0701e00.htm.

9. The estimate that coal produces 20 percent of the world's greenhouse gas emissions is part of "Coal and Climate Change Facts," an informational posting from the Pew Center on Global Climate Change, available at www.pewclimate.org/global-warming-basics/coalfacts.cfm.

10. The 2007 *Environmental Assessment of Plug-In Hybrid Vehicles* by the Electric Power Research Institute and the Natural Resources Defense Council is

at http://mydocs.epri.com/docs/CorporateDocuments/SectorPages/Portfolio/PDM/PHEV-ExecSum-vol1.pdf.

11. I wrote "Dirty Power, Clean Cars: Even from Coal, EVs Are Cleaner" for NPR's *Car Talk* blog, and it was posted June 4, 2010, at http://cartalk.com/blogs/jim-motavalli/?p=208.

12. The estimate that California could have more electric car sales by 2015 than the next five states combined is extracted from the Center for Auto Research study, *Deployment Rollout Estimate of Electric Vehicles, 2011-2015*, January 2011, posted at www.cargroup.org/pdfs/deployment.pdf.

13. The analysis comparing the carbon output of battery cars with other vehicle types is from "How Green Is My Plug-In?" by John Voelcker, *IEEE Spectrum*, March 2009, posted at http://spectrum.ieee.org/energy/the-smarter-grid/how-green-is-my-plugin/0.

14. I wrote about Chattanooga's new smart grid for CBS Interactive's BNET Auto June 28, 2010, and it's posted at www.bnet.com/blog/electric-cars/evs-and-the-smart-grid-go-together-in-chattanooga-but-few-other-places/1837.

15. The Department of Energy's *Grid 2030: A National Vision for Electricity's Second 100 Years* report was published in July of 2003 and is online at www.oe.energy.gov/DocumentsandMedia/Electric_Vision_Document.pdf.

16. "GE's Smart Grid Gets Ready for Electric Cars (and Wind Power, Too)" was written for CBS Interactive's BNET Auto and posted by me December 8, 2009, at www.bnet.com/blog/electric-cars/ge-8217s-smart-grid-gets-ready-for-electric-cars-and-wind-power-too/1145.

17. "New York Auto Show: Ford, Microsoft and EVs" appeared on the *New York Times Wheels* blog March 31, 2010. Troy Batterberry, a Microsoft manager, said that the Hohm system can help reduce "traffic jams" on the grid. http://wheels.blogs.nytimes.com/2010/03/31/new-york-auto-show-ford-microsoft-and-e-v-s.

18. "CES: All Eyes on Ford's Electric Focus," by Caroline McCarthy," January 7, 2011, CNET.com, http://ces.cnet.com/8301-32254_1-20027811-283.html.

19. Nissan detailed the electronic applications on the Leaf in a July 27, 2009, news release posted at www.nissan-global.com/EN/NEWS/2009/_STORY/090727-01-e.html.

20. "Can You Charge an Electric Car."

21. "OnStar Teams Up with Google to Develop New Chevrolet Volt Smartphone Apps," by Viknesh Vijayenthiran, appeared May 18, 2010, at *Green Car Reports*, www.greencarreports.com/blog/1045204_onstar-teams-up-with-google-to-develop-new-chevrolet-volt-smartphone-apps.

CHAPTER SEVEN: *CHINESE PUZZLES*

1. "China's Car Industry Overtakes US," by Chris Hogg, BBC News, February 10, 2009, http://news.bbc.co.uk/2/hi/business/7879372.stm.

2. "The Transition to Electric Bikes in China: History and Key Reasons for Rapid Growth," by Jonathan Weinert, Chaktan Ma, and Christopher Cherry, *Transportation* 2007;304–318, http://wenku.baidu.com/view/577e3de9856a561252d36f5c.html.

3. "China's New Celebrity Car Salesmen," by Owen Fletcher, *Wall Street Journal China Real Time Report* blog, September 29, 2010. It's online at http://blogs.wsj .com/chinarealtime/2010/09/29/chinas-new-celebrity-car-salesmen.

4. The CNBC video that includes an in-the-air interview with Warren Buffett is online at www.cnbc.com/id/39418582/Warren_Buffett_to_CNBC_Decision_ to_Buy_More_BYD_Shares_Would_Depend_on_Price.

5. The information on BYD's Los Angeles plans is from a December 16, 2010, AP report, "China's BYD Auto, LA to Test Electric Car Fleet," posted at http:// abcnews.go.com/Business/wireStory?id=12409444.

6. "Bad Year for Buffett-Backed BYD," by Alex Crippen, CNBC.com, December 29, 2010, posted at www.cnbc.com/id/40840866.

7. "BYD Sales Fall Short of 2010 Target," *People's Daily Online*, January 6, 2011, http://english.peopledaily.com.cn/90001/90778/90860/7252244.html. According to the story, "Chinese automakers face a challenge from foreign car companies, including GM and Volkswagen AG, as rising incomes prompt shoppers to buy more expensive foreign models."

8. "China Charges Into Electric Cars" by Brian Dumaine, *Fortune*, October 19, 2010, http://tech.fortune.cnn.com/2010/10/19/china-charges-into-electric-cars.

9. Export/import data for the United States and China from the US Census Bureau can be found at www.census.gov/foreign-trade/balance/c5700.html#2010.

10. *Food and Agricultural Imports from China*, by Geoffrey S. Becker, Congressional Research Service, September 26, 2008. Online at www.fas.org/sgp/crs/ row/RL34080.pdf.

11. "Lead Paint Prompts Mattel to Recall 967,000 Toys," by Louis Story, August 2, 2007, *New York Times*, www.nytimes.com/2007/08/02/business/02toy.html.

12. I interviewed Paul Midler in early 2010 for CBS Interactive's BNET. "Poorly Made in China: Challenges for Auto Exports" is at www.bnet.com/blog/electric-cars/poorly-made-in-china-challenges-for-auto-exports/1340.

13. The Geely crash video was sourced from the Russian Autoreview.ru and is posted at www.youtube.com/watch?v=8vAN2cx2UIE. The 2009 crash video is sourced from Latinncap.com.

14. "Auto Special: Safety Test Proves Geely Has the Right Path to Improved Performance and Competitiveness," *China Daily*, January 14, 2011, posted at www.chinesestock.org/show.aspx?id=114170&cid=11.

15. "Volvo Mulls China-Made Cars for U.S." by Norihiko Shirouzu, *Wall Street Journal*, January 13, 2011, posted at http://online.wsj.com/article/SB100014240 5274870480360457607800287405280.html.

16. "Volvo to Sell C30 Electric Car in China," Reuters, April 22, 2010, posted at www.reuters.com/article/2010/04/23/us-autoshow-volvo-idUS TRE63M0BT20100423.

17. "Volvo to Sell 800,000 Cars Globally by 2020," AFP, February 25, 2011, posted at www.swedishwire.com/component/content/article/1-companies/8762-volvo-to-sell-800000-cars-globally-by-2020. The source for that prediction of huge growth is Volvo CEO Stefan Jacoby.

18. "What China and Israel Will Teach the World" by Shai Agassi, *Economist*, November 22, 2010, posted at www.economist.com/node/17493423.

19. "For the Coda, a Preface in Washington," by Matthew L. Wald, *New York Times Wheels* blog, September 16, 2010, posted at http://wheels.blogs.nytimes .com/2010/09/16/for-the-coda-a-preface-in-washington.

20. My story "Coda for Coda: Can It Survive Its CEO Resignation and an EV Production Delay?" appeared on CBS Interactive's BNET on November 19, 2010, and is posted at www.bnet.com/blog/electric-cars/coda-for-coda-can-it-survive-its-ceo-resignation-and-an-ev-production-delay/2690.

CHAPTER EIGHT:
ICELAND'S FAST TRACK

1. "Financial Crisis Causes Iceland's Government to Collapse," by David Blair, *Telegraph Online*, January 27, 2009, www.telegraph.co.uk/news/worldnews/ europe/iceland/4348312/Financial-crisis-causes-Icelands-government-to-collapse.html.

2. The story of the Electrovan, complete with evocative photos and cutaway drawings, is at www.hydrogencarsnow.com/gm-electrovan.htm.

3. I talked with Tom Sullivan for "A Private Plan for a Hydrogen Highway," published April 16, 2010, as the *New York Times Wheels* blog, available at http:// wheels.blogs.nytimes.com/2010/04/16/a-private-plan-for-a-hydrogen-highway.

4. Details of the fuel-cell-equipped whale-watching boat are in "Icelandic Energy: The Elding Project," Autodesk.com, posted at http://usa.autodesk.com/ adsk/servlet/item?siteID=123112&id=15383784&linkID=10386716.

5. My article "Iceland's Abundance of Energy" was published by *E—The Environmental Magazine* February 29, 2008, at www.emagazine.com/archive/4085.

6. *Two Billion Cars: Driving Toward Sustainability* by Daniel Sperling and Deborah Gordon (New York: Oxford University Press, 2009), p. 33. I met Panik at Daimler's Fuel Cell Project House in Nabern, Germany, near Stuttgart. "We have a schedule, and we are sticking to it," he said then. The Daimler fuel-cell cars he was talking about ran on liquid methanol and used an onboard reformer to extract hydrogen. Daimler has abandoned that complicated technology and now, like nearly all fuel-cell developers, relies on pressurized hydrogen.

7. I interviewed Pétur Albert Haraldsson in a Skype call on February 7, 2011.

8. I interviewed President Ólafur Ragnar Grímsson September 16, 2009. An account is at *The Daily Green* at www.thedailygreen.com/living-green/blogs/ cars-transportation/iceland-president-clean-cars.

9. Interview with President Ólafur Ragnar Grímsson.

10. "Northern Lights Energy Commits to Purchase 1,000 Amp Electric Vehicles," November 29, 2010, a press release posted on PR Newswire at www .prnewswire.com/news-releases/northern-lights-energy-commits-to-purchase-

1000-amp-electric-vehicles-110963329.html.

11. "Northern Lights Energy Commits."

12. The letter of intent to Cristiano Carlutti, vice president of sales and operations for Tesla Motors in Europe, is dated September 16, 2010.

13. I interviewed Sturla Sighvatsson during my visit to Iceland for the Driving Sustainability conference, September 18, 2010.

CHAPTER NINE: *ON THE ROAD*

1. The Department of Energy's report, *One Million Electric Vehicles by 2015*, was published February 9, 2011, at www.energy.gov/news/documents/1_Million_Electric_Vehicle_Report_Final.pdf.

2. *Plug-In Electric Vehicles: A Practical Plan for Progress*, School of Public and Environmental Affairs at Indiana University, February 2011, posted online at www.indiana.edu/~spea/pubs/TEP_combined.pdf.

3. "Wheego Electric Cars Targets Oregon with Salem Dealership and Small Supply," by Ted Sickinger, OregonLive.com, June 20, 2011, posted at www.oregonlive.com/business/index.ssf/2011/06/wheego_electric_cars_targets_o.html.

4. I wrote about the Nissan Leaf in a blog post for Mother Nature Network April 20, 2010, www.mnn.com/green-tech/transportation/blogs/the-nissan-leaf-lines-up-paying-customers.

5. "Can the Nissan Leaf Really Run 0-60 mph in 5 Seconds? Not Likely" by Sam Abuelsamid, *AutoBlog Green,* May 11, 2010. Posted at http://green.autoblog.com/2010/05/11/can-the-nissan-leaf-really-run-0-60-mph-in-5-seconds-not-likely. Nissan speculated that CBS confused the Leaf's zero-to-60 time with that of the 370Z gas sports car.

6. "Tesla's Electric Car for the (Well-Off) Masses," by Christopher Palmeri, *Businessweek,* March 27, 2009, posted at www.businessweek.com/bwdaily/dnflash/content/mar2009/db20090326_679423.htm.

7. I got Franz von Holzhausen's quote and some details about the Tesla Model S infotainment system from a video posted at TechCrunch on April 9, 2009. It's at http://techcrunch.com/2009/04/09/a-look-at-the-tesla-s-17-inch-haptic-entertainment-and-navigation-system.

8. A useful PowerPoint presentation in PDF format by Robert Wimmer of Toyota Motor North America on the operation of the FCHV-adv is posted at www.electricdrive.org/index.php?ht=a/GetDocumentAction/i/15322. It includes details on how the company plans to increase stack efficiency, durability, and range.

9. "Toyota Advances Hydrogen Fuel Cell Plans Amid Industry's Battery-Car Push," by Alan Ohnsman, Bloomberg.com, January 13, 2011. Posted at www.bloomberg.com/news/2011-01-13/toyota-advances-hydrogen-plans-amid-industry-s-battery-car-push.html. "I have high expectations for fuel-cell vehicles as a candidate for next-generation cars," Toyota's Takeshi Uchiyamada is quoted as saying. "Over the past several years, we've seen many of the outstanding technical issues solved."

10. *The Great Depression in America: A Cultural Encyclopedia,* Volume 1, by William H. Young and Nancy K. Young (Westport, CT: Greenwood Press, 2007), p. 34. "During the grimmest years of the crisis, the purchase of used cars actually exceeded that of new ones," the book says. The demise of Duesenberg is said, by some, to have left us with the term "doozie," derived from the car's nickname, Duesy.

11. My article on Barry Bernsten's attempt to launch an EV company was posted on Mother Nature Network, August 3, 2010. It's at www.mnn.com/green-tech/transportation/blogs/the-electric-vehicle-that-is-not-to-be-carmaker-lacks-connections-gi.

12. "Entrepreneur Gives Up Quest to Assemble Electric Cars," by Joseph N. DiStefano, *Philadelphia Inquirer,* July 21, 2010, http://articles.philly.com/2010-07-21/business/24967810_1_fisker-electric-cars-electric-vehicle.

CHAPTER 10: *EDEN ATTAINED?*

1. Evatran really *does* have technology like this. "Coming Soon: Wireless Electric Vehicle Charging," by Ariel Schwartz, *Fast Company,* July 28, 2010. It's posted at www.fastcompany.com/1675225/coming-soon-wireless-electric-vehicle-charging.

2. "Toothbrush Tech Helps Buses Go Green," by John Herskovitz, Reuters, March 10, 2010, posted at www.abc.net.au/science/articles/2010/03/10/2841709.htm. The Korean Advanced Institute of Science and Technology demonstrated the inductive charging technology on buses traveling around its campus. The principle is borrowed from sealed, water-resistant electric toothbrushes.

3. This exact technology was predicted as part of the General Motors Futurama exhibit at the 1939 World's Fair. Fourteen lanes of cross-country travel would move at 100 mph, with close spacing controlled by "radio beams." I wrote about this in my first book, *Forward Drive: The Race to Build "Clean" Cars for the Future* (San Francisco: Sierra Club Books, 2000). My only liberty in my imaginative scenario was increasing the cars' speed somewhat.

4. In New York State, a law requires drivers convicted of misdemeanor or felony drunken driving to install ignition interlock Breathalyzer devices for a minimum of six months. If they fail the test, the car won't start. I wrote about it for the *New York Times Wheels* blog on July 20, 2010. It's posted at http://wheels.blogs.nytimes.com/2010/07/20/new-york-requires-alcohol-interlocks-for-first-time-drunken-drivers.

5. "Nation's First Automated Highway System Demonstrated in San Diego," by David Banasiak, *Roads and Bridges,* August 1996. It's posted at www.roadsbridges.com/Nations-first-automated-highway-system-demonstrated-in-San-Diego-article457.

6. The account of my conversation with Chris Paine was published on the *New York Times Wheels* blog on December 15, 2010. It's posted at http://wheels.blogs.nytimes.com/2010/12/15/chris-paine-returns-with-revenge-of-the-electric-car.

7. "Report: Honda, Toyota Earning Profits on Hybrids," Green Car Congress, posted April 28, 2009, at www.greencarcongress.com/2009/04/report-honda-toyota-earning-profits-on-hybrids.html.

8. "Toyota, Lexus Hybrids Top 1 Million Sales in U.S.," Toyota news release,

March 11, 2009, http://pressroom.toyota.com/pr/tms/toyota/toyota-and-lexus-hybrids-top-one-85047.aspx.

9. My talk with Tesla's Cristiano Carlutti was posted on CBS Interactive's *Plugged In* blog on September 17, 2010, at www.bnet.com/blog/electric-cars/europe-proving-a-tough-nut-for-tesla-motors-to-crack/2298.

10. "Tesla Hires Apple, Gap Veteran to Revolutionize Car-Buying Experience," Tesla Motors news release, July 8, 2010. It's posted at www.teslamotors.com/about/press/releases/tesla-hires-apple-gap-veteran-revolutionize-car-buying-experience. Additional information related also came from "10 Questions for Tesla's New (and Apple's Former) Retail Chief," by Josie Garthwaite, *Earth-2Tech*, July 9, 2010, posted at http://gigaom.com/cleantech/10-questions-for-teslas-new-apples-former-retail-chief.

11. "10 Questions for Tesla's New (and Apple's Former) Retail Chief."

12. "Fisker Automotive Reveals Striking New Images for European Market," Fisker news release, September 30, 2010. Posted at http://www.facebook.com/note.php?note_id=127319660656634.

13. "Maritz Automotive Research Group Study Shows Growing Consumer Awareness About Alternative Fuel Vehicles," Maritz Research news release, posted January 7, 2011, at www.maritz.com/en/Press-Releases/2011/Maritz-Automotive-Research-Group-Study-Finds-Growing-Consumer-Awareness-Concerning-Alternative-Fuels.aspx.

14. The *Wall Street Journal Driver's Seat* blog opined, "Toyota's Prius Hybrid Is Real Star of 'The Other Guys.'" Author Dennis Nishi points out that Prius "never falters, deftly staying ahead of armed enemies in car chase after car chase. Not bad for a 110 horsepower subcompact that's rated at 46 mpg." The piece was posted August 13, 2010, at http://blogs.wsj.com/drivers-seat/2010/08/13/toyotas-prius-hybrid-is-real-star-of-the-other-guys.

15. "Survey: Americans Want Better Fuel Efficiency—But Don't Want to Pay Extra for It," *Consumer Reports* blog, posted at http://blogs.consumerreports.org/cars/2010/11/green-car-survey-americans-want-better-mpg-fuel-efficiency-but-dont-want-to-pay-extra-for-it.html.

16. "Zero-Emission Vehicle Regulations Get Tougher for 2012: California Dreaming: The New CARB Diet," by Keith Barry, *Car and Driver*, January 2011, posted at www.caranddriver.com/features/11q1/zero-emission_vehicle_regulations_get_tougher_for_2012-feature.

17. The December 2010 Roland Berger Strategy Consultants prediction about Chinese auto industry growth also concludes that sales growth will decline. It is posted at www.rolandberger.com/media/pdf/Roland_Berger_Market_Outlook_China_2011_20101222.pdf.

18. "International Energy Outlook 2010," US Energy Information Administration, May 25, 2010, www.eia.gov/oiaf/ieo/liquid_fuels.html.

19. *Oil Market Report*, International Energy Agency, January 18, 2011, posted at http://omrpublic.iea.org/omrarchive/18jan11full.pdf.

20. *World Energy Outlook 2010*, International Energy Agency, presented to the press November 9, 2010, and online at www.worldenergyoutlook.org/docs/

weo2010/weo2010_london_nov9.pdf.

21. IEA, *Oil Market Report*.

22. Intergovernmental Panel on Climate Change, "Observed Changes in Climate and Their Effects," *Climate Change 2007: Synthesis Report*, posted at www.ipcc.ch/publications_and_data/ar4/syr/en/spms1.html. I also edited a book entitled *Feeling the Heat: Dispatches from the Frontlines of Climate Change* (New York: Routledge, 2004) that detailed global warming effects that were then already under way.

23. *Storms of My Grandchildren: The Truth About the Coming Climate Catastrophe and Our Last Chance to Save Humanity*, by James Hansen (New York: Bloomsbury USA, 2009).

24. James Hansen, "Hansen On the Issues: The Coming Storms," posted at www.stormsofmygrandchildren.com/climate_catastrophe_solutions.html.

25. "Global Warming and the Pollsters: Who's Right?" by Lee Dye, ABC News/Technology, June 16, 2010. It's posted at http://abcnews.go.com/Technology/DyeHard/global-warming-polls-climate-change/story?id=10921583.

26. Chelsea Sexton's comments about EVs facing "a couple of rough years" were made in an e-mail to me, February 22, 2011.

BIBLIOGRAPHY

Boschert, Sherry. *Plug-In Hybrids: The Cars That Will Recharge America.* Gabriola Island, BC: New Society, 2006.

Bradsher, Keith. *High and Mighty: The Dangerous Rise of the SUV.* New York: Public Affairs, 2003.

Carson, Iain, and Vijay V. Vaitheeswaran. *Zoom: The Global Race to Fuel the Car of the Future.* New York: Twelve Books, 2007.

Edsall, Larry. *Chevrolet Volt: Charging Into the Future.* Minneapolis: MBI and Motorbooks, 2010.

Fletcher, Seth. *Bottled Lightning: Superbatteries, Electric Cars, and the New Lithium Economy.* New York: Hill and Wang, 2011.

Kettlewell, Caroline. *Electric Dreams: One Unlikely Team of Kids and the Race to Build the Car of the Future.* Boston: Da Capo, 2004.

Larminie, James, and John Lowry. *Electric Vehicle Technology Explained.* New York: John Wiley, 2003

Leitman, Seth, and Bob Brant. *Build Your Own Electric Vehicle,* 2nd ed. New York: McGraw-Hill, 2009.

Motavalli, Jim. *Forward Drive: The Race to Build "Clean" Cars for the Future.* San Francisco: Sierra Club Books, 2001.

Nerad, Jack. *The Complete Idiot's Guide to Hybrid and Alternative Fuel Vehicles.* New York: Alpha Books, 2007.

Shnayerson, Michael. *The Car That Could: The Inside Story of GM's Revolutionary Electric Vehicle.* New York: Random House, 1996.

Sperling, Daniel, and Deborah Gordon. *Two Billion Cars: Driving Toward Sustainability.* New York: Oxford University Press, 2009.

Yost, Nick. *The Essential Hybrid Car Handbook: A Buyer's Guide.* Guilford, CT: Lyons Press, 2006.

ACKNOWLEDGMENTS

FOR THIS BOOK TO WORK, I needed a lot of people to say yes when I asked them for test rides or interview opportunities. Fortunately, nearly everybody did—they wanted to tell the story of the electric car's rebirth as much as I wanted to chronicle it. Therefore, I'm indebted to the following road warriors, some of whom have since left their frontline posts: Kristen Helsel (Aero-Vironment); Jim Taylor, Steve Burns, and Mike Dektas (Amp); Paul Wilbur (Aptera); Rick Rommel (Best Buy); Julie Mullins and Shai Agassi (Better Place); Dave Buchko, Sean Lobosco, Richard Steinberg, and Tom Plucinsky (BMW); Michael Brylawski and John Waters (Bright Automotive); Stanley Young (California Air Resources Board); Byron Washom (University of California at San Diego); Lisa Bicker (CleanTECH San Diego); Anne Smith and Richard Lowenthal (Coulomb Technologies); Kevin Czinger and Matt Sloustcher (Coda); David Cole (Center for Auto Research); Rik Paul, Eric Evarts, David Champion, and Gabriel Shenhar (*Consumer Reports*); John DeCicco (University of Michigan); Jonathan Read (ECOtality); Cathy Milbourn (EPA); Charles Gassenheimer (Ener1); Russell Datz (Fisker); Jennifer Moore, Bill Ford, Sherif Marakby, and Tara Martin (Ford); Britta Gross, Rob Peterson, Larry Burns, Scott Fosgard, and Tony Posawatz (General Motors); Chris Naughton (Honda); Phil Gott (IHS Global Insight); James Bell (Kelley Blue Book); Jim Kliesch

(American Council for an Energy-Efficient Economy); Sascha Simon, Donna Boland and Nicole Weiss (Mercedes Benz); Steve Oldham, Katherine Zachary, and Mark Perry (Nissan); Larry Moulthrop and Mark Schiller (Proton); Andrew Tang (PG&E); Dave Mazaika (Quantum Technologies); Michele Tinson (Saab); Rachel Konrad, Khobi Brooklyn, and Ricardo Reyes (Tesla); Richard Canny, Brendan Prebo, and Brian Engle (Think); Wade Hoyt, John Hanson, and Jana Hartline (Toyota); Susan Nicholson (Wheego); Alex Campbell (Zap). The Society of Environmental Journalists, and its lively listserv, continue to inspire.

Very special thanks to the outsize personalities I featured in the book, including Christina Lampe-Önnerud (Boston-Power), Elon Musk (Tesla), Henrik Fisker (Fisker), Mike McQuary (Wheego), and Kevin Czinger (Coda). From the world of advocacy, Dan Becker (Center for Auto Safety), Luke Tonachel and Roland Hwang (Natural Resources Defense Council), Gina Coplon-Newfield (Sierra Club) and Jeff Gearhart and Charles Griffith (Ecology Center Auto Project) have always been there with information and good advice. Chelsea Sexton has been an invaluable source and confidant. Huge thanks, as always, to Ed Begley Jr., who invited me into his house and showed me how he recharges his electric Toyota RAV4. Ed's been driving electric cars since they were eccentric little cars with brand names like Taylor-Dunn.

My two years of writing and blogging about green cars was aided and abetted by some very able editors, many of whom let me go on leave to write this book. The sharp-penciled David Hamilton at CBS Interactive has taught me a lot about writing for an online business audience. I continue to learn from my longtime friends at the *New York Times*: Richard Chang, Jonathan Schultz,

Norman Mayersohn, Jim Schembari, Chris Jensen, and Jim Cobb. At the University of Pennsylvania's Wharton School, I'd like to thank Joanne Spigonardo and Eric Orts at the Initiative for Global Environmental Leadership and Mukul Pandya, Steve Guglielmi, and Steve Sherretta at *Knowledge@Wharton*. Also at Penn, Robert Giegengack is a fount of useful information. My life has been enriched by meeting my partner in business writing adventures, Jon Miller.

In Iceland, I thank Pétur Albert Haraldsson, Gísli Gíslason, Bradley Skaggs, and Sturla Sighvatsson.

I've had no end of fun collaborating with the certifiable crew at NPR's *Car Talk*. Yes, Tom and Ray Magliozzi are the same off-mike as on, and Doug Mayer and Doug Berman have kept me in line and allowed me to (dis)grace the blog. I've had a great, creative ride with Benyamin Cohen, the content editor of the fast-moving Mother Nature Network. Dan Shapley of The Daily Green has always been wonderful to work with. Former Daily Green editor Brian Howard and I were friends and coeditors at *E/The Environmental Magazine*, where I thank Doug Moss and Brita Belli. Mitch Lipka (now with Reuters) was a wonderful mentor for Sally Deneen and me at AOL's Green Police.

Green car colleagues who have shared knowledge and laughs with me include Sebastian Blanco (AutoBlog Green), Nick Chambers and Brad Berman (Hybridcars.com/Plugincars.com), and John O'Dell (Edmunds' Green Car Advisor). Filmmaker Chris Paine has offered plenty of insights, and I wish *Revenge of the Electric Car* every success.

A very special thanks to the astute John Voelcker, senior editor at High Gear Media and to Felix Kramer of CalCars.org for volunteering to read sections of the book—it was timely, gentlemen. It should be pointed out that without Felix, plug-in hybrids may never have happened at all.

At Rodale, I'd like to thank my excellent editors, Gena Smith and Colin Dickerman, who helped me produce a tighter book, and also Nancy E. Elgin, the most astute copy editor I've ever worked with.

My daughters Delia and Maya had plenty of pithy things to say about the green cars that provided transportation to them and their friends. And my wife, Mary Ann, earned my undying gratitude (which she already had) for realizing how important this all was to me, steering me through some crucial career decisions—and letting me go on the road.

INDEX